HOME IN FLORIDA

HOME
IN
FLORIDA

Latinx Writers and the Literature of Uprootedness

Edited by Anjanette Delgado

UNIVERSITY OF FLORIDA PRESS

Gainesville

26 25 24 23 22 21   6 5 4 3 2 1

LIBRARY OF CONGRESS CONTROL NUMBER: 2021944499
ISBN 978-1-68340-250-3

UNIVERSITY OF FLORIDA PRESS
2046 NE Waldo Road
Suite 2100
Gainesville, FL 32609
http://upress.ufl.edu

UF PRESS

UNIVERSITY
OF FLORIDA

CONTENTS

I dedicate my work on this book

To my sister, Yadira, my blood, my conscience.
And to Migdalia, my sister in uprootedness.

AD

INTRODUCTION

ANJANETTE DELGADO

I want to create a new body of work now, a literature of uprootedness about someone who's living in an environment that's not
his own. In truth, this isn't a personal calamity but a universal
one, because the world is full of people who aren't living where
they should be, and if they are they have to run away. All the
literature of this century is somewhat burdened by the theme
of uprootedness.

REINALDO ARENAS, interviewed by Anne Tashi Slater in 1983,
published in *The New Yorker*, December 5, 2013

Dear Person Now Reading This,

What an incredible word, isn't it? Uprootedness. People, driven to uproot themselves by a variety of circumstances: violence, imprisonment, hunger, and sometimes, but much less often, by an act of nature. To run away to another place. With other people. To attempt life in an environment not their own, a place not where they (or their ancestors) believed they belonged or thought they'd ever be.

In English, not many sources come up when one looks for the word "up-rootedness" in the context of literature, the 1983 interview with then recent Cuban émigré Reinaldo Arenas one of precious few at the time of this writing.

As with so many things, in Spanish it is the opposite, and the term is every-where. *La literatura del desarraigo.* There are anthologies devoted to it, thesis projects that discuss it, even newspaper columns. And yet the words are the same. Or maybe not. It occurs to me that in Spanish, the connotation of the word for uprootedness, *desarraigo*, includes what is left behind and does so with something close to a rebuke. *You left us and now you belong nowhere un-less we forgive you.* Meanwhile, uprootedness in English is more pragmatic and, by necessity, more forward-looking. *You are an uprooted being. Work hard, and we'll talk.*

It is that concept—uprootedness—that this book is mostly about. Even the word carries inside the tension of seeming to mean one thing in Spanish and something never quite the same in English, the word itself with its dual mean-ing the very essence of the world in which a Latinx immigrant lives.

Note I say "lives" and not "arrives," because you are an immigrant until well after your arrival. Because the experience of uprootedness is not one of a moment, of a beginning. Rather, it is a continuum of long and short lines connected in jagged ways, like a constellation in which you can find each im-migrant, like a star, closer to or farther from home, occupying its own dot on the spectrum of belonging.

Home in Florida: Latinx Writers and the Literature of Uprootedness, then, is about how that turmoil-uproot-transplant-reroot process changes and defines the human beings who go through it and then, as in this case, how some of them, literally, live to write about it. It is about how the result, the contributions of these uprooted people (and their descendants), reshaped by all that new rooting soil, that *enraizante*, in turn changes the people and places they learn to call home. Like you, maybe. But really, like all of us who live in the kind of places where, it seems, the dreams of the uprooted stop to rest more often, to catch their breath long enough to wonder, "What if I stayed? What if here could one day be my home?"

There's another big concept in the title of this book. Latinx. It is a term some people say shouldn't even exist. That it is a made-up thing. Something advertis-ers and politicians created in order to form a more powerful buying market, a more influential voting block than if considered by each individual country of origin. They are right, in a sense.

But that is the thing with creations. They live. Take hold. They come to mean something. For me, "Latinx" is the word that defines the collective immigrant experience of people who share a past.

What past? The colonization of our countries, of course. The Spanish language? The Catholic religion? Both were imposed on us. The inherent culture of corruption that is colonization was beaten in so early and so violently that the leftovers still remain in the constant political instability, in the ever-present teetering toward autocracy of so many of our countries once ruled by Spain and Portugal, in so many laws and official customs arranged so as to still be prone to the intrinsic exploitation of occupation.

But that past is also present in our culture. The one reflected in how we use the same ingredients but cook them in different ways. In the common celebrations, the superstitions, the things *abuelas* teach their American-born grandchildren every day in this country, whether they are from Cuba or from Argentina. From Mexico or Venezuela. Those are the things that remain and make us seem more similar than we are, at least to the untrained.

Meanwhile, language changes over time. It is why you need not speak Spanish yourself to be Latinx. Because what makes a Latinx person Latinx is experiential.

That is why the word "Hispanic" is inadequate to talk about uprootedness. You see, once born, Hispanics are Hispanic no matter where they go. But we are only Latinos *here*. In our countries we are Cuban, Argentine, Mexican. By virtue of sharing the immigrant experience along with our similar pasts, we become Latinos. People trying to make the "here" our home while offering the culture of the place we (or our ancestors) came from, the best of us, in exchange: our gift to this country. *Soy de allá, pero vivo aquí*, as writer Isvett Verde says in her essay of the same title. I've chosen. Here's where I want to be.

This is all, of course, not new. The experience of the writer is how we've always given context to literature (and to every art, really). Why else would it be important to study Russian versus French literature, to know how they differ? It is because the lived experiences of writers are what enlighten their histories, and our own. They are what makes life clear, what enriches our understanding of humanity. And isn't that why we read, in the end?

Let's return now to the continuum of uprootedness I mentioned earlier. What does it look like beyond abstractions, and how does it make this book you now hold in your hands, or on your device, different?

We might draw two points. One, located at the start, on the left side of what will be an uneven line, holds your recently uprooted: the soon-to-returns, the just-arrives, the what-have-I-dones, souls with turmoil tattooed in indigo on the whites of their eyes, their gaze always lost, their eyelids heavy from having to look inward to find what they never imagined they'd miss this much. If they are writers, they do not write. Not now. They first need a job, a physical address, a first paycheck with which to send money back home. Not now. Why write? Nobody knows them here. Who would translate and publish them? It's too soon. They've had no time to create community. They are surviving, and even those rules, they are still learning.

The other dot goes on the opposite end of the spectrum, the right side, where you have the people you think of when you hear the term "Latinx." Many are second generation. The rest have been here long enough. They may or may not speak Spanish. They have jobs and speak English better than most and, in the worst of cases, certainly enough to get by. They have made a choice, in their hearts this time, or their parents made it for them before they were born. If they are writers, you'll have heard about their writing. Not just because they are widely published and reviewed, recognized, as is the case with the majority of the less recent émigrés in this book, but because they've been here long enough to have found their people: other writers. They have a voice, and any sadness has been tempered, processed, written, and given a drawer. Sometimes close to the front door. Sometimes in the most hidden of bedrooms.

Between the two ends of this spectrum I've tried to describe for you are lines, jaggedly connected, a zigzag of them teeming with stars, each in a unique spot on the road to belonging, and shifting daily in one direction . . . or the other.

And so, what might make the experience of reading this collection different for you, dear Person, is that it includes writers from the entirety of the spectrum. The best Latinx voices from the right side you've read or been told to read. But *also* those new Latinx writers who fall under the fog of a category that is on the left side of the continuum. The ones who managed to write important stories for this collection with the fresh perspectives that not yet belonging gives them. The ones who wrote anyway when immigrant life told them "Not now." Their stories are the ones not often found in English-language anthologies like this one because our radars tend not to track the left side of the spectrum of uprootedness, when most writers are surviving and not writing, or at least not as much as they might have in their countries of origin, too broken to write after the long voyage here and the even longer goodbye to all that they left.

Here, you will also find writers who left us too soon, like Reinaldo Arenas,

Guillermo Rosales, and Judith Ortiz Cofer. Their stories, essays, and poems included serve as a window into the past of Florida, so we might judge what "Home in Florida" might have meant for a Latinx writer two or three decades ago and learn for ourselves the factors that made the uprooting of such gifted souls possible in some cases, tragically impossible in others.

Incredible word, uprootedness, isn't it? Always hiding inside itself the notion of home, which is the last big concept in this book: Home in Florida, or not.

To many of the writers in this book, Florida was destiny. They were not supposed to come here. Or if they were born here, they were supposed to have left a long time ago. Some, indeed, left and were back before they knew it. Others ended up here by mistake, or their parents did, and Florida, whichever one of its corners but more commonly the southern one, became a temporary place for waiting until it was safe to go back where they came from. Others left, unable to find their dreams, but most importantly, themselves, here.

Of course, for those who stayed, it wasn't an easy decision.

There was racism. There still is. It used to be in the signs reading "No Cubans. No Dogs" common in Miami Beach in the '70s and '80s. Now it is in the voice of the potential landlord who hangs up before you can tell her you also speak English.

There were riots stemming from the same racism when directed at others, most often, African Americans.

There was confusion and sometimes corruption, born of the mix of dreams and heat.

Look at them, tsk, tsk, the rest of country seems to say, at times. Is Florida even part of the United States?

It absolutely is. Home to 21.5 million people, out of which 5.8 million, 27 percent, are Latinos, according to preliminary numbers of the 2020 Census. That is diversity, and diversity is messy.

And I won't lie. Or say that what you've noticed isn't true. For many, Florida is a world of misplaced nostalgia. There are some Floridians who pine for the Blue Moon '50s and those twist-and-shout "Happy Days" of fifteen-cent malted shakes and places where everybody knew your name. They resent the change and the foreigners, even those who were born here, and work overtime to capture the Florida of the past that still lives in their hearts but wasn't really very happy for anyone else.

For others, the nostalgia is for a different place, one left behind, that also may or may not have existed, but where they experienced childhood, first love, family. These people struggle between memory and presence. Struggle to make this their forever home. To contribute to it. To learn from it. To share themselves with it. To belong beyond politics.

They come here, and they stay because once you are home, you don't leave if you can humanly avoid it.

Then there are the people who make it possible to stay. Sometimes they are native to Florida. Sometimes they, too, are immigrants, from another state or from another stage of life. Often they are not Latino. They are Caucasian, Black, Native American, Italian, Irish, and more. They know that on the other end of diversity and acceptance there is progress, vibrancy, flavor, economic progress, and yes, heightened positive cultural experiences, as in literature. The catch? The occasional chaos of change.

But they don't like the cold either, so there is that. They like being able to easily find a good Cuban coffee *colada* or *cortadito*. These Floridians love being open to the world and that Florida is not like any other state. They like having access to different cultures and might think about learning Spanish to go with their French. They are curious. They think Florida is big enough for all of us. They know we all have value. They say, "Why would I want everything to stay exactly the same? I'm not dead, you know?"

This mix of readers, you among them, dear Person still with me, is why this book is not limited, or even organized, by genre—fiction, nonfiction, poetry. But we did make sure to distinguish between fiction and nonfiction within each entry because, in narrative, when writers do their job, as they have here, the truth is stranger than fiction, and fiction is just the lie that tells a truth, as (transplanted) longtime Florida writer John Dufresne says in his book thus titled.

Instead, the works here are organized in the same experiential way in which rerootedness might occur, the emotional weight of each piece guiding the way, composed like a song on the spectrum of belonging with love letters to Florida, prose songs about Florida, rants and manifestos against Florida, jokes, lyric essays, cries and promises, real vows of the can't-quit-you kind, and short stories based on things remembered because they happened here and we had just arrived or had been here a long time and wondered, still, if we were home, if we would ever be. This, even if we were born here, but especially if we were not.

Some writers didn't stay. But those who did have gotten used to the angst of something (often, something weird) always happening in Florida: crocodiles who eat your breakfast, Miami blue butterflies migrating to Key West, robbers who come back and return the money when they realize they committed a theft on Good Friday. All of this distracting from another kind of angst over what is being buried by time, by a hurricane, a tornado, by water rising above you, all around you, around and over your home, as you struggle to claim the soil sliding away by naming, naming, naming in order to feel sheltered, protected, belonging, at home.

They don't want to be just another loud-talking Latinx person living in, where else? Florida. They want to give back. So they stay. They stay and one day something happens and they are shocked to know, to feel, they *are* home. They may still not be sure they belong here, but it's home. Somehow, Florida has seeped in. Gotten inside but good, like mold from the swamps. Inside even the skin/home they brought with them and carry around like backpacking snails. Like the laughter that surprises you, making you snort out loud before you've had a chance to think, hold back. Or like tears that have no reason for being, just that it's December and the Florida cold (that nobody else thinks is cold) makes you think of that other place that wasn't cold, or was colder, or was just cold enough and perfect in your memory. That moment . . . that is the moment these works seek. The moment we learned we were home. In Florida, despite it all, or because of it.

PATRICIA ENGEL is the author of *The Veins of the Ocean* (Grove, 2016), winner of the Dayton Literary Peace Prize; *It's Not Love, It's Just Paris* (Grove, 2013), winner of the International Latino Book Award; *Vida* (Black Cat, 2010), a finalist for the Pen/Hemingway and Young Lions Fiction Awards, a *New York Times* Notable Book, and winner of Colombia's national book award, the Premio Biblioteca de Narrativa Colombiana; and *Infinite Country* (Avid Reader, 2021), a *New York Times* bestseller. She is a recipient of fellowships from the Guggenheim Foundation and the National Endowment for the Arts. Her stories appear in *The Best American Short Stories 2017*, *The Best American Mystery Stories 2014*, *The O. Henry Prize Stories 2019*, and elsewhere. Born to Colombian parents, Patricia is associate professor in the MFA in Creative Writing Program at the University of Miami.

"La Ciudad Magica" is nonfiction.

> You overhear their lunch conversation, comparing nannies by country of origin. "I prefer the Panamanians and Nicaraguans," says one woman, picking at her salad, "because they know their place. They don't try to get too friendly with me. I hate that."
>
> From "La Ciudad Mágica"

LA CIUDAD MÁGICA

You see them walking along the shaded perimeters of parks, dressed like nurses in pressed white uniforms, pushing strollers, talking to the babies in their care. You see them sitting together on benches near the playground, watching the children on the swings, occasionally calling to them not to climb so high on the jungle gym.

You see them walking along the road, carrying the child's backpack on the way home from school, while the child walks a few steps ahead, laughing with a friend. You see these women waiting outside of karate and ballet class, sitting in church pews beside the children on Sundays.

You see these women at the supermarket, pushing the cart down the aisle, the child perched atop the seat, legs dangling between the metal rails, while she pulls food from the shelves to buy and prepare for the family. You see these women sitting at the end of tables in restaurants, keeping the children entertained with coloring books and video games, cutting their food into small pieces, whisper-begging the child to take another bite, so as not to interrupt the parents' dinner conversation.

You see these women in the morning, as early as sunrise, stepping off the bus from the downtown terminal, walking quickly along the avenue to arrive at the place of their employment in time to wake the children, feed them breakfast, and get them ready for school.

You see these women in the evening, sitting five to a bench beneath the bus stop shelter, shielding themselves from the summer sun or from the winter rain, waiting for the bus to come to take them home.

*

A group of mothers dressed in exercise clothes, adorned with jewelry and painted with makeup, gather for lunch at a café in Coral Gables—where streets lined with ficus and poinciana trees have Spanish names like Valencia, Minorca, and Ponce de León.

You overhear their lunch conversation, comparing nannies by country of origin.

"I prefer the Panamanians and Nicaraguans," says one woman, picking at her salad, "because they know their place. They don't try to get too friendly with me. I hate that."

Another woman jumps in. "Oh, you mean when they address you directly? My God, it's like, 'Who gave you permission to open your mouth?'"

"Brazilians are just crazy, and you can't trust Colombians or Ecuadorians. They steal and they'll flirt with your husband," offers another woman. "Don't even bother trying them out. And Guatemalans come with too many problems. They're always crying about something. Like, hello? I hired a nanny, not a charity!"

The women laugh, then brag to each other how their children are fluent in Spanish, and though it annoys them that now the nannies and their offspring can have private conversations, at least it's still cheaper than hiring an American babysitter or paying an agency commission for a European au pair.

*

Tuesday morning at a bakery in The Roads.

Two men ahead of you on the counter line catch up after not having seen each other in a while.

One man tells the other he and his family plan on moving away soon.

"We're tired of feeling like foreigners around here. You can't go anywhere in this city without hearing Spanish spoken. I don't want my children growing up around that."

He says they're thinking about moving north to Broward or Collier County. "Somewhere spic-free."

"But they're everywhere," his friend laughs. "You can't escape them."

"We want to get away from the Miami kind. They're the ones taking over."

Then each man takes his turn at the counter, ordering a dozen empanadas to go.

*

After eight days at sea, twenty-four Cuban migrants making their way to Florida shores on a shabby vessel spot the Coast Guard in their wake. They throw themselves into the water and climb the American Shoal Lighthouse six miles off the coast of Sugarloaf Key, hoping it will amount to having touched dry land. It takes an entire day for officials to coax the Cubans off the red iron lighthouse rails. They are detained for a month until a judge rules that the lighthouse, despite its name, does not count as U.S. soil. The Cubans will be repatriated and will likely serve prison sentences for having fled their island.

*

The Magic City.
La Puerta de las Américas.
The Capital of Latin America.

*

The rainbowed Brickell Avenue highrises made as famous as the flamingos in the opening credits of *Miami Vice* are now tiny folds in a much taller and more congested panorama of mirrored towers that glisten like machetes; the Miami that cocaine and money laundering built.

Brickell Avenue snakes into Biscayne Boulevard, cutting through downtown, a place everyone but the diamond and drug dealers used to avoid, now lined with new condos and chic restaurants, with a view of the restored waterfront parks, unfolding along the bay into urban pockets where longtime residents have been edged out by developers and hiked rents, christened with catchy names and written about in travel magazines as the trendy new neighborhoods to explore.

*

Far down Biscayne, in a sleepy subdivision built along the Intracoastal, your friends Joe and Nicole live in a small stucco house with a red-shingle Spanish roof. Their next-door neighbors recently moved out so their baby could pursue a career in toddler modeling in Atlanta. A single guy in his forties moved in a few weeks later.

You all assume he's a bachelor because of the different girls coming to the house. Young, beautiful. Some in fancy cars. Others dropped off. There is a girl who arrives on a skateboard. Another, on her own Ducati.

One day while barbecuing in the backyard, Joe decides the neighborly thing is to invite the bachelor over.

The guy arrives and drinks tequilas around the patio table till long after dark.

At one point he leans over to you and says, "I hear you're Colombian. I've got a couple of Colombian girls working for me. They're the best. Second only to the Russians."

You ask what sort of business he's in.

"Film production."

"What kind of films?"

"Well, not really films, per se. More like video production. For the internet."

Another tequila and the guy admits he's running a porn studio out of his house. Each bedroom outfitted with lights and cameras operated from a central control room. The girls perform for subscription internet channels. Most have loyal followings and do private shows, sometimes alone, sometimes with each other.

"Where do you find these girls?" is all you think to ask.

"It's easy. One girl tells another. I've got a waitlist thirty girls deep."

He pats your hand as if to assure you.

"Believe me, it's all perfectly legal. I don't hire minors. I leave that to the guys up in Fort Lauderdale."

*

In the mailroom of your apartment building, you say hello to another resident checking her box near yours. She's the type who complains about anything. The weather. The color of the paint on the walls. A speck of lint on the lobby floor. "This country is screwed," she always says, "especially Florida." She kicks herself every day for moving down from Delaware twenty years ago and constantly threatens to go back.

"How's work?" you say.

She's a masseuse and tells you her least favorite clients are the "Latins" because they make her use the service entrance when entering their homes—the same door meant for the maids, cooks, and plumbers.

"Can you imagine?" she says, horror streaked across her face. "They treat me like a servant. They don't even want me to walk in the front door. They act like they own this city. They're so entitled. They've ruined Miami, turning it into their own colony."

"Now you know how it feels," you say, dropping your junk mail in the garbage.

Your neighbor stares at you, her pale cheeks flushed with anger, but says nothing in response and walks away.

*

There's a saying locals throw around:

The best thing about Miami is how close it is to the United States.

*

They come from other cities and from other countries, looking for paradise by the sea; looking to be South Beach models, to marry rich and become queens of Star Island, but instead find themselves in the republic of pills and powders and paid sex.

You see them standing outside of hotel lobbies on Collins Avenue, dressed in designer clothes, balanced on sharp high heels. Legs tanned and shiny. Breasts large and fake. You see tourist men come out of the building to look for a girl to take in to the hotel bar, or up to a room. You see red rented Ferraris pull up to the curb and the women step over to them casually, as if the man is just asking for directions, and then climb into the passenger seat. He doesn't even open the door for her.

You see them walking along Biscayne Boulevard, even in parts the city has worked so hard to clean up. You see them outside of the Wonderland strip club on 79th, ignored by cops patrolling the area, and among the homeless and stray dogs in the concrete yards beneath I-95 that use to hold the Mariel refugee tent city.

You see them standing outside the motels among teenagers smoking cigarettes and working as lookouts for drug dealers. You see them wandering the few vacant lots still left along the bay that haven't yet been bulldozed and flattened to make room for more skyscrapers; the ones where body parts often wash up—a hand, a foot, even a whole leg, that will remain forever unidentified.

You knew one of these girls once. A white Texan named Toni who worked a five-block stretch on lower Biscayne where your boyfriend at the time lived with his bandmates. She was always high and would get in the car of any guy who whistled her way, but always said hello and watched after you when you walked alone to your car late at night.

"This city's not safe for nice girls like you and me," she used to say.

One day her father came from Dallas to collect her. Everyone in the neighborhood heard her shouting that she didn't want to leave. You and your boyfriend watched from the second-floor window as she fell to her knees on the sidewalk and cried. But then her father scooped her up, embraced her long, and she let him take her home.

*

A dozen Cuban migrants land on the beach near your apartment building. They arrive in a motorless wooden boat loaded with broken paddles, empty water jugs, and a torn plastic sheet they used as sail during their two weeks at sea. They are sunburned and filthy, thin, their faces crusted with sea salt. A mob of beachgoers gather on the sand around them, welcoming them to Miami, offering the migrants their sunglasses, hats, towels, and shirts with which to cover their charred shoulders; water and beers from their coolers, until the police arrive to process them for amnesty, and release them to their relatives.

*

La Ciudad Mágica.
La Ciudad del Sol.
Cuba con Coca-Cola.

*

Down U.S. 1, past the waterfront mansions of Coco Plum and Gables by the Sea, the sprawling estates and ranches of Pinecrest, a few turns off the highway onto a narrow dusty road, you find people selling fruit out of tin shacks; papayas the size of footballs, guanábana, carambola, starfruit, and unbruised mangos, perfectly ripe, erupting with nectar.

Here you will drink straight from the coconut while, a few yards down, another vendor offers barbecued iguana—the same ones they sell in pet stores that owners grow bored of and release to the wild, and people in the suburbs pay to have removed from their property or wild hog, alligator, and diced python, served with hot sauce and rice, freshly hunted down in the Everglades.

Out here, you can pick out a pig from a corral and they'll slaughter it right in front of you, ready to take home, head and all, to roast for all your friends in your caja china; or you can whisper your request to a guy who knows another guy, and in a few minutes find someone to sell you horsemeat.

Out here you can watch a live dog fight, buy a peacock to take home and keep in your backyard to protect you from the evil eye of your enemies, have your illnesses cured by the polvos of a curandero, and a spell cast by a brujo so you'll be lucky in money and in love.

Nobody will ever know you were here.

*

The shrine to La Virgen de la Caridad del Cobre sits on Biscayne Bay, with its own replica of the Havana malecón. Elderly people are bused in daily from retirement communities and senior centers; families come together in pilgrimage from all over the state. Here, people gather to pray to Cuba's patron saint and to leave sunflowers for her other face, the orisha Ochún.

A year ago, on a day like any other, as the viejitos sat before the altar praying for freedom from Fidel, as they often do, President Obama entered the church unannounced, walked down the aisle, and knelt beside the faithful in the pews.

Your friend Alejandro's grandmother was there.

She said it was like seeing Jesucristo himself.

Alejo was born in Cuba and spent three months in a Guantanamo refugee camp before his family received permission to enter the U.S. His father worked as a dishwasher in Sweetwater. His mother sold watermelons at the intersection of 87th Avenue and Coral Way. He's a lawyer now and plans on running for a public office.

"Why do you think Obama came that day?" he says. "It's because every politician knows that without the abuelos of Miami in your pocket, you won't make it to the corner."

He says there are other major Latino cities. Los Angeles. Houston, San Diego. Even Chicago and New York. But none like Miami, where a national minority is the ruling majority, with sixty-seven percent of the population, where the money and the political power sits firmly in Latino hands.

"Miami is the city of the future," Alejo says, "and in a few years, the rest of the country will finally catch up."

*

Your Miami begins in New Jersey where you were raised far from the ocean in an Anglo suburb near woods and mountains, speaking Spanish among family and close friends, while outside your home, classmates and townspeople mocked the color of your skin and your parents' accents, asking with suspicion how they managed to come to this country, and they'd answer that they came on a jet plane.

Your only community was your family. From the world beyond your tíos and primos, you were made to understand, before you could spell your own name, that even if you were born in this country, even if you speak the language, you will always be an outsider; this country will never belong to you.

Your Miami begins in New York, where you moved to at eighteen, lived in different downtown apartments and tried on different lives for over a decade before finally deciding to leave.

Your Miami begins in the Andean highlands, across the mountainous cordillera, low in the valleys of the Río Cauca, and deep in the wetlands of the Orinoco; before Bolívar, before the conquest, before Colombia was Colombia, when you were Muisca and spoke Chibcha; and before that, it begins across the Atlantic, on the northern coast of Africa.

Your Miami begins in Puerto Rico, where your older brother was born, and before that, it begins in the other América, where you father worked since age fourteen to support his family of eleven in Medellín; where your parents married in a chilly church in Bogotá; your Miami begins in Colombia, the country your parents loved but left, like so many others, so you, the child they did not yet know they would have, might have a chance at something more.

*

After they settled in the United States, as soon as they could afford it, your father took your mother on vacation to Miami. There is a photograph of her leaning on a crooked palm tree in the last pink hour before sunset. She stares at your father, who holds the camera. She is barely twenty-two. Her long hair colored a rusty red, still pearl-skinned from the lifelong overcast of Bogotá despite her indigenous blood.

There is a picture of you holding your father's hand a decade later; you, a child of two or three years old. Your mother took the photograph from the beach while your father led you into the shallow and flat edge of the ocean. He stands above you like a tower; you, in your red gingham baby-bikini. They tell you that you hated the ocean when you first felt it on your skin. You tried to stomp and slap it away. You cried and reached for firm land. But then something changed and you began to swim on your own before you could speak full sentences. And then they couldn't pull you out of the water.

As you grew older, despite the years you spent in other cities, feeling their claim on you, you knew Miami would one day be your home, at least for a little while.

You are not a refugee, but here in Miami you believe you have found a sort of refuge.

*

You walk along a nature trail in one of the city's spectacular ecological reserves, canopied with thick banyans and mangroves lining a lagoon. As you pass him standing on the edge of the trail, an old man with a thick belly and a T-shirt crescented with pit stains calls you over to him and points out a fat, furry, golden weaver, what locals call "lighting spiders," centered on a web shining like glass in the fractured sunlight.

"That is one big spider," you say.

"I used to practice shooting on them when I was a kid. Till I got bitten by one and my hand swelled so much the skin split like a banana peel."

He misses the old Miami, he says, when it was vast and empty, and you could walk for miles from what's now the Palmetto Expressway to Diner Key and not run into a soul.

"Now it's crazy and crowded and full of foreigners. It's like watching your first love turn into a junkie and finding her begging for pennies under the highway."

You tell him you still think there's a lot of beauty to Miami. Just look around.

"You didn't grow up around here. I can tell."

"That's right. I didn't. But I've lived here for twelve years so far."

"You're real brown. How'd you learn to speak English so good?"

You look back at the spider and then at the man, tell him to have a nice day, continue on your way down the trail, leaving him alone by the trees.

The man calls after you.

"You watch out for those big spiders, girl. Miami is dangerous territory. Remember, there are people like me out there."

NATALIE SCENTERS-ZAPICO is a poet, educator, and activist from the sister cities of El Paso, Texas, USA, and Ciudad Juárez, Chihuahua, Mexico. She is the author of *Lima :: Limón* (Copper Canyon, 2019) and *The Verging Cities* (Colorado State University Press, 2015). Her books have been reviewed widely in prominent periodicals like the *New Yorker*, *New York Times*, and *Washington Post* as well as platforms like NPR. Natalie's poems have been published and anthologized in a wide range of nationally and internationally distributed journals including *Poetry*, *Paris Review*, *Kenyon Review*, and *Best American Poetry 2015*. She is the winner of awards and fellowships from CantoMundo (2015); PEN/America, the Great Lakes Colleges Association, and the Lannan Foundation (2017); and a Ruth Lilly and Dorothy Sargent Rosenberg Fellowship from the Poetry Foundation (2018). She was a finalist for the Kingsley Tufts Poetry Award and the International Griffin Poetry Prize (2020).

Scenters-Zapico is an assistant professor of poetry at the University of South Florida in Tampa, where she lives with her husband, José Ángel Maldonado, an assistant professor of cultural rhetorics in USF's Department of English.

because he's a citizen de los united estates.

I got a stove this big, a refri this full, a mirror

just to see my pretty face.

From "My Macho Takes Care of Me Good"

NOTES ON MY PRESENT: A CONTRAPUNTAL

I write my body, as border between

    We have some bad hombres here

this rock & the absence of water.

    & we're going to get them out.

I cut myself with a scimitar,

    When Mexico sends its people,

as political documentation.

    they're not sending their best.

How do you write about the violence

    They're not sending you.

of every man you've ever loved?

    They're sending people

Macho, you

    that have lots of problems

breathe bright in the neocolony,

    & they're bringing those problems to us.

a problem of Empire pulling

    They're bringing drugs. They're bringing

the capitalist threads of my border.

    crime. They're rapists.

Empire: you were so sterile

    Mexico's court system is corrupt.

& shiny with your dead man's coins

    I want nothing to do with Mexico

& castration, your white roses

    other than to build an impenetrable

& that trash bag full of a Mexican

    WALL & stop them from ripping

woman's dark hair. Empire: you

    off U.S. I love the Mexican people,

made us hungry for the glint

    but Mexico is not our friend.

of machismo, the dim glare

    They're killing us at the border

of marianismo. Tonight on TV,

& they're killing us on jobs & trade.

muted montages of the largest

FIGHT! Happy Cinco de Mayo!

ICE raid in Texas. I drink

The best taco bowls are made

pink champagne in a hotel bar,

in Trump Tower Grill. I love Hispanics!

& correct the pronunciation of my name.

MY MACHO TAKES CARE OF ME GOOD

because he's a citizen de los united estates.
I got a stove this big, a refri this full, a mirror
just to see my pretty face. He says:

My name's on this license. I drive la troca,
so you don't have to, mija. I am a citizen
de los united estates. Because he's a citizen,

we are muy lejos de dios, but we love
los united estates. I don't wash laundry with cakes
of jabón zote, because my macho

takes care of me good. I bring my macho
Nescafé, American made, because he's a citizen
de los united estates. I ask for feria to go to a doctor,

& he says: *Ingrata, you're not sick.*
I clean chiles, then rub my eyes—
¡Siempre llora-lloras, chillona!

& he's right, I lloro-lloro sin saber
por qué. I bring my macho smoke in a glass
& smooth every shirt with my new electric iron.

He says: *No hay nadie en casa. Why wear*
clothes at all? So I don't. I fry chicharrones.
Hiss-hiss, across my bare skin. *Bang-bang,*

my macho's fists on the table. He wants más, más,
y más in his united estates. I give him all of me
served on a platter from back home:

plump, cracked, and ready-made. *Crunch-crunch,*
eats my macho. *You married him,* says my mother,
& he takes care of you good in his united estates.

BUEN ESQUELETO

Life is short, & I tell this to mis hijas.
Life is short, & I show them how to talk
to police without opening the door, how
to leave the social security number blank
on the exam, I tell this to mis hijas.
This world tells them I hate you every day
& I don't keep this from mis hijas
because of the bus driver who kicks them out
onto the street for fare evasion. Because I love
mis hijas, I keep them from men who'd knock
their heads together just to hear the chime.
Life is short & the world is terrible. I know
no kind strangers in this country who aren't
sisters a desert away, & I don't keep this
from mis hijas. It's not my job to sell
them the world, but to keep them safe
in case I get deported. Our first
landlord said with a bucket of bleach
the mold would come right off. He shook
mis hijas, said they had good bones
for hard work. *Mi'jas, could we make this place*
beautiful? I tried to make this place beautiful.

NILSA ADA RIVERA writes about gender and diversity is-sues. She is the former managing editor of *The Wardrobe* and the nonfiction editor of *Doubleback Review*. Her work appears in *Huff-ington Post*, *50 GS Magazine*, *Six Hens Literary Journal*, *Assay: A Journal of Nonfiction Studies*, *Selkie Literary Magazine*, *Quillkeepers Press*, and *Writing Class Radio*. She is an MFA candidate in nonfic-tion at Vermont College of Fine Art, was born in New York, of Puerto Rican ancestry, and lives in Riverview, Florida.

"I Write to Mami about Florida" is nonfiction.

How could you just leave me by myself? And in Miami?

From "I Write to Mami about Florida"

I WRITE TO MAMI ABOUT FLORIDA

November 30, 1990

Querida Mami,

Where are the green mountains and the rivers in Miami? I only see factories and warehouses here; my sole distraction is the constant back and forth of the trucks. I can't play on the street because you think a truck will hit me or someone will steal me. You don't trust the warehouse owners who come to work in their BMWs or Benzes, lock their doors, and leave before the sun disappears. Or the men who walk down the street so drunk or high their blank eyes can only manage to gawk at us.

    The rainwater that gets in through the windows of our apartment has replaced my favorite river. How is this better than living in the mountains next to a river in Puerto Rico? I know you had to leave Papi because he's too mean, but I miss the hills, the scents of oregano and coffee, and the river. I miss the wind hitting my face when I rode my bike down the hill while my friends screamed and laughed. I even miss Papi's beer and nicotine smell. I miss the times you and I sat together overlooking the mountains so green it seemed God had thrown an emerald blanket over the world. Unlike you, the only reason Miami makes my heart beat like a drum is because my birth mom and sisters are here. I hope Reina finally realizes that I'm her daughter too.

Xoxo,
Your confused granddaughter

June 27, 1991

Querida Mami,

My sisters finally took me to the bay today. The whole ocean was there, right in front of us. If we lived in the bottom of the ocean, I wouldn't have to lose my accent or deal with Reina's drunkenness. We would have food, a sand castle, and the dolphins could take us anywhere we wanted to be without us ever needing money. Wouldn't that be awesome?

How come we live in Miami if Reina and I were born in NY? I don't know if I would've liked NY. I love Puerto Rico. Maybe it's because of all those years I lived there or because it was your home. Despite Papi, you seemed happier there, and I was too. I guess because that's where your family is. It was the only place I felt at home and I miss home. My consolation is that in Miami the ocean is closer.

Xoxo,
Your adjusting granddaughter

January 13, 1992

Querida Mami,

How could you just leave me by myself? And in Miami? I'm only fourteen and you die. You've abandoned me just like Reina did. I thought it was us against the world forever. I know my real mom is here, in this stupid place, but she's always drunk or high. You were not just my grandmother; you were my true mother.

Xoxo,
Your ditched daughter

July 16, 1992

Querida Mami,

Reina kicked me out. I don't know where I'm supposed to go. Maybe I'll go to the bay. I told you she doesn't love me. How could you have loved this place? How could you have loved her?

Xoxo,
Your homeless daughter

March 4, 1993

Querida Mami,

A few months ago, I moved in with my boyfriend. He has his own apartment. He's a little mean like Papi, but at least, I have a bed now. I miss Puerto Rico so much. My room, my bed, my friends, you.

I turned fifteen today. Sorry I don't write often. I don't know where these letters will end. I'm sending them to our old address in PR. I guess I have to accept that you'll never get them, but I'm writing them anyway.

Xoxo,
Your birthday girl

January 30, 1995

Querida Mami,

I learned that men hurt too much. Is this what you meant when you said not to smile at or trust them? I know men are like this in PR too. I know Papi was like this, but at least in PR, I had family. I had you. Don't say I have my real mom because I don't. She's in another world, a world where smoke is oxygen, liquor is water, and drug is her nourishment.

I have a son now, Kervin. My world is made of bottles filled with WIC formula, twenty-five cent jars of baby food and water, ripped T-shirts to make diapers, and the search for a new home. Your grandson sleeps in my friend's apartment while I work at a bar. The owner knows I'm seventeen, but she lets me work anyway. Soon, I'll have my own apartment, hopefully somewhere far away from Florida, and no man will ever hit me or my son.

Miami is so rough. Its streets are hot and hungry. Hungry for my body, my mind, my life, and my freedom. The streets are always dirty, dirty needles and pipes, dirty clothes, dirty cardboards, and overgrown grass that lets me hide in it so I can sleep for a few hours before dawn. I miss my bed and the sounds of coquís, and of course, you. Why did you leave me here?

Xoxo,
Your lost girl

August 29, 1998

Querida Mami,

I tried to steal my way out of Miami. I was tired of the BMWs and Benzes passing by while my son and I slept in a stolen Honda with broken windows. Every morning before the sun rises over Publix's parking lot, a man in a truck leaves a pallet of fresh bread and pastries, and I steal some of it. Kervin is four now. He's tired of the pastries. He wants nuggets and fries, but I can't steal those.

Some places in Miami are clean. Coral Gables, I just learned, has safe parks with trimmed landscapes and water fountains. Their playgrounds don't get vandalized. Their houses have gardens full of orchids and colorful flowers, no boys standing on the corners, no young girls pushing strollers down the streets, no men smoking crack or drinking beers. Women in designer dresses and heels walk down long strips of sidewalk with elegant jewelry shops and clothing boutiques while they hold hands with their girlfriends or their men in polo shirts and linen suits. If there's a woman pushing a stroller, it is one of those fancy bassinets or a three-wheel stroller in which the baby looks like propped-up royalty. Everyone smiles and no one cries while shopping.

The cars are different too. I didn't see any broken-down Hondas or Toyotas. Even the banks in Coral Gables have more money. I know you taught me that envy is a sin and I should be humble, but Mami, we're hungry for a better life. Have you ever been so hungry you want to knock the food off someone's plate?

Well, I won't see any parks for a while, and I might lose my son. Miami's a poor person's trap, and I'm now snared in its claw. I'm sorry. Please send your blessings from above. We need them.

Xoxo,
Your caged girl

June 16, 2000

Querida Mami,

I still miss you and the mountains. Remember how I used to run barefoot to the river? Miami is changing and I am too. I have a job now and I'm going to college. I bought a hoopty with the financial aid refund. It's a shitty car, but it takes me to work and school.

The street is not my home anymore. Now, I live in a mobile home. Do they have trailer parks in Puerto Rico?

It's not as clean as Coral Gables or Kendall (another upscale community), but some of my neighbors grow flowers in their mini-gardens. I even bought your favorite violet orchid and put it in a tree by my mobile home. My trailer is baby blue like the sea. Maybe I finally found my spot in the bottom of the ocean, but you are still missing.

My neighbors are Puerto Ricans, Cubans, Peruvians, Dominicans, Haitians, Blacks, Hondurans, and even Whites. Every day, I walk around the trailer park smelling the blended scents of our lives. Mrs. Monica makes her beans with oregano, garlic, and onions. I can smell those beans a block away. Mr. Jones's always grilling BBQ ribs. Lucia's sweet pink roses soften the humid air. Nancy is always making cafecito. The coffee is not like the one in Puerto Rico, but it reminds me of it. Most people here are nice to me. They give me advice, bring my son and me food, and even come by to see how I'm doing.

I'm saving my money, Mami. My life is safer now, but soon it will be even better. Soon I'll never have to worry about being on the streets again.

Xoxo,
Your trailer park chick

March 4, 2003

Querida Mami,

In the last three years, I got married, had another son, and bought a house. Today is my 26th birthday, and I just closed the purchase of this house.

I wish you were alive to meet your grandsons, Kervin and Gio. I still miss you and PR. I wish I could visit the island, but I barely make enough to pay the mortgage. Some people call it living paycheck to paycheck. I call it dying with each bill.

Sometimes, I overdraft my bank account or don't pay the light bill so I can take my kids to the Miami Zoo in Kendall or to Rapid Waters in West Palm Beach. The cost of gas, food, admission fees, and any other fun activities or toys the boys want can amount to a good two hundred dollars. That's the whole light bill money. Driving to these attractions is expensive and far, but it's worth the gas, even if the car breaks down sometimes. I should be more responsible, but Mami, the boys have to know that Miami is more than the hood. That way, they'll dream of getting out. Hope is a fertilizer for motivation, and so is desperation, but I don't want them to know despair.

Not everyone accepts us in some neighborhoods. We visited a waterpark and they said we couldn't go in because we weren't residents of the City of Miami Shores, even though we live a block away from it. It's impossible for me to afford a house there, so we go to the beach. Miami Beach is better than that small waterpark could ever be. You never got a chance to visit the places that make Miami easier to digest so I still don't know why you loved it so much.

Xoxo,
Your irresponsible girl

December 29, 2007

Querida Mami,

It's when I get separated from a man that I remember how much you suffered, and the men-lessons you tried to instill in me. I should've listened better. I just got a divorce. He wasn't helpful to me or nice to Kervin, but I tried my best to make it work. I don't know how you did it. So many years with Papi. I think I understand why you brought me to Miami. You wanted to leave Papi and you tried to get Reina to take care of me. Of course, you didn't realize how addicted to drugs and alcohol she was.

Just like you, I've learned the hard way that when a woman leaves a man, even if it's for the best, she's always bound to suffer. If not for the loss of his love, it's because her children will miss him, or because the bills will need him.

A lot of people are losing their homes. The economy recently crashed for some people, but for others like me, it has always been broken. I won't return to the streets. No matter what. I'll fight for this house.

Miami has changed so much since you were here. Developers are building more condominiums. More people are moving here. The hood is being pushed north. The roads are still horrible. Crime is worse. The sea is claiming its land back, streets are getting flooded. This is a place of memories for me. A place that with a rough hand raised me. Miami crushed my soul, my mind, and my body, transforming me into a strong woman who will fight for what she wants. I doubt you ever imagined the effects Miami would have on me, but I'm finally becoming the woman you wanted me to be.

Xoxo,
Your determined woman

February 27, 2009

Querida Mami,

I wonder what my life would've been like if you had stayed in New York or
Puerto Rico. I make a bit more money now and can travel without worrying
about my car breaking down or running out of gas. In one day, I can get
a cafecito and buttery tostadas in Little Havana and watch the cruises
departing South Pointe. For lunch, I can go to Little Haiti for Chef Creole's
juicy oxtails. I can drive to Hialeah to buy clothes, and drive back fighting
with bad drivers while listening to bachata. Aventura Mall has my go-to
movie theater. Peruvian restaurants have the best ceviche. After that, I can
end my day reading at Books and Books, a local bookstore. In one day, I can
travel the world. The kids and I even visited the North Pole. Well, really just
Santa's Enchanted Forest.

I'm starting to think that to truly enjoy and love Miami, I have to have
money. This is the first time I can breathe Miami's air without suffocating. I
can almost smell the scent of home in the air without wanting to run.

Xoxo
Your traveling daughter

September 20, 2011

Querida Mami,

I finally made it out of Miami. I didn't go far: Orlando. I remember Papi
and you said you didn't like Orlando because it was deserted, but there are
more people now and the theme parks are fun. Supposedly, there's less crime.
Teenagers are dying in Miami by the dozen. I'm scared for my boys.

Orlando has its charms. The other night we heard a racket outside. When
my new boyfriend and I checked, it was hard to decipher the dark shadows
moving in our backyard. Then I saw it. A dark-haired hog at least four feet
long. Its long tusks reached its cheeks. The other feral hogs were smaller.
There must've been at least six or seven of them, Mami! Can you believe that?

By the time we figured it out, my boyfriend, my two sons, and I were
standing outside staring at them like if we were at an attraction park.
Kervin said, "Watch how they're going to run now," and ran back inside to
get his BB gun. I guess that's the Puerto Rican in him. The first shot startled

them. The second shot made the biggest hog dash toward him. We ran inside so fast we almost stumbled on each other. We had no other choice but to watch the hogs foraging our backyard from behind the sliding door. Feral hogs are not native of Florida, or North America for that matter. They were brought here by Spanish conquistadores or early European settlers. The hogs are immigrants like so many people in Florida. They have adapted, evolved, and survived. They've made the United States, and Florida, their home.

Slowly, I'm realizing Florida is my home too. Despite all the years of trying to leave, I'm still here, adapting, evolving, and surviving. The fight to survive and the constant evolution are common themes for almost everyone in Florida, a constant reinvention of who we are. A local business can be the shop around the corner for years and just when we're comfortable with its existence, it's gone. We must constantly adapt to new businesses and new neighborhoods. We are always forced to figure out who we are in relation to the various cultures and our roots. Through each reinvention, we hold on to whatever seems most concrete. We hold on to the ocean surrounding us, to the constant fight to survive, and to the memories we have made here.

Florida claims us too.

Somehow along the journey, I lost parts of me. I don't think in Spanish anymore. Don't remind me that I'm a second-generation American. I was holding on to my Puerto Rican roots as hard as I could. This land changes you, though. The boys don't speak Spanish. I'm trying to teach them how to remain Puerto Rican, but am I still Puerto Rican?

I've evolved into part White, Cuban, Peruvian, Honduran, and Dominican. I can prove it. I easily eat like a white person. I'm going vegetarian. It would've driven you nuts for me not to eat pernil or any meat. If I want to enjoy my evening, there are a thousand restaurants ready to serve me. I only go to Dominican hair salons because they understand my curls and know how to get rid of them. If I don't have Cuban cafecito, I get a headache. Even my boys are half-Cuban. Whenever I want seafood, I think Peruvian ceviche. I don't think I could live without these cultures.

When I don't recognize myself, I cook arroz con gandules while listening to salsa, just to inject some boricua back into my soul. I sometimes read in an hamaca and pray to Yemayá. Still, I fear, I'm losing you, your scent, your essence.

Xoxo,
Your diluted Puerto Rican

February 14, 2012

Querida Mami,

I'm getting married to a Florida native today. Does that mean I will never leave Florida? I'm in love, but I've learned love is temporary and Florida isn't. Florida is here to stay despite all the ecological predictions.

Xoxo,
Your married woman

May 20, 2014

Querida Mami,

I'm back in Miami. Orlando is too calm for me and I need to remember how to fight, how to survive. I miss the family, the cultures, even the traffic. I especially miss the ocean.

Xoxo,
Your Miami chick

July 16, 2020

Querida Mami,

The boys (well, Kervin's a young adult now, really) and my husband wanted to leave Miami. For the first time ever, I didn't. They didn't even care where we moved as long as we moved. They are concerned with the increased crime in Miami. Between cops and robbers, the most important men in my life thought they might lose their lives. Of course, we still lived in the hood so it's a possibility I didn't want to think about, but had to acknowledge.

So I found a compromise: Tampa. A city where diversity paints a mosaic picture; where people can be who they are and still connect with one another. There're Dominican salons, Vietnamese nail shops, Mexican taquerías, Puerto Rican restaurants, Cuban coffee stands, white bookstores, and soul food. These cultures are all part of me now.

In Tampa, the sun stays out even while it rains. The rain chooses which streets it will wet and which ones it won't touch. Palm trees fall with the faintest winds. Animals make themselves known and respected. Lizards still freeze and fall from the sky, and frogs invade homes. There's traffic and just the right dosage of meanness. Here in Tampa, I still see the fight in people's eyes. I still notice the frustrations that come from knowing that we could all be somewhere else, that Florida isn't the vacation paradise that we imagined. And yet, we still chose it as our home. Sometimes, I look at the ocean and it is as if the Mother Goddess had thrown a foaming blue serape over the land so I would know: I am finally home.

Xoxo,
Your Florida resident

JUDITH ORTIZ COFER was a critically acclaimed and widely published poet, novelist, and essayist. She was born in Hormigueros, Puerto Rico, but moved to the mainland when her military father was transferred to Paterson, New Jersey, and transplanted the family there. She spent her childhood and, indeed, her adult life, traveling frequently to and from Puerto Rico and the different parts of the country in which she lived, wrote, spoke, and taught, including the ten years she spent in Florida in the 1970s. She wrote extensively about the challenges of identity as a Puerto Rican, a woman, and a writer in the United States. She earned a BA in English from Augusta College in Georgia and an MFA in English from Florida Atlantic University, and she did graduate work at Oxford University. She was the lauded Regents and Franklin Professor of Creative Writing at the University of Georgia, where she taught literature and creative writing. In 2010, Ortiz Cofer was inducted into the Georgia Writers Hall of Fame for her mastery in exploring the incongruences and gaps that arose from her divided cultural origins. More about her life and works is available at http://judithortizcofer.english.uga.edu

"The Cruel Country (Excerpt 68)" is nonfiction.

Homesickness is called a sickness for a reason.

From "The Cruel Country (Excerpt 68)"

THE CRUEL COUNTRY (EXCERPT 68)

Homesickness is called a sickness for a reason. It can be either brief or chronic, and when it becomes a permanent part of one's life, as it must have for my mother and perhaps my father, it turns into what has been labeled by sociologists as cultural grief or bereavement, and by my native culture as *la tristeza*— that is, a sense of loss that does not abate. In trying to understand what my parents must have felt when they left their culture as young people, I researched cultural grief, "el duelo cultural," and found a list of symptoms and behaviors familiar from our early lives on the mainland. In Spanish, the symptoms sound like a religious litany: *el duelo por la familia y los amigos, el duelo por la lengua, el duelo por la cultura, el duelo por la tierra, el duelo por el contacto con el grupo étnico, el duelo por los riesgos físicos, el duelo por la pérdida del proyecto migratorio, el duelo por no poder regresar.* Grief over the loss of family and friends, over the loss of the mother tongue, over the loss of culture; grief over the loss of the homeland, over the loss of contact with your ethnic group, over the fear of physical danger; grief over the loss of the original dream, and the grief of no possible return.

EL OLVIDO

It is a dangerous thing
to forget the climate of your birthplace,
to choke out the voices of dead relatives
when in dreams they call you
by your secret name.
It is dangerous
to spurn the clothes you were born to wear
for the sake of fashion; dangerous
to use weapons and sharp instruments
you are not familiar with; dangerous
to disdain the plaster saints
before which your mother kneels
praying with embarrassing fervor
that you survive in the place you have chosen to live:
a bare, cold room with no pictures on the walls,
a forgetting place where she fears you will die
of loneliness and exposure.
Jesús, María, y José, she says,
el olvido is a dangerous thing.

VERA (HERNÁN VERA ÁLVAREZ) was born in Buenos Aires in 1977. A writer, cartoonist, and frequent editor, he studied literature at Florida International University and has, for years, taught creative writing for a variety of institutions, among them Miami Dade College's Koubek Center. He is the author of the poetry collection *Los románticos eléctricos* (Sudaquia, 2020); the novel *La librería del mal salvaje* (SED, 2018), which won a Florida Book Award the following year; the short-story collections *Grand Nocturno* (SED, 2016) and *Una extraña felicidad (llamada América)* (SED, 2012); and the graphic story collection *¡La gente no puede vivir sin problemas!* (Press Join, 2000). He has edited the anthologies *Don't Cry for Me, América* (Ars Communis, 2020), *Escritorxs salvajes* (Hypermedia, 2019), *Miami (Un)plugged* (SED, 2016), and *Viaje One Way* (SED, 2014). He lived in the United States for eight years as an undocumented immigrant, working in shipyards, in the kitchen of a nightclub, in discotheques, and in construction. Vera lives in Miami.

ANDREÍNA ELENA FERNÁNDEZ was born in Maracaibo, Venezuela. She received her master of arts in women's studies and a graduate certificate in Latin American studies from the University of Florida. It is thanks to her parents, María Antonietta and Jorge, and the vibrant and complex Latinx communities of Florida that she is able to provide this translation.

"Rite of Passage" is nonfiction, translated from the Spanish by Andreína Fernández.

Everything was pastel. Everything heat and tropical humidity.

From "Rite of Passage"

RITE OF PASSAGE

1.

I thought having a family meeting on an afternoon in the middle of June was strange. Then my mother announced we'd travel, first to Miami, and then to Orlando, on our way to Disney World. Until then, we'd spent our vacations at my grandparents' house in the south of Argentina. My mom would stay with us for the week of Christmas and New Year's, then go off, do her own thing. Being a divorced mom of two in a city like Buenos Aires was exhausting. She needed a break from the grind. Still, an out-of-nowhere trip to Miami seemed weird. Could it be the preamble to a serious revelation? To the confessing of an illness, perhaps? At the time, Miami was, to me, just a television series I enjoyed. One that later became a diffused pop culture memory. I don't think even my sister, who was three years younger than me, had thought once about Disney before that afternoon. Then my mom announced that her partner, Sergio, would be joining us.

2

It took us two days to get to the United States because of an issue with the airline labor union that resulted in a layover in Asunción del Paraguay. An enormous portrait of dictator Alfredo Stroessner greeted you as soon as you got through customs. It read "Aeropuerto Internacional Presidente Stroessner," so there'd be no doubt as to who was in charge. Guarding the portrait were young men dressed as soldiers holding automatic weapons, their gaze both distrustful and goading. The heat was intense. It suffused the mood of passengers stuck in a city that chose to welcome them with the worst possible first impression of South America, probably the reason no one complained, too drained to make their misery evident in any way beyond the fear on their faces. A small Volkswagen van transported us to the hotel. We passed low-ceilinged houses, poorly lit streets, gloomy trees.

3

The American breakfast was the first of many luxuries I would discover in Miami. And yet, Miami Beach felt small, even provincial, the slow passage of time disturbed only at dusk when the sound of ambulance sirens became constant. Back then, the city was still a place where retirees chose to live out their final years. Everything was pastel. Everything heat and tropical humidity.

4

I don't remember going to the beach. For some reason, my memory did not safeguard that instant Polaroid. Instead, it kept one of a pool filled with burnt-pink-skinned tourists speaking English, and another of a blonde girl my age pacing the edge of the pool, and in which it is particularly clear I long to come close, talk to her in Spanish.

5

My mother's partner kept attempting to engage me in common complicity. It was different with my sister: her need for a father figure could forgive any disappointment, any heartbreak. Sergio loved my mother and never did anything improper, but he displayed character traits I've always condemned in men: a toxic masculinity, the garish display of money, anger at life.

This trip was the closest thing I had had to a model of what a family was, and I detested it.

6

Other snapshots:

A man with Beckett's face (it is only now that I make this connection in order to describe him) talks to himself on a downtown street.

The silver dollar I get back as change after inserting a five-dollar bill into a Coca-Cola vending machine.

A teenager spray-painting the side of a bus and an old man who scolds him and receives a "Fuck you" in response.

7

There is another image that remains though the years. When I left Buenos Aires in May 2000, I remembered it and it seemed a good reason to return to Miami. There are two girls on the bus. They have very black hair and very white skin (I suspect they're Cuban). They speak and move their hands expressively. They laugh like they know how beautiful they are. They switch from English to Spanish seamlessly as they talk. The linguistic switch is not an act, it is something natural to them. It is an experience I have never lived.

8

My memory of being bored in Disney World also remains. I am a lucky man: in the twenty years I've lived in Florida, I've never had to return. The unending lines for access to rides endured under insane levels of heat must have taken their toll, I'm sure, but more, still, the empty enjoyment that I felt even as a child, the sense of being in a hypocritically happy world.

There was another incident. I am leaving the theater after watching a special 3D edition of *Moonwalker*, the movie's protagonist, the teen idol of the moment . . . Michael Jackson. The draw of it is wearing glasses that allow you to discover special effects embedded in the movie. The glasses are made of plastic and have to be thrown into a bin to be recycled after the movie. I forget to do this, take them with me. Some time passes and I am walking, crossing the park, when two theater employees approach me. Without a word, they snatch the glasses right out of my hands.

9

Restaurants in Disney are so expensive, Sergio complains. We eat hamburgers from McDonald's. My mom takes photos, laughs at the quaintness of the place. Here she doesn't have the time to argue like she does at home. I want to write my dad in Paris to inform him of all I am seeing, of my discomfort, and how lucky he is to live in Europe. On the way back to the hotel I send him a postcard. Just a few lines, more for my own sake than to know how he is.

10

At the hotel they offer an excursion to Key West. In a show of advertising seduction, they inform us Key West is the US place closest to Cuba and of the possibility of visiting the house in which Ernest Hemingway lived. I have not yet read his books, but I did watch a television adaptation of *For Whom the Bell Tolls*.

The next day we travel on a jitney. The passengers are a retired English couple, a thirty-something German man, Dutch newlyweds, a French woman and her young son, two African American women with a young girl, and us, Argentines. The excursion's organizer (and bus driver) is a middle-age American woman. During the trip, we make friends with the French woman and her son. There is a scheduled stop at a seafood restaurant. The French woman confesses to us that the English retirees scolded her for sharing a table with Latinos, being European.

The monotonous route of similar houses, gas stations, palm trees, and the malfunctioning air conditioning make the trip unbearable.

Key West is the picture postcard of a Southern town. Enormous houses with white picket fences and perfectly manicured lawns. At Hemingway's house there are cats and more tourists. As night falls, we head over to the final scheduled activity of the trip: dining at a bar with live music. I think the band plays country music. Sergio doesn't want to pay the tour company the agreed-upon rate. The broken air conditioner and the shady nature of the bar are reason enough for him. The woman gets nervous, is on the verge of tears. Some men approach us. My mother speaks to Sergio, and pays.

11

The Miami of the late '80s is quite different from that of tragic 2020. Because of the virus, the city is no longer. The large shopping centers look as abandoned as cathedrals from another era. I live a few blocks from the Design District, a place previously devoid of charm that over the past few years has transformed into one of the places that most attracts tourists and millionaires, housing international brands such as Tiffany & Co., Rolex, Yves Saint Laurent, and so many others.

Their store windows display awesome products no one can afford to buy, not only because we can only go outside, leaving our homes, to buy basic necessities such as food, but because of fears that, any moment now, the economy could enter a twilight zone.

Within two days, the state of Florida's website for handling unemployment claims crashes. By that Thursday, there are 300,000 newly unemployed workers. The governor announces there isn't enough money for all of them.

Yesterday, a neighbor bought himself a gun. He is afraid people from poor neighborhoods will come to rob him if things get worse. Another asks me how likely is the possibility he'll have to pay a fine if he fails to pay rent this month.

I am lucky, I have not lost my job. I can teach both my university course and my creative writing workshop via Zoom. Today, a student who missed a deadline excused himself cleverly: "Every day is the same day." Over the summer, FIU informs me classes will continue online.

Curfew begins at ten. A strange silence roams the empty streets. Only police cars circulate, but not our streets. Instead they circle the Design District's purses and watches.

At night, there are no performances on balconies and no applause: people stay locked inside watching Netflix. There is fear and air conditioning.

REINALDO ARENAS was born in Cuba in 1943. A young man in 1959, when a revolution placed Fidel Castro in power, he became increasingly disenchanted with the regime's homophobic rhetoric and policies. In 1963 he moved to Havana, where he worked as a researcher and later as editor and journalist for the literary magazine *La Gaceta de Cuba*. His first novel, *Celestino antes del alba* (Unión de Escritores y Artistas de Cuba, 1967; republished as *Cantando en el pozo* and translated as *Singing from the Well*, Penguin, 1988), was his only book published in Cuba. When open persecution of homosexuals began in the 1960s and 1970s, he rejected the revolution and was no longer allowed to publish his increasingly critical writings on the island. His second and best-known novel, *El mundo alucinante* (Diógenes, 1969; translated as *Hallucinations: Being an Account of the Life and Adventures of Friar Servando Teresa de Mier*; also published as *The Ill-Fated Peregrinations of Fray Servando*, Penguin, 2001), was smuggled out of the country and published abroad.

During the mid-1970s, Arenas spent three years in prison for his writings and open homosexuality. He came to Florida as part of the Mariel boatlift, and by 1980 he was publishing new work: the novella *La Vieja Rosa* (Arte, 1980; translated as *Old Rose*, Grove, 1994) and the novel *Otra vez el mar* (Argos Vergara, 1982; translated as *Farewell to the Sea*, Viking Adult, 1985), a manuscript once confiscated by the Cuban government. The heterogeneous collection of poetry, essays, and letters *Necesidad de libertad* (Kosmos, 1986) was followed by the novels *La loma del ángel* (Dador/Quinto Centenario, 1987; translated as *Graveyard of the Angels*, Avon, 1987) and *El portero* (Dador, 1989; translated as *The Doorman*, Grove, 1991). Suffering from AIDS and too sick to continue writing, Arenas died by suicide in New York, where he had relocated, in 1990.

In a farewell letter to the Miami newspaper *Diario las Américas* he wrote, "My message is not a message of failure, but rather one of struggle and hope. Cuba will be free. I already am." By the time of his death, he had completed nine novels, an autobiography, scores of poems, plays, and short stories, and dozens of political and literary essays. Among his posthumously published works are *Viaje a la Habana: Novela en tres viajes* (Mondadori, 1990) and the autobiography *Antes que anochezca* (Tusquets, 1992; translated as *Before Night Falls*, Viking, 1993), which was made into an Academy Award–nominated film in 2000.

DOLORES M. KOCH was a Cuban American literary critic and translator who was a pioneer in the genre of microfiction. Koch was born in Havana, Cuba, in 1928. She received her PhD in Latin American literature from the City University of New York, and in addition to her work on microfiction, she translated into English several important Spanish-language works, including those of Laura Restrepo, Jorge Bucay, Alina Fernández, Emily Schindler, Enrique Joven, and her compatriot Reinaldo Arenas, whose work *Before Night Falls* was adapted into a film of the same name. Her article "El micro-relato en México: Torri, Arreola, Monterroso y Avilés Fabila," published in 1981, is the first critical work on microfiction found in the Spanish-speaking world. Koch died at her home in New York on June 11, 2009.

"The Glass Tower" is fiction, translated from the Spanish by Dolores M. Koch.

As he listened to the music, Alfredo placed his hand against the outside wall of the house, and the stillness of the night conspired with the garden and the thickness of the wall to give him a sense of security, of peace almost, that he had not experienced for many years, too many years. . . . Alfredo would have preferred to remain there, outside the house, alone with his characters, listening to the music from far away.

From "The Glass Tower"

THE GLASS TOWER

Ever since he had arrived in Miami, after the veritable odyssey of escaping his native country, noted Cuban author Alfredo Fuentes had not written a single line.

For some reason, since the day he arrived—and it had already been five years—he had found himself accepting all kinds of invitations to speak at conferences, to participate in cultural events or intellectual gatherings, and to attend literary cocktail and dinner parties where he was inevitably the guest of honor and, therefore, never given any time to eat, much less to think about his novel—or perhaps story—the one he had been carrying around in his head for years, and whose characters, Berta, Nicolás, Delfín, Daniel, and Olga, constantly vied for his attention, urging him to deal with their respective predicaments.

Berta's moral integrity, Nicolás's firm stance against mediocrity, Delfín's keen intelligence, Daniel's solitary spirit, and Olga's sweet and quiet wisdom not only clamored for the attention that he was unable to offer, they also reproached him constantly, Alfredo felt, because of the time he was spending with other people.

Most regrettable of all was that Alfredo hated those gatherings, but was incapable of refusing a gracious invitation (and what invitation isn't gracious?). He always accepted. Once there, he would be so brilliant and charming that he had earned a reputation, particularly among local writers, as a frivolous man who was something of a show-off.

On the other hand, if he were to turn down invitations to such gatherings at this point, everyone (including those who were critical of his excessive talkativeness) would consider it evidence of inferior breeding, selfishness, even a false sense of superiority. Thus, Alfredo found himself caught in an intricate web: he was well aware that if he continued to accept the endless flow of invitations, he would never write another word, and if he didn't, his prestige as a writer would soon fade into oblivion.

But it was also true that Alfredo Fuentes, rather than being at the center of those obliging crowds, would have much preferred to be alone in his small apartment—that is, alone with Olga, Delfín, Berta, Nicolás, and Daniel.

So pressing were his characters' appeals and so eager was he to respond, that just a few hours earlier he had vowed to suspend all social activities and devote himself entirely to his novel—or story, since he didn't yet know exactly where all this might lead him.

Yes, tomorrow he was definitely going to resume his solitary and mysterious occupation. Tomorrow, because tonight it would be practically impossible for him not to attend the large party being given in his honor by the grande dame of the Cuban literary circles in Miami, Señora Gladys Pérez Campo, whom H. Puntilla had nicknamed, for better or for worse, "the Haydée Santamaría of the exile community."[*]

This event, however, was not merely cultural, but also had a practical purpose. Gladys had promised the writer that she would lay the foundation, that very evening, for a publishing house that would print the manuscripts that he had, at great risk, smuggled out of Cuba. Alfredo, incidentally, didn't have a penny to his name and this, of course, could give him a tremendous financial boost, as well as help to promote the works of other important but still unknown writers less fortunate than Alfredo, who already had five books to his credit.

"The publishing project will be a success," Gladys had assured him on the phone. "The most prominent people in Miami will support you. They will all be here tonight. I am expecting you at nine, without fail."

At five to nine, Alfredo crossed the vast, manicured garden toward the main door of the Pérez Campo mansion. The scent of flowers swept over him in waves, and he could hear pleasant melodies emanating from the top floor of the residence. As he listened to the music, Alfredo placed his hand against the outside wall of the house, and the stillness of the night conspired with the garden and the thickness of the wall to give him a sense of security, of peace almost, that he had not experienced for many years, too many years. . . . Alfredo would have preferred to remain there, outside the house, alone with his characters, listening to the music from far away. But, always keeping in mind the solid publishing project that would perhaps one day allow him to own a mansion like this one and that could also mean the future salvation of Olga, Daniel, Delfín, Berta, and Nicolás, he rang the doorbell.

Before one of the maids (hired specially for the reception) could open the door, an enormous Saint Bernard belonging to the Pérez Campos lunged toward him and began licking his face. This display of familiarity from the huge dog (which answered to the name of Narcisa) encouraged similar shows of affection from the other dogs, six Chihuahuas who welcomed Alfredo with a chorus of piercing barks. Fortunately, Gladys herself came to the rescue of her guest of honor.

Fashionably attired—although rather inappropriately for the climate—in an ankle-length skirt, boa, gloves, and a large hat, the hostess took Alfredo's arm and led him to the most select circle of guests, those who would also be most interested in the publishing venture. Gladys, at once solemn and festive, introduced him to the president of one of the city's most important banks (in his imagination Alfredo saw Berta making a face in disgust); to the executive vice president of the Florida Herald, the most influential newspaper in Miami ("A horrible, anti-Cuban paper," he heard Nicolas's voice saying from a distance); to the governor's personal assistant; and to an award-winning lady poet ("A couple of serious bitches," Delfín's sarcastic voice piped in loud and clear). The introductions continued: a distinguished minister, who was a famous theology professor as well as the leader of the so-called Reunification of Cuban Families. ("What are you doing with these awful people?" Daniel shouted desperately from far away, causing Alfredo to trip just as he reached out for a famous opera singer's hand and fall instead directly into the diva's ample bosom.) Gladys continued with her introductions as if nothing had happened: a famous woman pianist, two guitarists, several professors, and finally (here Gladys assumed a regal bearing), the Countess of Villalta. Born in the province of Pinar del Río, she was an elderly woman, no longer in possession of lands and villas, but still holding fast to her splendid title of nobility.

As he was on the point of bowing discreetly before the countess, Alfredo sensed that the characters of his budding opus were again urgently demanding his attention. And so, as he kissed the lady's hand, he decided to search for the pen and paper that he always carried in his pocket, in the hope of being able to jot down a few notes. But the countess misconstrued his intentions.

"I certainly appreciate your giving me your address," said the lady, "but, as I am sure you will understand, this is just not the right moment. I do promise to send you my card."

And with that, the countess turned to the award-winning poetess, who had witnessed the scene and, apparently trying to help Alfredo, offered a suggestion. "Now that you've almost finished writing your address, why don't you give it to me? I do want to send you my latest book."

And instead of taking the notes his characters demanded (by now Olga was moaning and Berta screaming), Alfredo had no choice but to write his address on the piece of paper.

Trays brimming with assorted cheeses, hors d'oeuvres, pastries, and drinks were being passed around. Trays that, amid new greetings and inquiries, Alfredo saw approach and then disappear without ever having a chance to sample from them.

At midnight Gladys announced that, in order to make the gathering more intimate, they would all move to the glass tower. This elicited a very pleased Aaah! from the guests (even the countess joined in), and, led by their fashionable hostess, they set off immediately.

The glass tower, circular and transparent, rose at one side of the house like a gigantic chimney. While the guests climbed laboriously up the spiral staircase (except the countess, who was transported in a chair designed especially for this purpose), Alfredo again heard his characters' urgent cries. Imprisoned in Holguín, deep in the Cuban countryside, Delfín begged not to be forsaken; from New York, Daniel's groans sounded aggravated and menacing; from a small French village, Olga, sweet Olga with her pages still blank, looked at him with a combination of reproach and melancholy in her eyes; meanwhile Nicolás and Berta, right there in Miami, angrily demanded immediate participation in the narrative that he had still not begun. To appease them momentarily, Alfredo tried to raise his hand in a gesture of understanding, but, as he did this, he accidentally tousled the pianist's elaborate coiffure, and she in turn gave him an even more hateful look than Berta's.

By now they had all reached the glass tower. Alfredo was expecting the real conversation to begin at any moment; that is, they would finally start talking about the publishing plans and the first authors to be published. But just then, Gladys (who had changed into an even more sumptuous gown without anyone noticing) gestured with an elegant wave of her hand for the musicians to start playing. Soon the bank president was dancing with the wife of the executive vice president of the Florida Herald, who, in turn, began dancing with the governor's assistant. A college professor deftly whirled around the room in the strong arms of the opera singer, outclassed only by the celebrated poetess, who was now performing a prize-winning solo. Between the clicking of her heels and the frenetic undulations of her hips and shoulders, she careened over to Alfredo, who had no recourse other than to join the dance.

When the music ended, Alfredo thought that the time had finally come to discuss the central issue of the gathering. But at another signal from Gladys, the orchestra struck up a dance number from Spain. And even the most reverend minister, in the arms of the old countess, dared to venture a few parsimonious steps. As the dancing continued and the opera singer began to show off her high notes, Alfredo was sure he could hear quite distinctly the voices of his characters, now at very close range. Without interrupting his dance, he passed close by the glass wall and looked out into the garden, where he saw Olga, quivering desperately among the geraniums, begging to be rescued with silent gestures; farther away, by the perfectly trimmed ficus trees, Daniel was sobbing. At that moment, as the diva's notes reached a crescendo, Alfredo felt that he could no longer excuse his own indolence and, still dancing, he grabbed a napkin in flight and began desperately to scribble some notes.

"What kind of a dance is this?" interrupted the executive vice president of the Florida Herald. "Do you also keep a record of your dance steps?"

Alfredo didn't know what to say. On top of it all, the pianist's stare, suspicious and alert, made him feel even more vulnerable. Wiping his brow with the napkin, he lowered his eyes in embarrassment and tried to pull himself together, but when he looked up again, there they were, Nicolás, Berta, and Delfín, already pressing against the glass walls of the tower. Yes, they had gathered here from different places to pound on the windowpanes and demand that Alfredo admit them (infuse them with life) into the pages of the novel—or story—that he had not even begun to write.

The six Chihuahuas began barking excitedly, and Alfredo thought that they too had seen his characters. Fortunately, however, their barking was just one of Gladys's bright ideas (or "exquisite touches," as the countess called them) to entertain her guests. And entertain them she did when, following her steps and the beat of the orchestra drums, the Chihuahuas surrounded the Saint Bernard, Narcisa, and, standing on their hind legs, imitated complicated dance steps with Narcisa herself as the central figure. For a moment, Alfredo was sure he saw a sadness in the eyes of the huge Saint Bernard, as the dog looked over at him. Finally, the audience burst into applause, and the orchestra shifted to the soft rhythms of a Cuban danzón.

Berta, Nicolás, and Delfín were now pounding even harder on the windows, while Alfredo, becoming more and more exasperated, whirled around in the arms of the award-winning poetess, Señora Clara del Prado (haven't we mentioned her by name yet?), who at that moment was confessing to the writer how difficult it was to get a book of poetry published.

"I know exactly what you mean," Alfredo agreed mechanically, distracted by his characters, who were now struggling on the other side of the glass like huge insects drawn to a hermetically sealed streetlamp.

"You couldn't possibly understand," he heard the poet's voice counter.

"Why not?"

By then, out in the garden, Daniel and Olga had begun sobbing in unison.

"Because you are a novelist and novels always sell more than poems, especially when the author is famous like you. . . ."

"Don't make me laugh."

By now Daniel's and Olga's sobs were no longer sobs at all but agonized screams that ended in a single, unanimous plea for help.

"Rescue us! Rescue us!"

"Come on," urged the celebrated poetess, "stop acting so modest and tell me, just between you and me, how much do you get a year in royalties?"

And as if the screams coming from the garden weren't enough to drive anyone out of his mind, Nicolás and Berta were now trying to break through the glass walls of the tower, with Delfín's enthusiastic encouragement.

"Royalties? Don't make me laugh. Don't you know that there's no copyright law in Cuba? All my books were published in other countries while I was still in Cuba."

"Rescue us, or we'll break down the door!" This was, without a doubt, Berta's infuriated voice.

"They're all thieves, I know that. But other countries don't have to abide by Cuban law."

With their bare hands and then their feet, Berta and Nicolas were beating on the glass wall, while the screams coming from the garden grew louder and louder.

"Other countries will adopt any law that allows them to plunder with impunity," Alfredo asserted clearly, ready to abandon the poetess in order to save his characters, who seemed, strangely enough, to be gasping for air, although out in the open.

"So how are you planning to get funding for the great publishing house?" inquired the award-winning poetess with an ingratiating twinkle, before adding in a conspiratorial tone: "Oh, come on, I'm not going to ask you for a loan. I only want to publish a little volume of mine. . . ."

Somehow—Alfredo could not figure out exactly how—Berta had managed to slip one hand through the glass and, right in front of her astonished creator, turned the lock and opened one of the tower windows.

"Look, lady," Alfredo said curtly, "the fact is I don't have any money. As far as the publishing house is concerned, I am here to find out how everyone here plans on establishing it and whether I can get my books published, too."

"We've all been told that you are going to be the backer."

At that moment, Delfín slid down the tower and was now hanging dangerously by his fingers from the edge of the open window.

"Watch out!" Alfredo screamed, looking toward the window and trying to avert his character's fall.

"I thought we poets were the only crazy ones," said the lady poet, staring intently at Alfredo, "but now I see that novelists are too—perhaps twice as crazy."

"Three times as crazy!" proclaimed Alfredo, running to Delfín's aid at the window, just as Berta González and Nicolás Landrove entered the room.

Alfredo felt embarrassed to have Nicolás, Berta, and Delfín Prats (whose life he had just saved) see him surrounded by all these people instead of being at work with them; therefore, feeling more and more under pressure to remove himself and his characters from the scene, he decided to say goodbye to his hostess and to the rest of the guests instead of waiting for the famous discussion to begin. Followed by Narcisa, who was now intent on sniffing his leg, he walked over to them.

But a strange tension permeated the tower. Suddenly nobody was paying any attention to Alfredo. Worse, he seemed to have become invisible. In her tinkling tones, the award-winning poetess had just communicated something to Gladys and her friends, and they all made faces as if surprised or offended. Alfredo did not need a writer's observational skills to realize that they were talking about him, and not favorably.

"He'd better leave!" he heard Gladys Pérez Campo mutter in a low, indignant voice.

But even if he understood (albeit with some measure of surprise) that those words referred to him, Alfredo felt so confused that he was not able to absorb them. Besides, the words had not been spoken directly to him, although they were certainly intended for his ears. Gladys's good manners and social standing would not allow her to make a public scene, much less force one of her guests to leave. Therefore, still with the intention of rescuing his characters (who were now, for their part, completely ignoring him), Alfredo pretended not to have noticed and tried to blend in with the conversation. But the countess gave him a look of such withering scorn that the confused writer took refuge in a corner and lit a cigarette. But wouldn't it be a sign of very poor breeding to leave without saying goodbye to the host and the other guests?

On top of everything else, right at that moment Delfín Prats opened the door to the spiral staircase, and Daniel Fernández and Olga Neshein came in. Holding hands and not even looking at Alfredo, they joined Nicolás Landrove and Berta Gonzáiez del Valle, both of whom had already had a few drinks and were well on their way to getting drunk. Once again Alfredo felt Narcisa's tail brushing against his legs.

The five characters of his story (by now, at least, he knew that these people were worth only a story) took great pleasure in walking around the room, eyeing everything with a mixture of curiosity and calculation. Alfredo concentrated all his energy on trying to make them leave. But they just would not obey. On the contrary, they mingled with the most prominent of the guests, the true elite, introducing themselves to one another, bowing and curtseying and exchanging pleasantries.

From the corner where he was hidden behind a huge tropical palm and obscured by the smoke from his cigarette, Alfredo carefully observed his five characters and discovered that none was dressed as he had decided. Olga, supposedly shy and sweet, had arrived wearing too much makeup and a tight miniskirt; she was gesticulating wildly, making faces and laughing too hard at a joke that the director of Reunification of Cuban Families had just told her. Meanwhile, Berta and Nicolás, the paragons of "unshakable integrity" according to Alfredo's vision of them, were kowtowing outrageously to the governor's assistant. At one point, Alfredo even thought he overheard them asking for a small business loan to open a pizzeria in the center of the city. For his part, Daniel ("the introverted, solitary one") had already introduced himself as Daniel Fernández Trujillo and was telling the award-winning poetess such off-color stories that the old countess had discreetly moved to another seat. But insolence seemed to have met its master in the talented Delfín Prats Pupo. While downing a beer (his fifth? his seventh?) straight from the bottle, he mocked his creator, that is, Alfredo Fuentes, in a manner that was not only grotesque, but also almost obscene and ruthless. With diabolical skill, Delfín Prats Pupo imitated Alfredo, exaggerating all of the writer's tics, gestures, and idiosyncrasies, including his manner of speaking, walking, and even breathing. Only then did Alfredo realize that he sometimes stammered, that he walked with his stomach thrust forward, and that he was bug-eyed. And as he watched his favorite character mock him, he also had to endure more face-licking from the passionate Saint Bernard.

"The worst thing of all is that for all his pretensions and ridiculous posturing as a brilliant author, he has no talent whatsoever and can't even write without making spelling mistakes. He often misspells my first family name and writes it without the t," concluded Delfín Prats Pupo, so as not to leave any doubt on the matter.

And everyone laughed, again producing a strange sound like the tinkling of wine glasses.

Increasingly nervous, Alfredo lit another cigarette, which he quickly dropped on the floor when Delfín Prats Pupo, mimicking his every gesture, began to light one too.

"Sir, would you please pick up that butt?" one of the nearest servants reprimanded him. "Or are you trying to burn the carpet?"

Alfredo bent down to do as he was told and, while in that position, verified that the peculiar tinkling sound was produced by the tittering voices of the guests as they whispered, glancing at him with contempt. He brusquely extricated himself from the Saint Bernard's legs, as the dog howled pitifully, and approached the guests to try to figure out what was going on. But as soon as he joined the group, the governor's assistant, without looking at him, announced her immediate departure.

Suddenly, as if propelled by a spring, the guests decided it was time to leave. The countess was carried away in her imposing chair, while most of the guests kissed her hand, which was now transparent (at least to Alfredo). The famous opera singer was also leaving, on the (truly transparent) arm of the bank president. The minister turned to go while keeping up a lively conversation with the pianist, whose face was becoming more and more shiny and brilliant. When the award-winning lady poet left with Daniel Fernández Trujillo's arm around her waist, Alfredo saw the young man's hand sink effortlessly into her translucent body (although Daniel Fernández Trujillo's hand soon became invisible as well, and both figures fused into one). The black musicians were also leaving, led by Delfín Prats Pupo, who jumped around among them cheerfully, producing the familiar tinkling sound, while mimicking the gestures of the writer, who could do nothing to stop him. Olga Neshein de Leviant left with a mathematics professor, their hands entwined. In the midst of this stampede, Berta González del Valle stuffed her handbag with French cheeses, and Nicolás Landrove Felipe carted away the candy, both of them oblivious to Alfredo's signals and the protests of the hostess, Gladys Pérez Campo, who, on her way out in the company of her Chihuahuas, threatened to call the police. But her voice faded away into an imperceptible tinkling.

Within a few minutes, the hostess, the guests, and even the hired staff had disappeared, along with the characters of the story, and Alfredo found himself alone in the huge mansion. Disconcerted, he was getting ready to leave when the thunder of trucks and cranes reverberated through the building.

Suddenly the foundations of the house began to move and the roof disappeared; the carpets rolled up automatically; the windowpanes, freed from their casements, flew through the air; the doors left their frames; the paintings came off the walls; and the walls, moving at an unbelievable speed, vanished, along with everything else, into a huge truck. As everything disassembled and packed itself (the whole garden with its plastic trees, walls, and air fresheners was already moving out), Alfredo saw that the mansion had been nothing more than an enormous prefabricated cardboard set that could be installed and dismantled quickly, and that one could rent for a few days or even a few hours, according to the ad on the side of the large truck in which everything was being carted away.

In a flash, the site where the imposing mansion had stood became nothing but a dusty embankment. Standing at the center, still perplexed, Alfredo could not find (it no longer existed) the path that would take him back to the city. He walked around aimlessly, thinking about the story he had never written. But an enthusiastic bark pulled him out of his meditation.

Exasperated, Alfredo began running, but the Saint Bernard, evidently more athletic than the writer, caught up with him quickly, knocked him down, and began licking his face. An unexpected joy came over Alfredo when he realized that her tongue was indeed real. He pulled himself together and got up. Caressing Narcisa—who followed him faithfully—he abandoned the site.

Miami Beach, April 1986

* Haydée Santamaría was the director of the government publishing house, La Casa de las Americas, who decided which books would be published in Cuba.

Born in Cuba and raised in Miami, **ISVETT VERDE** focuses on the Latino experience in the United States. Isvett serves as editor and writer for the *New York Times* opinion section. She attended Florida International University, where she majored in French literature, and she received a master's in Spanish journalism at the CUNY Graduate School of Journalism. She was part of the award-winning team that in 2015 exposed labor and health practices detrimental to workers in New York City's nail salons, but she has also written about avocado dyes and Walter Mercado, the astrologer so dear to Latinx hearts.

"Soy de allá, pero vivo aquí" is nonfiction.

When I was older, I learned what it was like for my dad during those weeks when we didn't know if he was alive or dead. Unsure if he'd ever see us again, he would lock himself in the bathroom of Caridad's house every night, stare at a photo of my mom and me, and cry.

From "Soy de allá, pero vivo aquí"

SOY DE ALLÁ, PERO VIVO AQUÍ

Growing up, I'd break into a cold sweat anytime the rumor circulated that Fidel Castro was dead.

To me, his death meant having to leave our house in Miami and returning to an island that was supposed to be home, but that I barely remembered. "I don't know anyone there," I'd think. "Where will I go to school? Where will we live?"

To me, Cuba was a collection of my parents' memories. Tobacco farms, childhood homes, a large extended family which included my older half-sister; I could imagine all of these things, these people, but I had no tangible connection to them.

In those days, the Cuban government forbade those of us who'd left from coming back to visit. We could only call our extended family, which meant a very expensive five minutes of shouting into the phone before the call inevitably dropped. Our letters were filled with old news by the time they were unfolded by our loved ones' hands.

I was born in a hospital in Guanajay, Cuba in July 1979. Approximately nine months later, a group of Cubans crashed a bus through the gates of the Peruvian embassy in Havana, setting in motion a chain of events that would forever alter the lives of hundreds of thousands of families.

My dad, desperate for a way off the island, tried to make his way into the embassy. But when he returned that night, unsuccessful, my mom was relieved. She'd been afraid that if he got in, she'd never see him again. Not long after, Fidel announced that anyone who had relatives who could come get them was free to leave from the Mariel port.

My mom had never dreamed of leaving. She was 17 at the time and Cuba was the only home she had ever known. "You'd hear these terrible rumors about what life was like here," she told me. But my dad was resolute. Communism was not for him. He didn't see a viable future for us, for me, in Cuba. Caridad, my great-aunt, would send letters with photos that spun a story of what life was like in *el exilio*. My mom drew comfort from these photos. "Maybe it's not so bad there," she thought.

Our relatives in Miami pooled their money to buy a boat to come get us. It began to sink shortly into the journey, nearly killing everyone on board, or so family legend goes. Eventually, they paid a man named Nano $1,000 each—a small fortune in those days—to take my dad, my mom, and me to Miami.

On June 19, 1980, my mom and dad were sitting on the porch after dinner when a police officer on a motorcycle with a sidecar rode up to the house. He had a list of people bound for the United States and asked if my dad was home. It was time for him to leave.

My mom was absolutely gutted as he rode away with nothing more than the clothes he was wearing. For weeks, there was no news of him. Then my mom got the news: he had made it safely to the United States. When I was older, I learned what it was like for my dad during those weeks when we didn't know if he was alive or dead. Unsure if he'd ever see us again, he would lock himself in the bathroom of Caridad's house every night, stare at a photo of my mom and me, and cry.

A month to the day later, it was our turn to leave. My mom had enough time to pack 30 jars of baby food, saltines, clothes for me and 100 Cuban pesos. We waited 12 days in a camp at the Mariel port before leaving. I got a fever. Guards strip-searched my mom and confiscated her money.

Finally, we crammed into a boat with 300 other people and set sail from Mariel around three in the morning on July 31. My mom remembers looking at the darkness, at the vast ocean on the horizon and the people throwing up all around her and thinking to herself, "My god, what have I done?"

In the end, we made it. My dad, a mechanic by trade, had immediately found a job when he arrived. They both worked hard, took English lessons, bought a home and opened a business. My sister was born. Life went on. In Florida.

But that didn't stop them from longing to go back. I remember every New Year's party would end with Willy Chirino's song "Nuestro día (ya viene llegando)," which translates to "Our Day Is Coming." My parents' eyes would get misty as they wondered if this would be the year we would be reunited with our family in Cuba.

In 1994, we were finally able to go back and visit. I had nine days to build a lifetime of bonds and memories, to get to know my older sister and grandparents and cousins. It was not enough time, but it was all we had.

I'm an adult now. When I heard the news that Fidel Castro had died, I didn't break into a cold sweat. After all these years, it felt almost anticlimactic. My parents have lived in Miami longer than they lived in Cuba. In many ways, the island now feels just as foreign to them as it does to me. This is home now.

We won't get back all those years that we missed with our loved ones, some of whom have passed away. I'll never know what my grandmother's morning routine was. What her life was like when she was a kid. Why my grandfather chose to be a baker.

My story is not so different from what so many other refugees experience: the feeling of being suspended between two worlds and not quite belonging in either. Castro's brand of Communism pitted neighbor against neighbor, disrupting family bonds, friendships, and the very fabric that held together the community.

Cuba is no freer today than it was when he was alive. But when he died, I did listen to Chirino's song on repeat, banged pots in the streets of Miami in spirit. Our day had finally come.

JOSÉ IGNACIO VALENZUELA is a prominent and prolific Chilean writer with outstanding contributions in film, literature, television, and theater. Recently named by the *New York Times About.com Magazine* as one of Latin America's best ten writers, his works include more than twenty-five published books, among which the bestsellers *Trilogía del Malamor*, *El filo de tu piel*, *La mujer infinita*, *Mi abuela, la loca*, and *Mi tío Pachunga* stand out. The script for his movie *La sangre iluminada*, coauthored with the Mexican director Iván Ávila, won recognition at the Sundance Festival in 2001. *Miente*, another movie he wrote, was selected by Puerto Rico to be its entry to the 2008 Oscars. *Amores*, a TV series Valenzuela created and wrote in 2004, was nominated for an Emmy award. And in 1999 he won the Grand Jury's Award in Cannes for his script *Los pioneros del fin del mundo*. His telenovelas *La casa de al lado* and *Santa Diabla*, both produced by Telemundo, have been broadcast throughout the world, breaking audience records. In 2021 Netflix streamed his new series *¿Quién mató a Sara?* and he began developing a series for Sony International Television based on his book *El filo de tu piel*. Valenzuela has taught screenwriting throughout Latin America, including universities in Mexico, Chile, the Dominican Republic, and Puerto Rico. More about him can be found at https://www.chascas.com.

Please see translator ANDREÍNA FERNÁNDEZ's bio on page 38.

"A Matter of Time" is fiction, translated from the Spanish by Andreína Fernández.

> The woman dreamed in vibrant color. She saw enormous roots, like wooden snakes, grow from her feet and sink into the earth in search of water and minerals. She was happy.
>
> From "A Matter of Time"

A MATTER OF TIME

AUTHOR'S NOTE: They say it's only a matter of time until a city gets under your skin and becomes part of your DNA. Someone said that to me at the airport, the first time I left Chile, around 1995, heading to Mexico City, where I was supposedly going to live for a year. When I arrived at my destination, I was stunned by the disproportion, the immensity of the city that seemed never ending from inside the taxi taking me to the hotel. "I'll never be able to feel like I belong in a place like this," I thought to my dismay. But it did not go that way: my twelve-month stay was prolonged a little over a decade. When I left Mexico City for New York, the entire country was tattooed on my body, in my way of speaking, in my culinary tastes, in my view of the world. They say that it's also only a matter of time until you start to love an unfamiliar place, one that categorizes us as foreigners. How much time passes in "a matter of time"? Months? Years? Decades? I admit that when I came to live in Miami, my first reaction was to once again utter the phrase "I'll never be able to feel I belong in a place like this." I don't like the beach, the heat gives me migraines, the mosquitos maliciously follow me around, the lizards, crocodiles, and iguanas horrify me, I refuse to step foot in a shopping mall, hurricanes render me paralyzed, and I have never gotten on well in areas that are predominantly politically conservative. And Miami encompasses all of that. I was only supposed to live in this city while writing a 120-episode telenovela. But here I am, nine years and six telenovelas later, with two hurricanes in my body, various anthologies of political debates in my repertoire, completely accustomed to the heat, somewhat reconciled with the world of scales and reptiles, taking allergy pills daily in order to survive the mosquitos, and without having stepped foot on a beach or in a mall. That "matter of time" necessitated almost a decade for me to reconcile with a city that I always felt was fake and with which I didn't mix well from the beginning. That is why I wrote this story. Because many days I felt like the protagonist of the story: making superhuman efforts to belong and put down roots in a place that did not seem to be made for me. In the case of my heroine, the end of her struggle is something more intense than what I could bear. I suppose that is what literature is for: to help you make peace with that which exceeds you, that which is larger than your own existence, and that escapes your small, mortal control. And from that experience I gain two great lessons: that I could not have survived Miami without writing about her and without converting her into the stage of many stories. And, further, that, for me, there is no better place to reside than fiction. Welcome, all, to the Miami of my imagination.

*

The first bud grew out of her pinky finger. It was the slight, novel throbbing that caught her attention. Surprised, she brought her fingertip up to her eyes and confirmed her theory: the smell of flowers wafted from her skin. The woman smiled. That night, before falling asleep, she found another: it was near her elbow. She mentioned the good news to her husband, and he said something to her that she didn't quite understand. She asked that when the moment arrived, he be attentive that she had everything she needed. He again responded in his strange tongue and continued with what he was doing. The woman dreamed in vibrant color. She saw enormous roots, like wooden snakes, grow from her feet and sink into the earth in search of water and minerals. She was happy.

When she awoke, the first thing she did was run to the bathroom and take off her nightgown. She had to cover her mouth with both hands to contain shouts of joy. Her body was covered in small spots the colors of nature: some green, others yellow, and some blueish hues. Finally. It was happening. What she had wished for years was finally being granted to her. She looked at the growth on her pinky. The skin was so tight that you could begin to guess the colors of the flower that would soon bloom. She couldn't wait. Using nail scissors, she made a small cut into that spot on her skin. She did not bleed; on the contrary, a purple fan opened its petals and even revealed a leaf with perfect edges and veins. The woman could not hold back her tears of joy.

That day she went out with an enormous smile on her lips. She greeted the man who sold magazines on the corner and did not care that he responded in that language she did not understand. She affectionately patted her neighbor's son on the head, that little pestering kid who always laughed at her as she walked down the stairs of the building. Somehow, her neighborhood seemed even more beautiful to her now. It was only a matter of time, she told herself as she made her way to the vegetable stand and the smell of a spring garden permeated the air around her. It was only a matter of time.

She decided to prepare a dinner fit for kings. She wanted to celebrate what was happening. She was going to grab a knife to cut a tomato but had a problem: the flower on her pinky had grown enough to stand on its own, and it impeded her ability to use her hand fully. The bud on her elbow had also opened and a shaky sprig peeked out from under the sleeve of her dress. She felt the pressure of hundreds of new buds against the fabric of her clothes. So, she filled the bathtub and stepped in, naked. And she stayed there, smiling, excited, allowing each pore to open and close its mouth, drink the water that it so badly needed. It was then that she discovered the first root unroll from her toes and shake around in the air, searching for its own sustenance.

She went out to the balcony and grabbed the first pot she could find. Coming in contact with the soil, still cool from the morning dew, calmed its hunger for minerals. She left her foot there, half sunken into the planter. She had to take off the thin robe that covered her because the water had animated every zone of her body and now hundreds of leaves, stems, and petals danced to the rhythm of the wind and her breath. She became restless. How would she get on with her normal life? How would she explain to her husband that she just wanted to put down roots in this distant country that he had brought her to, and that she had followed him to, just as she had been taught that an obedient and devoted woman had to do? She tried to remove her foot from the pot, but immediately felt a sharp shock in her leg.

Her husband found her half-hidden behind her own foliage. He did not care. He never listened to reason, he just wanted to have dinner. She dragged herself toward the kitchen. With pain in her body and soul, she had to break away from the soil to which she had tethered herself in order to avoid staining the tiled floor. That night, the sheets suffocated some of the flowers and branches, and she had a shortness of breath. She could not sleep, much less dream. No matter how much she tried, she could not cry: all the water in her body was being urgently distributed to the stems damaged by the bedspread.

The next day, her body hurt. As soon as her husband left, she went out to the balcony in search of morning dew, warm rays of sun, and the damp soil in her planters. She thought about the groceries she needed to buy, vegetables, some bread, a bit of meat, but just the thought of having to go down the stairs toward the street made her whole body shudder. She felt her roots crash against the inner walls of the pots, desperate to cover more ground. But there was none. The woman opened her mouth and tossed in a handful of soil, but that was not enough either. She let some fruit-filled branches hang down to the balcony below. The smell of oranges and apples diffused through the air, carried away by the wind. She could hardly see anymore: a forest of weeds and honeysuckle emerged from her chest and covered her neck and head. She felt the chair crack below her from her own weight. Her last thought was of the groceries she still had not gotten and her desire to put down roots in that country she had never managed to love.

Her husband found someone who would come to cook for him each day. He did not bother to water the mess of vegetation that hung like a green cascade from the balcony. He left it like that, at the mercy of the wind, the rain, and the birds that made nests between the branches and the flowers. It did not matter to him when he saw it dry out little by little, when autumn stripped off the leaves, and the winter finished destroying the last of the growths that strained to survive. The same person who came to cook for him begrudgingly cleaned the mess of dried petals, broken stems, and withered soil that remained.

When the man married the maid, he promised her, in his own language, that soon, very soon, they'd put down roots in that unfamiliar land. It was only a matter of time.

GUILLERMO ROSALES was born in Havana in 1946. There, he wrote *El juego de la viola*, a finalist for the much-lauded Casa de las Americas Award. In 1979 he fled Castro's regime and exiled himself in Miami. He had, years before, been diagnosed with schizophrenia. In Miami, he very briefly lived with relatives before turning to halfway houses, "those marginal refuges where the desperate and the hopeless go." That quote is from his novel *La casa de los náufragos* (Siruela, 2003), published in English as *The Halfway House* (New Directions, 2009), which was informed and inspired by his experiences in those South Florida homes. A gut-turning, deeply disturbing work that might just be the best novel ever written about Miami, it was published posthumously, after Rosales destroyed almost everything he had ever written and died by suicide in 1993. *Publishers Weekly* gave it a starred review, extolling it as "a frightening, nihilistic cousin of *One Flew Over the Cuckoo's Nest.*" Another work that escaped the flames was a collection of short stories based on *El juego de la viola*; the collection was published in Spanish by that title (Universal, 1994) and in English as *Leap Frog and Other Stories* (New Directions, 2013). *Leap Frog* and *The Halfway House* were translated by Anna Kushner.

The daughter of Cuban exiles, ANNA KUSHNER was born in Philadelphia and has been traveling to Cuba since 1999. She has translated the novels of Norberto Fuentes, Marcial Gala, Leonardo Padura, Guillermo Rosales, and Gonçalo M. Tavares as well as two collections of nonfiction by Mario Vargas Llosa.

"The Halfway House" is fiction, translated by Anna Kushner.

"You'll be fine here," my aunt says. "You'll be among Latinos."

From "The Halfway House"

THE HALFWAY HOUSE

(AN EXCERPT)

The house said "BOARDING HOME" on the outside, but I knew that it would be my tomb. It was one of those marginal refuges where the desperate and hopeless go—crazy ones for the most part, with a smattering of old people abandoned by their families to die of loneliness so they won't screw up life for the winners.

"You'll be fine here," my aunt says, seated at the wheel of her straight-off-the-assembly-line Chevrolet.

"You'll understand that nothing more can be done."

I understand. I'm almost grateful that she found me this hovel to live in so that I don't need to sleep on benches and in parks, covered in grime and dragging sacks of clothes around.

"Nothing more can be done."

I understand her. I've been admitted to more than three psychiatric wards since I've been here, in the city of Miami, where I arrived six months ago, fleeing the culture, music, literature, television, sporting events, history and philosophy of the island of Cuba. I'm not a political exile. I'm a complete exile. Sometimes I think that if I had been born in Brazil, Spain, Venezuela or Scandinavia, I would have also fled those streets, ports and meadows.

"You'll be fine here," my aunt says.

I look at her. She gives me a long, hard look. There's no pity in her dry eyes. We get out of the car. The house said "Boarding Home." It's one of those halfway houses that pick up the dregs of society. Beings with empty eyes, dry cheeks, toothless mouths, filthy bodies. I think such places exist only here, in the United States. They're also known simply as homes. They're not government-run. They're private houses that anyone can open as long as he gets a license from the state and completes a paramedic course.

" . . . a business just like any other," my aunt explains to me. "A business like a funeral home, an optician's, a clothing store. You'll pay three-hundred dollars here."

We opened the door. There they all were: René and Pepe, the two mentally retarded men; Hilda, the decrepit old hag who constantly wets herself; Pino, a gray, silent man who just glares at the horizon with a hard expression; Reyes, an old one-eyed man whose glass eye constantly oozes yellow liquid; Ida, the grande dame come to ruin; Louie, a strong American with greenish-yellow skin who constantly howls like a mad wolf; Pedro, an old Indian, perhaps Peruvian, silent witness to the world's evils; Tato, the homosexual; Napoleón, the midget; and Castaño, a ninety-year-old geezer who can only shout "I want to die! I want to die! I want to die!"

"You'll be fine here," my aunt says. "You'll be among Latinos."

We go on. Mr. Curbelo, the owner of the Home, is waiting for us at his desk. Did I find him repulsive from the very beginning? I don't know. He was fat and shapeless, and was wearing a ridiculous tracksuit made all the worse by a juvenile baseball cap.

"Is this the man?" He asks my aunt with a smile on his face.

"This is him," she responds.

"He'll be fine here," Curbelo says, "like he's living with family."

He looks at the book I'm carrying under my arm and asks, "Do you like to read?"

My aunt responds, "Not only that. He's a writer."

"Ah!" Curbelo says with mock surprise. "And what do you write?"

"Bullshit," I say softly.

Then Curbelo asks, "Did you bring his medicines?"

My aunt looks in her purse.

"Yes," she says. "Melleril. One hundred milligrams. He has to take four a day."

"Good." Mr. Curbelo says with a satisfied face. "You can leave him then. We'll take care of everything else."

My aunt turns to look into my eyes. This time, I think I see the slightest trace of pity.

"You'll be fine here," she assures me. "Nothing more can be done."

My name is William Figueras, and by the age of fifteen I had read the great Proust, Hesse, Joyce, Miller, Mann. They were for me what saints are to a devout Christian. Twenty years ago, I finished writing a novel in Cuba that told a love story. It was the story of an affair between a communist and a member of the bourgeoisie, and ended with both of them committing suicide. The novel was never published and my love story was never known by the public at large. The government's literary specialists said my novel was morose, pornographic, and also irreverent, because it dealt harshly with the Communist Party. After that, I went crazy. I began to see devils on the walls, to hear voices that insulted me—and I stopped writing. All I produced was a rabid dog's froth. One day, thinking that a change of country would save me from madness, I left Cuba and arrived in this great American country. There were some relatives waiting for me here who didn't know anything about my life and who, after twenty years of separation, barely knew me anymore. They thought a future winner was coming, a future businessman, a future playboy, a future family man who would have a future house full of kids, and who would go to the beach on weekends and drive fine cars and wear brand-name clothing like Jean Marc and Pierre Cardin. The person who turned up at the airport the day of my arrival was instead a crazy, nearly toothless, skinny, frightened guy who had to be admitted to a psychiatric ward that very day because he eyed everyone in the family with suspicion and, instead of hugging and kissing them, insulted them. I know it was a great disappointment for everyone, especially for my aunt who was expecting something great. They got me instead. An embarrassment. A terrible mark on this fine Cuban petit bourgeois family with their healthy teeth and buffed fingernails, radiant skin, fashionable clothes, who were weighed down by thick gold chains and owned magnificent cars of the latest make and spacious houses with well-stocked pantries and central heat and air-conditioning. That day (the one on which I arrived), I know that they all eyed each other with embarrassment, made some scathing comments and drove off from the airport without any intention of ever seeing me again. And that's the way it's been. The only one who remained faithful to the family ties was this Aunt Clotilde, who decided to make herself responsible for me and kept me at her house for three months, until the day when, at the advice of other friends and relatives, she decided to stick me in the halfway house: the house of human garbage.

"Because you'll understand that nothing more can be done."

I understand her.

This halfway house was, originally, a six-room house. Perhaps it was once inhabited by one of those typical American families who fled Miami when the Cubans fleeing communism began to arrive. Now the halfway house has twelve tiny rooms, with two beds in each room. In addition, it has an ancient television set that's always broken, and a kind of living room with twenty folding chairs that are falling apart. There are three bathrooms, but one of these (the best one) is reserved for the boss, Mr. Curbelo. The toilets in the other two are always clogged since some of the residents stick in them old shirts, sheets, curtains and other cloth materials that they use to wipe their behinds. Mr. Curbelo does not give us toilet paper, although he is supposed to by law. There is a dining room, outside the house, tended by a Cuban mulata with scores of religious necklaces and bracelets whose name is Caridad. But she doesn't cook. If she were to cook, Mr. Curbelo would have to pay her an additional thirty dollars per week, and that's something Mr. Curbelo would never do. So Mr. Curbelo himself, with his bourgeois little face, is the one who makes the stew every day. He makes it in the simplest way, by taking a handful of peas or lentils and dropping them (plop!) in a pressure cooker. Maybe he adds a little garlic powder. The rest, rice and a main dish, comes from a home delivery service called "Sazón," whose owners, knowing they're dealing with a nut house, pick the worst they have and send it over any which way in two huge greasy pots. They should send enough food to feed twenty-three people, but they only send enough for eleven. Mr. Curbelo thinks this is enough and no one complains. But if a complaint does arise, then Mr. Curbelo, without even looking at the person, says, "You don't like it? Well if you don't like it, leave!" But . . . who's going to leave? Life on the streets is hard. Even for crazy people whose brains are on the moon. And Mr. Curbelo knows this and repeats, "Leave, quickly!" But nobody leaves. The complainer lowers his eyes, grabs his spoon and goes back to swallowing his raw lentils silently.

Because in the halfway house, no one has anyone. Old Ida has two kids in Massachusetts who want nothing to do with her. Quiet Pino is all alone and doesn't have anyone at all in this huge country. René and Pepe, the two mentally retarded guys, could never live with their weary relatives. Old one-eyed Reyes has a daughter in Newport that he hasn't seen in fifteen years. Hilda, the old lady with cystitis, doesn't even know her own last name. I have an aunt . . . but "nothing more can be done." Mr. Curbelo knows all of this. He knows it well. That's why he is so sure that no one will leave the halfway house and that he will continue to receive the checks for $314 that the American government sends for each one of the crazy people in his hospice. There are twenty-three nuts: $7,222. Plus, with another $3,000 that comes from I don't know what supplemental source, it comes to $10,222 a month. That's why Mr. Curbelo has a well-appointed house in Coral Gables and a farm with racehorses. That's why he spends his weekends perfecting the fine art of deep-sea fishing. That's why his kids' photos appear in the local paper on their birthdays, and he goes to society parties wearing tails and a bow tie. Now that my aunt is gone, his face, once warm, eyes me with cold indifference.

"Come along," he says dryly. He takes me down a narrow hallway to a room, number four, where another crazy guy is sleeping with a snore that reminds me of an electric saw.

"This is your bed," he says, without looking at me. "This is your towel," and he points at a threadbare towel full of yellowish stains. "This is your closet, and this is your soap," and he takes half a piece of white soap from his pocket and hands it to me. He doesn't say another word. He looks at his watch, realizes how late it is and leaves the room, closing the door behind him. Then I put my suitcase on the floor, place my small television set on top of the armoire, open the window wide and sit on the bed assigned to me with the book of English poets in my hands. I open it at random, to a poem by Coleridge:

God save thee, ancient mariner!
From the fiends that plague thee thus!—
"Why look'st thou so?"—With my cross bow
I shot the Albatross.

The door to the room suddenly opens and a robust figure, with skin as dirty as puddle water, comes in. He has a can of beer in his hand and takes several sips from it while giving me the once-over out of the corner of his eye.

"You're the new guy?" he asks after a while.

"Yes."

"I'm Arsenio, the guy who takes care of things when Curbelo leaves."

"Okay."

He looks at my suitcase, my books and stops at my small black-and-white TV set.

"Does it work?"

"Yes."

"How much did it cost you?"

"Sixty dollars."

He takes another swig, without taking the corner of his eye off of my TV set. Then he says, "Are you going to eat?"

"Yes."

"Then get going. The food's ready."

He turns around and leaves the room, still drinking from his can. I'm not hungry, but I should eat. I only weigh 115 pounds, and I tend to get woozy. People on the street sometimes yell *Worm!* at me. I throw the book of English poets on the bed and button up my shirt. My pants swim around my waist. I should eat.

I head toward the dining room.

Miss Caridad, the one in charge of distributing food to the crazy people, points out the only open spot to me. It's a seat next to old one-eyed Reyes, and across from Hilda, the decrepit old hag whose clothes reek of urine, and Pepe, the older of the two mentally retarded men. They call this table "the untouchables' table," since no one wants to be with them when it's time to eat. Reyes eats with his hands, and his enormous glass eye, as big as a shark's eye, constantly oozes watery pus that falls down to his chin like a large yellow tear. Hilda also eats with her hands and does so reclined in her chair, like a marchioness eating delicacies, so that half of the food ends up on her clothes. Pepe, the retarded guy, eats with an enormous spoon that looks like a spade. He chews slowly and loudly with his toothless jaw, and his whole face, up to his large popping eyes, is full of peas and rice. I bring the first spoonful to my mouth and chew slowly. I chew once, three times, and then I realize that I can't swallow it. I spit everything out onto my plate and leave. When I get to my room, I notice that my TV set is missing. I look for it in my closet and under the bed, but it's not there. I go in search of Mr. Curbelo, but the person sitting at his desk now is Arsenio, the second in command. He takes a swig from his can of beer and informs me,

"Curbelo's not here. What's up?"

"My TV set has been stolen."

"Tsk, tsk, tsk," he moves his head in despair. "That was Louie," he then says. "He's the thief."

"Where's Louie?"

"In room number three."

I go to room number three and find Louie the American, who howls like a wolf when he sees me come in.

"TV?" I say.

"Go to hell!" He exclaims, furious. He howls again. He throws himself at me and pushes me out of the room. Then he shuts the door with a loud slam.

I look at Arsenio. He smiles. But he hides it quickly, covering his face with the beer can.

"A sip?" he asks, holding the can out to me.

"No thanks, I don't drink. When will Mr. Curbelo be in?"

"Tomorrow."

Great. Nothing more can be done. I go back to my room and let myself fall heavily on the bed. The pillow stinks of old sweat. The sweat of other nuts who have been through here and shriveled up between these four walls. I throw it far away from me. Tomorrow I'll ask for a clean sheet, a new pillow and a lock to put on the door so that no one enters without asking first. I look at the ceiling. It's a blue ceiling, peeling, overrun with tiny brown cockroaches. Great. This is the end of me, the lowest I could go. There's nothing else after this halfway house. Just the street and nothing more. The door opens again. It's Hilda, the decrepit old hag who urinates on her clothes. She has come in search of a cigarette. I give it to her. She looks at me with kind-hearted eyes. I notice a certain beauty of yesteryear behind that revolting face. She has an incredibly sweet voice. With it, she tells me her story. She has never married, she says. She's a virgin. She is, she says, eighteen years old. She's looking for a proper gentleman to marry. But a gentleman! Not just anyone.

"You have beautiful eyes," she says sweetly to me.

"Thank you."

"You're welcome."

I slept a little. I dreamt I was in a town in the provinces, back in Cuba, and that there wasn't a soul in the whole town. The doors and windows were wide open, and through them you could see iron beds with very clean, tightly pulled white sheets. The streets were long and silent, and all of the houses were wooden. I was running around that town in distress, looking for anyone to talk with. But there was no one. Only open houses, white beds and total silence. There wasn't a single hint of life.

I awoke bathed in sweat. In the bed next to me, the crazy guy who was snoring like a saw is awake now and putting on a pair of pants.

"I'm going to work," he tells me. "I work all night at a pizza place and they pay me six dollars. They also give me pizza and Coca-Cola."

He puts on a shirt and slides into his shoes.

"I'm an old slave," he says. "I'm reincarnated. Before this life, I was a Jew who lived in the time of the Caesars."

He leaves with a slam of the door. I look at the street through the window. It must be midnight. I get up from the bed and go to the living room, to get some fresh air. As I pass Arsenio's room, the hospice manager, I hear bodies struggling and then the sound of a slap. I continue on my way and sit in a tattered arm chair that reeks of old sweat. I light a cigarette and throw my head back, fearfully remembering the dream I just had. Those white, tightly made beds, those wide open solitary houses, and I, the only living being in town. Then I see somebody coming out of Arsenio's room. It's Hilda, the decrepit old hag. She's naked. Arsenio comes out behind her. He's naked too. They haven't seen me.

"Come on," he says to Hilda in a drunk voice. "No," she responds. "That hurts."

"Come on, I'll give you a cigarette." Arsenio says.

"No. It hurts!"

I take a drag of my cigarette and Arsenio discovers me among the shadows.

"Who's there?"

"Me."

"Who's me?"

"The new guy."

He mutters something, disgusted, and goes back inside his room. Hilda comes over to me. A ray of light from an electric street lamp bathes her naked body. It's a body full of flab and deep valleys.

"Do you have a cigarette?" she asks in a sweet voice.

I give it to her.

"I don't like getting it from behind," she says. "And that pig!" she points to Arsenio's room. "He only wants to do it that way."

She leaves.

I lean my head against the back of the armchair again. I think of Coleridge, the author of "Kubla Khan," whose disenchantment with the French Revolution provoked his ruin and sterility as a poet. But my thoughts are soon cut off. A long, terrifying howl shakes the boarding home. Louie, the American, shows up in the living room, his face bursting with rage.

"Fuck you up the ass!" He screams at the street, which is empty at this late hour. "Fuck you up the ass! Fuck you up the ass!"

He slams his fist against a mirror on the wall and it falls to the floor in pieces. Arsenio, the manager, says lazily from his bed,

"Louie, you *cama* now. You *pastilla* tomorrow. You *no jodas más.*"

And Louie disappears into the shadows.

RICHARD BLANCO, a Florida International University alumnus, was selected by President Obama as the fifth inaugural poet in U.S. history, joining the ranks of such luminary poets as Robert Frost and Maya Angelou. He was the youngest and the first Latino, immigrant, and gay person to serve in such a role. Born in Madrid to Cuban exile parents and raised in Miami, the negotiation of cultural identity characterizes his many collections of poetry. He has also authored the memoirs *For All of Us, One Today: An Inaugural Poet's Journey*, and *The Prince of Los Cocuyos: A Miami Childhood*. Blanco is associate professor of creative writing at Florida International University.

I have captured you in English at the kitchen table

waiting for the *café* to brew, the milk to froth,

and your life to adjust to your life. In English

From "Translation for Mamá"

WHEN I WAS A LITTLE CUBAN BOY

O José can you see . . . that's how I sang it, when I was
a *cubanito* in Miami, and *América* was some country
in the glossy pages of my history book, someplace
way north, everyone white, cold, perfect. *This Land
is my Land,* so why didn't I live there, in a brick house
with a fireplace, a chimney with curlicues of smoke.
I wanted to wear breeches, and stockings to my *chins,*
those black pilgrim shoes with shiny gold buckles.
I wanted to eat yams with the Indians, shake hands
with *los negros,* and dash through snow I'd never seen
in a one-horse hope-n-say? I wanted to speak in British,
say really smart stuff like *fours core and seven years ago*
or, *one country under God, in the visible.* I wanted to see
that land with no palm trees, only the strange sounds
of flowers like petunias, peonies, impatience, waiting
to walk through a door someday, somewhere in God
Bless America and say, *Lucy I'm home, honey. I'm home.*

TRANSLATION FOR MAMÁ

What I've written for you, I have always written
In English, my language of silent vowel endings
never translated into your language of silent h's.

    Lo que he escrito para ti, siempre lo he escrito
    en inglés, en mi lengua llena de vocales mudas
    nunca traducidas a tu idioma de haches mudas.

I've transcribed all your old letters into poems
that reconcile your exile from Cuba, but always
in English. I've given you back the *guajiro* roads
you left behind, stretched them into sentences
punctuated with palms, but only in English.

    He transcrito todas tus cartas viejas en poemas
    que reconcilian tu exilio de Cuba, pero siempre
    en inglés. Te he devuelto los caminos guajiros
    que dejastes atrás, transformados en oraciones
    puntuadas por palmas, pero solamente en inglés.

I have recreated the *pueblecito* you had to forget,
forced your green mountains up again, grown
valleys of sugarcane, stars for you in English.

    He reconstruido el pueblecito que tuvistes que olvidar,
    he levantado de nuevo tus montañas verdes, cultivado
    la caña, las estrellas de tus valles, para ti, en inglés.

In English I have told you how I love you cutting
gladiolas, crushing *ajo*, setting cups of *dulce de leche*
on the counter to cool, or hanging up the laundry
at night under our suburban moon. In English,

    En inglés te he dicho cómo te amo cuando cortas
    gladiolas, machacas ajo, enfrías tacitas de dulce de leche
    encima del mostrador, o cuando tiendes la ropa
    de noche bajo nuestra luna en suburbia. En inglés,

I have imagined you surviving by transforming
yards of taffeta into dresses you never wear
keeping *Papá's* photo hinged in your mirror,
and leaving the porch light on, all night long.

he imaginado como sobrevives transformando
yardas de tafetán en vestidos que nunca estrenas,
la foto de papá que guardas en el espejo de tu cómoda,
la luz del portal que dejas encendida, toda la noche.
Te he captado en inglés en la mesa de la cocina
esperando que cuele el café, que hierva la leche
y que tu vida se acostumbre a tu vida. En inglés
has aprendido a adorar tus pérdidas igual que yo.
I have captured you in English at the kitchen table
waiting for the *café* to brew, the milk to froth,
and your life to adjust to your life. In English
you've learned to adore your losses the way I do.

SILENT FAMILY CLIPS

The projector whirls like a tiny, black time-machine
on the coffee table, a cone of light shoots the dark,
opens a hole in the living room wall like a portal
into lives I never knew, years I don't remember living.
1970 is about ten seconds long featuring a version
of my brother I never loved, content with hitting
a ball against the graffiti on a city wall, twenty years
before we'd learn to be brothers | the wall breaks
to Miami beach waves dissolving at my *abuela's* feet,
sauntering down the shore with beauty pageant steps
her bathing cap flowers fresh as the Art Deco facades
shimmering behind her | fading away to my *abuelo*
standing on the boardwalk at orthodox attention,
his hair once as black as the black of his oxfords,
the circles from his *tabaco* like tree rings dating him
and filling the frame with smoke | the smoke clears
to a mist floating above Niagara Falls, the deluge
a backdrop to a woman who must be my mother,
donning a magenta blouse scribbled with paisleys,
a string of plastic teal beads like a candy necklace
competing against the golden mums and the clock
in a knot garden where she's never been a widow
standing next to *papá* | he speaks into the camera,
but the film is silent, cloud shadows darken over
his dark lips, a voice I can't hear forever | forever
there is a room strung with banners and balloons,
a birthday cake circled by faces like stained glass
lit by dim candle light, faces not yet loved or lost
by a boy who is me | I watch myself close my eyes,
take a breath, make a wish I will never remember.

Pulitzer Prize–winning journalist LIZ BALMASEDA is a story-teller at heart. In an eclectic career that began in the 1980s, she has worked as a foreign correspondent, magazine writer, television field producer, newspaper reporter, metro columnist, food editor, dining critic, and more. It was as a metro columnist for the *Miami Herald* that she won the 1993 Pulitzer Prize for commentary and in 2001 shared a second Pulitzer for breaking news coverage. She has authored and co-authored several books, including the memoir of Miami's doctor to the homeless, Pedro José Greer (*Waking Up in America*, 1999, Simon and Schuster), the memoir of television anchor María Elena Salinas (*I Am My Father's Daughter*, 2007, HarperCollins), and a novel (*Sweet Mary*, 2009, Simon and Schuster). The winner of a Hispanic Heritage Award for writing excellence, she also worked as an associate producer on the HBO film *For Love or Country*, the story of jazz trumpeter Arturo Sandoval. In 2006 she joined the *Palm Beach Post*, where she is food and dining editor. In 2015 the Cuban-born Balmaseda joined presidential inaugural poet Richard Blanco as a founding board member of the Bridges to Cuba literary website (BridgesToCuba.com); fellow board members include the authors Sandra Cisneros, Nilo Cruz, and Edwidge Danticat. Balmaseda resides in Palm Beach Gardens, Florida.

"Hialeah, Isla Mía" is nonfiction.

> In suburbia, the elements against us seemed more visible. May-be it's because I was a young newspaper reporter covering the Mariel Boatlift and the anti-immigrant backlash it sparked, but the messages were hateful: forget your native land, your first language, your family's culture. Stop obsessing over historical heartaches. Melt into the pot. Such messages seemed alien in Hialeah, a city that refuses to melt into any damn pot.
>
> From "Hialeah, Isla Mía"

HIALEAH, ISLA MÍA

I blame a plate of croquetas for the barbarity I'm about to commit in Hialeah. I can't help it. They're too damn adorable, plump, crispy, golden, and they refuse to be ignored. How could I not glamour-shoot them, capture them in the sunlight streaming through the café storefront as if they're wearing a lamé sash proclaiming "Miss Municipio de Puerto Padre"?

Back in my old Hialeah days, nobody would consider a random croqueta worthy of such exile beauty-queen treatment. My people might have laughed at the sight of me: angling the phone just so, resisting that first hot bite, that only truly worthy bite. Everybody knows the flavor lifespan of a croqueta is five minutes max. You devour them fresh from the fryer while they're still fluffy. A cold or even room-temp croqueta is nobody's pleasure. There's an urgency to some of the best bites in Cuban American cuisine. Like Hialeah itself, they shine best in the immediate. Sandwiches must be toasty. Tostones must be hot and crisp. Batidos de trigo must be freshly blended—nobody wants a shake with puffed-wheat sediment at the bottom of the glass.

So, Mami, Papi, Abuelo, Abuela, all the saints enshrined on Hialeah lawns, and anyone else who may wonder how a child of this City of Progress could grow up to Instagram a croqueta like it's a celebrity with all the time in the world, please look away.

Truth be told, I feel like an interloper in this strip-mall café. I drove more than eighty miles south to reach Hialeah, a near Key West-to-Havana distance from my home two counties to the north. I scribbled a list of such places on the back of an envelope, curious to see what los foodies de Hialeah were gorging on these days. This café is the first stop on an impromptu gastronomic swing through my childhood city, a moveable buffet that included an Elena Ruz sandwich sweetened with guava jam, a creamy malanga soup, a bacalao croqueta so delicious I wanted a dozen of them, and a frothy orange and papaya shake at a frenetic counter where a sign announces the best batidos anywhere.

And here, in this storefront café, I search the gastro-pubby menu for signs of my old Hialeah before giving in to the tweaked-Cuban novelty vibe. I order ropa vieja served in Chinese-style steamed buns and these preening, ham-and-Swiss orbs they call Medio Día Croquettes.

This is one of those newish spots serving Cuban food a branding expert might call "reimagined." The décor is a mashup of industrial USA and sepia Havana. Into this setting walks a young couple seeking a venue for their daughter's First Holy Communion celebration. They chat up a helpful thirty-something manager (or maybe owner) about the possibilities. Overhearing snippets, I gather the manager has hospitality experience that extends beyond this tiny spot. He offers to close part of the café to accommodate the party and suggests a "family-style menu" service.

"¿Qué cosa es eso—family es-tile?" asked the young mother.

The helpful manager gives a logistical explanation, describing the placement of large sharing platters of each dish along the center of the tables.

"Oh, like at home," says the mother.

Like at home, but formalized. During my Hialeah years, circa 1965 to 1978, family-style wasn't a restaurant meal option. It was a nightly rotation of fricasé, potaje, bistec empanizado, and daily arroz shared in the gaze of a gold-framed Last Supper painting that dominated our dining room. It was weekend comelatas in the yard, birthday parties with syrupy Cuban cakes, and baby showers featuring the most delicious chicken salad in the world, the one my mother and aunts made by kitchen-table assembly line, tossing pulled chicken with apples, potatoes, hard-boiled eggs and mayo, and decorated with olives, sweet peas, and strips of fancy pimiento. Sure, there were Cuban restaurants. But the meals that really mattered, be they informal suppers or Saturday pachangas, happened at home. And the feasts, lovingly cobbled from humble ingredients and backyard fruit, were epic.

I've conjured an image of my Hialeah years from pops of memory. I've sifted through boxes of old photos, hoping to fill in the details and find confirmation of the house as I remember it, the decorations, food, and fashion. But the city captured in those photos is a funky haze, washed out in the pastel filters of the 1960s and the burnt siennas of the 1970s. My memories are sharper. I see the handmade tablecloth stretched beneath the familiar composition of palomilla steaks, golden onions, white rice, and fried plantains. I see the baby-blue pantsuit my mom made for me to wear to guitar recitals. I see our late-1960s living room hopping with grownup party guests, women in palazzo pants and tangerine lipstick, men in polyester safari jackets, Johnnie Walker sloshing around in their thick cocktail glasses, all shimmying to Joe Cuba's big boogaloo hit "El Pito." I can hear the chorus resound all over the house, from the Last Supper wall to the Don Quixote–themed bar in the Florida room: "I'll never go back to Georgia! I'll never go back!" Hialeah is where I came to understand on certain party nights how it's possible to dance and cry at the same time.

"La gente de Hialeah," my relatives would say when we walked into family gatherings in Sweetwater or Westchester. It was as if we were visitors from another land, one more concentrated in its identity and Cubanía. If it wasn't back then, it would become so: nearly three-fourths of the population is Cuban or Cuban American, making Hialeah the most Cuban city in the USA.

Life in my Hialeah was cloaked in nostalgia, one I couldn't fully understand but one I felt to the point of tears. I'd well up at the Cuban national anthem and every time they played "Cuando salí de Cuba," the schmaltziest of exile anthems, at local variety shows. My parents brought me from Cuba to Miami when I was ten months old. I did not know Cuba. But the fog of Cuba? *That* I knew well.

Years after we moved away, a bizarre newspaper assignment about a roofer who had been fined an exorbitant amount for dumping toxic waste led me back to my old house in Hialeah by sheer coincidence. The house now belonged to the delinquent roofer. The rooms that were once filled with suppertime chatter, my mother's cherished decorations, my younger siblings' favorite toys, and Fania tunes were now scattered with haphazard furnishings. It had become a house of frowning people who, for some reason, placed their young son in a playpen covered by a net to secure him. Essentially, the invaders of my childhood home had caged their kid in the middle of the living room. My chest tightened at the sight of it all. I continued my interviews as best I could, all the while desperate to get out of there. I feared one more minute there would ruin the house of my memories. My parents never returned to Cuba because they knew the island would be nothing like they remembered it. Leaving the delinquent roofer's house that night, I could understand why.

As I drive through today's Hialeah, it feels as if I'm traveling two cities at once, the traffic-choked one unfolding before me and the one that drifts in as street numbers and facades nudge a reverie. In each corner, a hidden city.

There's the pool where I learned to swim and the leafy street where I learned to play the guitar. There's the parking lot by Milander Park where I learned to dance Cuban during practice sessions for a friend's quinces party. Thanks to the choreographer's eclectic tastes and my quinceañera friend's super-Cuban parents, we learned a range of moves, from the starched traditional danzón to the hip-swiveling, Cuban-style Mozambique.

There's the school where I learned to speak English. For that, I thank a devoted young teacher who made special flash cards for me, visited my house to check on my reading progress, and prepared me to compete in the first-grade spelling bee. It was a long shot, but I took home the little First Place trophy. It would be decades before I learned the reasons Miss Sussman took such an interest in me, the only Spanish-speaking kid in her class. She reached out to me one day at work and filled in the details I had not grasped as a child. She said she protected me because I was "a Cuban refugee girl in a redneck town" and she worried about me. I'm not sure she realized just how powerful her protection would be. Her gift of the English language would become my amulet against the bigots I'd encounter throughout my career.

There's the school sidewalk where I practiced reciting Robert Frost's poem "Stopping by Woods on a Snowy Evening" on my way to a fourth-grade poetry challenge. I still remember the darkly majestic scene it evoked on my sunny walk in Hialeah.

Hialeah is the island we constructed between sacks of arroz blanco and sheets of palomilla steaks cut from bola entera, from spelling bee trophies and the stray threads from la factoría that clung to my mother's work blouse. And it wasn't easy to leave it. When my father, an enterprising salesman who dreamed of more spacious digs for us, announced we'd be moving to a new house in Kendall, it felt like a new exile. We'd leave our tight community, our walking-distance friends and relatives, the landmarks that told our family story, for a house with a pool in suburbia. Leaving Hialeah was like leaving behind the frame that held together our family's identity.

In suburbia, the elements against us seemed more visible. Maybe it's because I was a young newspaper reporter covering the Mariel Boatlift and the anti-immigrant backlash it sparked, but the messages were hateful: forget your native land, your first language, your family's culture. Stop obsessing over historical heartaches. Melt into the pot. Such messages seemed alien in Hialeah, a city that refuses to melt into any damn pot. They were nothing but waves crashing against the malecón of the island we built. We could see them, regard them as curious, maybe even fascinating, but know they wouldn't erode what kept us afloat. In a city that runs on the immediate, that's how we became americanos—by refusing to be moved by such noise. To understand Hialeah's pull, one must understand this.

I often think about my old city now that I'm almost ninety miles away in a very different city, where Cuban chatter is as rare as a decent croqueta. Sometimes I feel I live a translated life or one that might have required subtitles in my old Hialeah. The memories of those childhood years still anchor me, and they still flood me. And sometimes the feeling is pure "Cuando salí de Cuba."

YADDYRA PERALTA is a poet and writer whose work has appeared in *SWWIM, Miami Rail, Ploughshares, Tigertail, Abe's Penny, Hinchas de Poesia,* the *Miami Herald,* and the anthologies *Eight Miami Poets* (Jai Alai, 2015) and *Ghazals for James Foley* (Hinchas, 2015). She is coauthor, with illustrator Elina Díaz, of the book *Anxious Art: A Creativity Journal to Help Calm You* (Mango, 2019). She holds an MFA in creative writing from Florida International University and has taught writing at Miami Dade College and Homestead Correctional Institution and for O, Miami Poetry Festival's Sunroom project. Peralta was assistant director of the Palm Beach Poetry Festival from 2015 to 2018 and is a book editor living in Miami, Florida. She was born in Honduras.

"From Las Colinas to Carol City and Back: Variations on a Theme of Acculturation" is nonfiction.

It was Mamá's mission to sell moving to America to us kids. Everything would be cleaner, faster, larger.

From "From Las Colinas to Carol City and Back: Variations on a Theme of Acculturation"

FROM LAS COLINAS TO CAROL CITY AND BACK: VARIATIONS ON A THEME OF ACCULTURATION

1.

The world before America was a rush of green.

I lived down in the front yard's grass with the sensitive plants—abrir cerrar abrir cerrar—
I lived with the ants, watching them carry crumbs from the kitchen to the utility room and out through a crack under the door that led to Father's garden.
From the ground I watched the birds; I barely had the language to name them, but I loved their song more than any other sound.

Beyond everything, the mountains.

2.

It was Mamá's mission to sell moving to America to us kids. Everything would be cleaner, faster, larger. The only part of it that sounded remotely interesting to me was the lie (or my misunderstanding) that the elementary school had a café. I imagined something very European—delicate pastries and complicated cakes behind glass. Children with espressos in little white cups congregating at tables discussing the latest dilemmas like which El Chavo del Ocho character was least likable. A seductive scene worthy of a picture book.

3.

A grown woman in a yellow dress barefoot on a yellow-tiled porch, sometimes just standing, sometimes lying in a hammock all day.

In the distance, Pico Bonito covered in her majestic greenery, her upper reaches sometimes obscured by clouds.

Time is elastic—we could do this forever—I submerge completely in this act of wondering.

What hides in the cloud forest that is stranger than my mind?

I am in the land of my people. Alternate universe me.

4.

To step from the kitchen, to the utility room, and out into the alley leading to the backyard. The lawn pulled up in patches for Father's new garden. The replacement soil spilling from stacked bags is a maw-like black unlike the exposed clay-colored that's been living here. I take a fistful of each, to taste the two. I want to know the difference.

5.

We ended up in what my mother called Opa Locka, based on the neighborhood's proximity to the small airport. It was really Carol City, and years later, Miami Gardens.

We stayed with Mamá's schoolmate Merly. She was una hondureña too—olanchana—with rural origins like my mother, but now wore her hair feathered and blond-tipped like a character out of *Dynasty*. Her husband and three children were a decidedly American family. I mean, no one spoke Spanish. Their English left their mouths in large blocky letters. The carpets were wall-to-wall. Syndicated sitcoms played on the Florida room TV all afternoon. Merly and her husband and his parents each had a relatively new and spotless Cadillac. The cars, the carpeting, the kitchen phones, the smell of newness permeating what seemed like a life of ease.

A short time later, we had our own house, a rental, at the other end of the neighborhood. No A/C, a shed full of spiderwebs and dusty old suitcases, a pendulous beehive right outside the door to the back porch. My sister and I watched *Little House on the Prairie*. This American neighborhood in northwest Dade County was not too different than that more distant and vast Minnesotan frontier. This neighborhood in the dark, sleeping soundly inside night's alligator mouth, was a forlorn wilderness of isolated houses, except our food came in cans and frozen boxes.

6.

In the land of my people, cilantro, remolacha, rábanos still dusted with soil.
In the land of my people, sugarcane and watermelon: treasures from the elders.

Pomegranate jewels spill forth from my grandmother's hands and into my mouth. The little globules, a journey of questions.

In this land, the toucans fly free, and the bellbird's cry is an alarm call that wakes us all from the long deep dream.

7.

Before heading to the airport, I refuse to leave behind my favorite pillow. You're going to lose it, Tia Jenny warns. She takes the pillow from my arms, sews it shut inside its pillowcase, and when she's done, she hands it back.

There have always been dreams in which my voice is taken from me. In the atmospherically dark and busy restaurant—memory-banked from some old American movie—I am two or three and so invisible to my parents. I slip away to explore, enchanted by the tinkling symphony of clinking glass and silverware. Just as I turn back, I find myself inside a clear Lucite cube—trapped, a moth under an overturned glass. My silent wails are limitless. I open and open my mouth, but the world goes on. I see my parents and they do not see me. Many dreams, many variations of this being buried alive under all of the world's loam while holding on to a single pillow.

On the flight from Tegucigalpa to Miami, I question whether we're breathing in real air. Are we flying through time and space? The flight attendants float up and down the aisle in bright orange uniforms, tending to our minor needs.

8.

My mother, five siblings, and I can afford to do two things for what she calls "diversión." One is visiting the Opa Locka Flea Market, where we are allowed to have small disposable treasures like plastic bird-shaped water whistles and the occasional more practical item like clear bubble umbrellas. During our first hurricane season, my sister and I sneak out during rainstorms and stand in the front yard like little spacewomen protected by the clear domes. We stare out at our new wild home, teeming with life—the verdancy of weeds, the bougainvillea overtaking the wobbly chain link fence. Spiny orb weavers, lizards and frogs, the occasional snake. (At night, in the deepest silence, this tangle of nature seems to live inside too.)

On Sundays we start attending la iglesia mormona in Hialeah. There the boys and the girls do Bible study separately. An accordion partition wall divides the two groups at our age level, and I think so much of this partition as we study Adam and Eve, Cain and Abel. Biblical pairs traversing the foreign lands of neatened history.

9.

What does it mean to be in the land of my people? It does not mean I know the names of all the living things. It means I do not need to. The language lives inside me, divorced from meaning: mecate, petate, cipote—the words colored by sounds—jaguar y guacamayo macao. Emerald words multiplying in the mouth, until the words themselves are my mouth. In the end, who needs a head to weigh her down?

10.

A paleta from the Oso Polar ice cream man on a bike. The sharp smell of cold from his cooler, a fathomless portal to the North. As he hands me the treat, I anticipate the sudden rush of sugar and aromatic vanilla overtaking my senses. On the white paper wrapper, two polar bears in the sun hoisting their paletas in the air like champagne glasses during a toast.

[Erased from my memory because I was too young to read: the full brand name of the Honduran ice cream company, Oso Polar American Ice Cream.]

11.

There are many theories regarding an immigrant's process of assimilation. Sociologist Milton Gordon offers seven stages. The first is acculturation—when the subject or group adopts the language, dress, and customs of the dominant culture.

My father joins us several months later in Miami. New house rule, no Spanish in the house. This will help us all become more American. The problem is not simply the loss of language, but our specific corner of it. Not just the rhythms of Nahuatl-derived words like aguacate and zacate (wild grass!) peppered in, but the singsong birdieness of the Spanish of my mother's people. And what of my father's languages? His Spanish touched by the swinging rhythm of his Bay Island Creole English?

12.

I do not know my people.

The pictures painted are with words and words of words. Pictures made with eyes closed, with disjointed memories as models. Trees live without birds here. And there are those you think you love who feel like zoo exhibitions when trapped in your gaze.

13.

Roatán. The clarity of her warm waters. The first time I visit without my parents, my grandparents are living without hot water and have limited electricity. My first night, I awake to pure black. No nightlights or street lights to remind you of the living. Despite a panic that wakes up the entire house, I am not allowed to sleep with a flashlight as I do back home. Each night I am there, I open my eyes and try to breathe into the black, the knowledge that even if my eyes grow accustomed, I will not recognize the shapes of this life.

14.

I am the worst reader in my class for all of the first and the second grade. Once I start to catch up, I spend our once-a-week visit to the school library with biographies of monster-movie actors Bela Lugosi, Lon Chaney, and Boris Karloff. I can speak English pretty well but am so painfully shy I'd sometimes rather pee my pants than ask to go to the bathroom in the adjoining sixth-grade classrooms.

One of the first books I check out on my own is a biography of Abraham Lincoln. I am drawn mostly to his childhood—the story of poverty and long hard days, the spare log cabin, homework by candlelight—I swallow it all like everyone before me, the immensity of meritocracy, the desire to work at being so unabashedly normal and American. I pick up the idea that literacy is somehow tied to self-flagellation. I spend many nights in palimpsestic Miami neighborhoods surrounded by books.

DANIEL RESCHIGNA was born in Buenos Aires in 1970 and has lived in Miami since 2005. He is a songwriter and storyteller, an avid guitar player, a trusty handyman, and a self-taught pizza maker as well as a slow reader and a fierce soccer defender. His most important role is that of dedicated husband and father.

Originally from Argentina, MARTINA LENTINO grew up in Miami, Florida. She is an MA student at the Institute of Fine Arts at New York University, focusing on modern and contemporary art of Latin America.

"Ziploc" is fiction, translated from the Spanish by Martina Lentino.

In this city, the odds of a woman, a cool night, and a fireplace coinciding are akin to winning the lottery. I lit the chimney and the flames blazed crazy, like the Cordoban's.

From "Ziploc"

ZIPLOC

The street was scorching. I confirmed it the very day I arrived when I touched the pavement with my hand. It burned. After barely walking around the block, I came back inside, desperate for some cool air, drank a glass of water, and called her. I told her I'd seen huge houses, brand new cars, no buses, few trees, and sidewalk paths that were nothing like ours. I also told her the heat, the humidity, here were crazy, that I seemed to be the only one getting around on foot, and that I missed her.

Over the next few months, I would call Julia several times a day. After about three weeks, the good vibe was over and the arguments began. Among her many complaints: how this was not the original idea, how she'd known this would happen, how I had said it would only be for three months and what was she supposed to do in Miami. We were both right. We both had our reasons. Meanwhile, I wrote songs while learning to say unfamiliar words like arepa, arrechera, traba, rola, parche, coladita, chamo, marico, yuca and to live with the guilt that I couldn't shake. I was not as happy as I looked in photos; decided to try therapy via Skype.

Friday afternoons, I'd close all the blinds in the apartment, light a nag champa, and peering into the small Skype app window on the screen of my laptop, talk to the beard of a psychologist who, every so often, managed to reach basic conclusions:

"Your decisions point to a desire of being alone."

A couple of weeks in, I'd figured out his tricks. They were always the same. Five minutes before the end of each session, he'd ask me something and close with:

"But don't answer me now, let's sit with that unease until next Friday."

Then I would bid goodbye to the low-resolution beard, more frustrated than before, and with even more questions.

Julia came to visit, if only to confirm that things weren't going to work out, that she didn't see herself in Miami. I had bought her a blue used Kia. It ran well but she wanted no part of it, never even gave it a test drive.

Sixty nights. We took pictures on the beach, in the New York snow, wearing "Happy 2006" party glasses on Broadway, naked in Sanibel, home making milanesa de soja, in line to see Cirque du Soleil, smoking in Fort Lauderdale. Before she left, we printed copies for each other; I put mine in a Ziploc bag. The image I remember most is one where I am drying myself off in the bathtub and she is leaning against the door frame, crying.

Years later, I moved to Biscayne and 71st. Clothes, guitar, speakers, mattress, table, chairs, TV, laptop, and toaster. Everything fit in two trips of a van.

The new house was old and too big for me alone. The first thing I did was put on Spinetta and boil water in the kettle for mate, a sort of ritual to make myself comfortable within those walls. At night, I would hear sounds in the other bedroom, in the kitchen, the attic, in my head.

Everyone said the house had good energy, even the plumber. Wood floors, lots of windows, and an impressive chimney in the middle of the living room.

The usual friends and acquaintances came to the housewarming party, like the recording engineer turned realtor from Cordoba, who I have to admit was the only one who ever knew how to work the chimney.

"Allow me," he boasted, and no one dared dispute him the task.

It was cold, it doesn't matter how cold, it was chilly and the Cordoban's fire delivered hours of warmth and laughter.

A month later, Linda, a journalist from the *Miami Herald* I had a crush on, came to visit. In this city, the odds of a woman, a cool night, and a fireplace coinciding is like winning the lottery. I lit the chimney and the flames blazed crazy, like the Cordoban's. As I started to heat a can of Hunt's tomato sauce in the kitchen, I noticed a strange fog. I looked up and the cloud of smoke in the living room was so dense I couldn't see Linda. We opened windows. I coughed. She must've too.

On another occasion, I invited my friends and the Cordoban. He didn't get back to me, so, once again, smoke, coughing, and two weeks of airing out the house.

I called the only person I could find who thought it was a good business idea to specialize in chimneys in a tropical city. The man who arrived was the typical sixty-something from Maine who zeroes in on Florida to live out his last years.

"How you doin' sir?" he must have said, and seconds later he was crawling through the ash with his impeccable apron as if it were his intention to dirty it. He examined this and looked at that, but everything was fine. "I see no problem," he said and quizzed me to see if, at least in theory, I knew how to make a fire. Then he gave me a pat on the back and left without charging me.

The third cloud of smoke I inhaled before coughing it back up all by myself, but it no longer mattered to me. I felt at home.

Six months later, I met Sonia. She and her eight-year-old son moved into the second bedroom. Sonia and I fell in love in the summer, and by the time winter arrived, we could argue in English, in Porteño, and in Colombian. The house was no longer too big, and we couldn't agree on the placement of the television or the new sofa. I wanted to get rid of the chimney, but Sonia did not. I did. She didn't.

When Dora was born, we adopted a pet. I learned to change diapers and to go on walks twice a day. I had never had a dog. One night, I came home from work and the dog was wagging his tail with my passport between his teeth. He'd chewed it up like he'd done to the legs of the table, the chairs, the sofa cover, and every photo in the Ziploc.

It was cold and Sonia insisted we finally use the chimney.

"We can have him neutered," I told her as we watched the fire grow and the sparks fly.

"We can also burn photos," she said, just before the smoke enveloped us for the last time.

CARIDAD MORO-GRONLIER was born in Los Angeles, California, to Cuban immigrant parents who relocated to Miami, Florida, in 1979. She is the author of *Tortillera* (Texas Review, 2021), winner of the TRP Southern Poetry Breakthrough Prize for Florida, and *Visionware*, published in 2009 by Finishing Line as part of its New Women's Voices Series. She is a contributing editor of *Grabbed: Writers Respond to Sexual Assault* (Beacon, 2020) and associate editor of *SWWIM Every Day*, an online daily poetry journal. Moro-Gronlier is the recipient of an Elizabeth George Foundation Grant and a Florida Individual Artist Fellowship in poetry. Her work has been nominated for two Pushcart Prizes, the Best of the Net, and a Lambda Literary Award. Her work can be found at *Best American Poetry*, *Rhino*, *Go Magazine*, *West Trestle Review*, *Fantastical Florida*, *Notre Dame Review*, and other publications. A career educator, Moro-Gronlier has been honored as the recipient of an Educational Leader Award from Unity Coalition for her work with LGBTQ youth and as a Francisco R. Walker Teacher of the Year nominee for Miami-Dade County Public Schools, where she is a dual-enrollment English professor in conjunction with Florida International University. She resides in Miami, Florida, with her wife and son.

> You have come as if this place
> could sustain you, retain the whole
> of you, the stamp and edge of you,
> but Los Estados Unidos will never be home.
>
> From "Topography"

ANALFABETA

It took a while for Abuela to figure out that an F
on my report card did not stand for Fantástico,
her experience with school limited to fourth grade
back in the days of wooden rooms and rulers that beat
knowledge into those bold enough to opt for ignorance.

Abuela kept what she could from el colegio en el campo—
arithmetic, the alphabet, penmanship that wobbled
long before her arthritis set in. She would not stand for less
than my best which is why she beat my ass with her chancleta
when she learned I'd been lying about my ease with fractions and P.E.

You would have thought her a dignitary the day she walked
into my 6th grade classroom, staccato heels, her good black dress
ironed crisp as a dollar, all for a date with Mrs. Dempsey
who looked at us down the long slope of her nose and began
to tear me down in tea-time tones that forgot to mention

she sometimes slipped and called me 'Spic,' how she pounced
when I spoke to my friends in Español. Abuela caught most
of the words Dempsey lobbed her way, but didn't say a thing
just glared at me every second she endured the shame of
my shortcomings, as personal as the fine stitch of her heirloom DNA,

as if she alone were to blame for the thrust of my chin, the purse
of my lips, the crossbones of arms I strapped to my chest as the words
too smart for her own good lingered in the air like the bells
that ruled our days, which is when Abuela finally stood, said the words
that set me straight—Neber too esmart, mi niña, neber too esmart!

WET FOOT, DRY FOOT, 2002

We watch the rush hour spectacle
from our living room exile,
plush and merciless as the helicopters
that swivel between palm trees and swoop in
for the next great shot.

Amid feet pounding pavement, bodies
scatter across the Rickenbacker Causeway
but only her polished onyx face anchors the screen—
dressed up for a new life in buttercup yellow organza
awash on the gangplank, her soles sway
sheathed in lace-rimmed socks, white patent leather
Mary-Janes too big for her feet, starched
ribbons braided through her hair.

We don't ask what it cost,
her Sunday best—

not Abuela who buys those same itchy dresses at La Canastilla Cubana
for my cousins in Havana now that lace and church have gone black market;

not Papi who once ran from hammer-fisted rednecks
eager to knock his accent right out of his mouth;

not Mami who collects pantyhose and Kotex
for her best friend, Teresita, whom she had to leave behind.

It's easier that way, easier to overlook her
space on the freighter, so much like the one
that ferried cousin Pepito to Key West during El Mariel,
easier to complain about the invasion of Key Biscayne
where work wizened nannies speak Creole now
that Español has moved into the zip code.

We do not speak of travesties—
Wet Foot, Dry Foot,
white face, black face,
tic-tac-toe of policy.

We do not ask if she dreams of Griot,
soil culled vegetables, a brand-new doll
dressed in buttercup yellow.

Only human when it comes to our own,
we watch and know she'll be returned
to Port-au-Prince, sea weary, sweat-drenched
dress a ruined souvenir strapped to her back.

TOPOGRAPHY

After Ana Mendieta, Siluetas Series, 1980

You have come to make sense
of this land, to lie within
a canyon of want, stake a spot
of stone with the weight of your bones.

You have come to plant
your body in this cracked earth,
parched streambed that survives
on the memory of water.

You have come as if this place
could sustain you, retain the whole
of you, the stamp and edge of you,
but Los Estados Unidos will never be home.

You have come to leave
your impression in the ground,
a reminder of what is left after
the stripping away of root, seed and soil—

cavern, chronicle, chasm.

LEGNA RODRÍGUEZ IGLESIAS, born in Camagüey, Cuba, in 1984, is a prize-winning poet, fiction writer, and playwright. Her work includes the poetry books *Mi pareja calva y yo vamos a tener un hijo* (Liliputienses, 2019), *Miami Century Fox* (Akashic, 2017), and *Transtucé* (Casa Vacía, 2017); the short-story collections *La mujer que compró el mundo* (Los Libros de La Mujer Rota, 2017) and *No sabe/no contesta* (La Palma, 2015); and the novels *Mi novia preferida fue un bulldog francés,* (Alfaguara, 2017), *Mayonesa bien brillante* (Hypermedia, 2015), and *Las analfabetas* (Bokeh, 2015). Among her literary awards are the Centrigugados Prize for Younger Poets (Spain 2019), the Paz Prize (National Poetry Series, 2017), the Casa de las Américas Prize in Theater (Cuba, 2016), and the Julio Cortázar Ibero-American Short Story Prize, 2011). *Spinning Mill*, a chapbook of her work, appears in English translation (CardBoard House, 2019, translation by Katerina González Seligmann). Rodríguez Iglesias lives in Miami, where she writes a column for the online journal *El Estornudo*.

Please see translator ANDREÍNA FERNÁNDEZ's bio on page 38

"I Came to Miami Because I Was Told This Was Where My Son Lived" is nonfiction, translated by Andreína Fernández.

One comes filled with excited anticipation, wrecked by emotion. Some habits fade in time. Others fail to die.

From "I Came to Miami Because I Was Told
This Was Where My Son Lived"

I CAME TO MIAMI BECAUSE I WAS TOLD THIS WAS WHERE MY SON LIVED

She told me good evening once more.

And although there were no children playing, no doves, no blue roofs,

I felt like the town was alive.

And that if I heard only silence,

It was because I was still not accustomed to the silence;

Perhaps because my head was filled with noises and voices.

Juan Rulfo, *Pedro Páramo*

Whoever arrives in a place called Miami at thirty-five has the right to write anything, whatever they want, however they want, and in the genre they please, about Miami or not, traversed positively by the experience or not, with anticipation or incredulity, with delirium or with reluctance, exposing themselves, shaking it all off, relieving themselves, because so what? in the end.

Because anyone who turns thirty-five in Miami deserves a happy birthday, at the very least the song, and they deserve it in their native language, out of tune, mortgaged, filled with an austere, frugal, precarious happiness. Congratulations on your day, dear so and so, may you spend it in health and joy, many years of peace and harmony happiness happiness happiness.

Whoever turns thirty-five in Miami deserves a bottle of rum, ay ay ay the bottle of rum. And they also deserve to buy themselves a scratch-off and win the lottery or to receive a call from an important editor telling them they'd like to buy the rights to their book, pay them the following number of dollars.

Let's suppose that it happens: the scratch-off. Let's suppose that someone turns thirty-five in Miami and wins five hundred dollars (which is not much at all) in one night, without lifting a finger, without a drop of sweat, putting in no mental effort whatsoever. The first thing they think is: I am going to save one bill in my wallet and I won't use it so that it can be my good-luck bill and attract more sibling bills or cousin bills, or, at least, members of the same family, surely.

Human thought in all its splendor, thinking of Miamian swine here. Splendorous. The thoughts of an adult birthday girl who only wants to blow out her candle and write, if possible, in the notes app on a phone she will have finished paying off in twenty-four months. Sound familiar? Who can relate?

Whoever reaches thirty-five in Miami forgets how to sing, forgets how to read, forgets how to write, forgets to drink coffee in the morning, forgets to drink water throughout the day, forgets to call their family on the phone, does not remember to shave their armpits, cannot remember what it's like to get drunk.

That person who has reached the same age her parents were not too long ago when she was a child does not save any bills in her wallet, more likely she spends them all immediately, on gasoline, or first exchanging them for quarters to go to the laundromat and wash her dirty rags. A laundromat is a dive. Who can relate?

I still don't know if it's a good thing to, once a year, read a bunch of pages from *Pedro Páramo*, top to bottom, but I do know that it is not a good idea to take *Pedro Páramo* to the laundromat with you and to read *Pedro Páramo* while parts that are called things like motor and gasket rotate, around and around: there is a sky and there is a state of coma. Definitely not good. As in nutritious, is what I mean to say. Like pumpkin, which no matter how many pieces of it you eat or how much pumpkin soup you drink, the stomach remains light, as if mildly empty, because pumpkin is little more than water, but water that contributes, that feeds, that nourishes.

Here, the context does not nourish. The context of exile in its fullest expression: a person carrying a bag full of dirty laundry, accumulated over a month to make the most of the trek and get it clean as fast (and as cheaply) as possible, their expenses, minimal, and their income even less. A person accustomed to a house with a Russian washing machine inside it, damaging both fancy clothes and everyday clothes, a washing machine all their own and also Russian, perhaps not even Russian, but certainly their own. Dilapidated, oxidized, and owned.

The next step after receiving a Social Security number and a work permit, after leasing an efficiency or studio or a room inside a house with its own separate entrance or without, after eating Chinese food and finding work at a Navarro, Burger King, or Walmart, is to wash the dirty clothes.

One-person rentals do not generally include the use of a washing machine. Tienes que ir al laundry, mi vida. You have to exchange a bill for quarters or get a laundry card, depending on the laundromat or system the laundromat uses. Because a recent arrival from Cuba or Haiti or Puerto Rico or Mexico is unlikely to rent an apartment with an in-unit washing machine. An in-unit washing machine is a luxury for a recent, insular, Caribbean immigrant's head in the clouds feet on the ground.

It is normal for people to still be at the laundromat well into the night, the small washing machines not allowing more than a few pounds of clothes, there are many people at the laundromat, some machines don't work. One arrives accustomed to washing clothes the white with the white, the colored with colored, and the work clothes reeking of food with other work clothes also reeking of food. One gets here filled with the manias, habits, and domestic customs grandparents teach grandkids. One comes filled with excited anticipation, wrecked by emotion. Some habits fade in time. Others fail to die.

I have searched (to no avail) for a photo of Alva Fisher showing Alva Fisher next to a washing machine so I can print it, frame it, and place it on a wall in my small apartment. Alva Fisher invented the washing machine in 1901 although she did not patent it until 1910. My maternal grandfather was born in 1919 and my maternal grandmother in 1923. I remember them washing and cooking in unison. They taught my mother to rinse clothes twice. They rinsed clothes in an aluminum basin on the patio under impossible sun. Around them, chickens, ducks, and even a pig. The sheets always came out extremely white.

What Alva Fisher did was invent a machine that would spin, shake, and throw around whatever was inside. It was as if Alva Fisher had purchased a scratch-off and won the lottery or received a call from an important editor telling her from that day forward everything would change.

Alva Fisher never imagined her invention would be reproduced into millions and millions of electric drums shaking the dirty clothes of immigrants in unison all over the world. Alva Fisher could not have imagined Miami would become a giant hub for washing machines mixing white clothes with colored clothes with work clothes that reeked of food.

You need to go to a laundromat, Alva Fisher. You have to take a bill and make change in quarters or get a laundry card and put the quarters into the little hole or the card into the narrow slot made for the card. You have to take a book with you to read while the drum rotates, shakes. An easy one. You need to grab a book that is not *Pedro Páramo*. Taking *Pedro Páramo* with you to the laundromat goes against basic human well-being. *Pedro Páramo* in a laundromat is suicide. A laundromat in *Pedro Páramo* would constitute a new literary genre.

The laundromats in Miami smell of Miami. The detergents and fabric softeners are products with ranges like android phones: high reach and low reach. It is rare to encounter high reach in a laundromat. The low reach, on the other hand, comfortably finds its home there.

The men and women who work in the laundromat providing their services to the clientele of the laundromat are the mirror image of their clients: tired faces alongside bulimic faces, indifferent faces alongside tired faces, bulimic faces alongside heads in the clouds. Feet on the ground proliferate in the laundromat. Everything there is feet on the ground.

I recommend doing as in Latino infomercials and listening to Shakira's album "Laundry Service," released in English in 2001, while at the laundromat waiting for the washer and dryer to finish. When people speak of washing machines in Miami, the dryer is implied. There are no clotheslines in Miami for recent arrivals. For there to be clotheslines it is necessary to also have a house with a patio and time, all of the time. In Miami there are washers and dryers.

Oddities:

1

The collection of Tana Oshima photographs on her private Instagram, selfies in a laundromat in New York, should illustrate my references, should form part of the poetics of laundry. If they do it. They don't do it. They do it. They do it poorly. I want to go to the laundromat with Tana Oshima. That's all.

2

I found out about Juan Gabriel's death at a laundromat. I could not take my eyes off of the television on top of the washing machine. Susana Pérez, the famous Cuban actress, was on all the time, promoting her cosmetic surgery clinic in Miami's Southwest. Susana Pérez's famous clinic called My Cosmetic Surgery, translates to Spanish as Mi cirugía cosmética. The ad song Susana Pérez sang sounded loudly in juxtaposition to the news of Juan Gabriel's death: three zero five two six four nine six thirty-six and sing along so that it sticks.

3

If the efficiency or studio or room with a private entrance also comes without a kitchen, hot plate, or coffee pot, you can go to the laundromat and get coffee there. There are machines that dispense American coffee, cappuccinos, mochas, and hot chocolate. All four drinks are a bit watery and have a strange Downy-like taste, but one shouldn't ask a coffee-dispensing machine for pears.

4

You can also have lunch at the laundromat. There are dispensers, also, for bags of chips, mariquitas with or without lime, cookies with or without cream, famous bars of chocolate like Snickers and Milky Ways. Frank Báez has a poem about Snickers and Milky Ways that is a marvel. I would say that some of Frank Báez's poems are good for reading while at a laundromat and others are not.

5

With time and a small hook to use as a tool one can become accustomed to the balls of other people's hair that accumulate under waiting chairs and in the corners of the laundromat, to the balls of other people's hair mixed with the gray lint that accumulates in the filters of the dryers of the laundromat and the clumps of other people's wet detergent that accumulate on the edges of the washing machines. Human beings are made to become accustomed to anything. Sound familiar? Who can relate?

When a (Cuban) emigrant arrives in Miami, they are asked why they came in myriad ways, as if their response could immediately confer on them the benefit of the doubt, the advantage of conviction. The question contains a rhetoric, a kind of intrigue that remits itself to the space of the paranoid, the ugly incomprehensible, the almost vernacular, the closed in. An intrigue that remains on the margins of individual narrative. An intrigue that annuls itself.

They are asked and challenged, pressed against the wall. Their answer should be, as it was in another time, energetic. I have never given an energetic answer, unless it is a writing in response to something, because what is energetic has to do with those obligatory parades of the first of May and with Fidel Castro's energetic speeches lasting hours, days, weeks, months, sixty-six years, the number of the beast. My answer, then, like it or not, has always been one of fiction.

Miami, December 14, 2019

13:11

ARIEL FRANCISCO is the author of *Under Capitalism If Your Head Aches They Just Yank Off Your Head* (Flowersong, 2022), *A Sinking Ship Is Still a Ship* (Burrow, 2020), and *All My Heroes Are Broke* (C&R, 2017). A poet and translator born in the Bronx to Dominican and Guatemalan parents and raised in Miami, his work has been published in the *New Yorker, American Poetry Review, Latino Book Review, American Poet's Magazine*, and the Academy of American Poets' "Poem a Day" series, and featured by the New York City Ballet and elsewhere.

. . . I hope every crab in the world marches into your home

From "They Built a Margaritaville on Hollywood Beach Which Was Once My Favorite Place in the World and Now I Can't Go Back Because It's Unrecognizable So Fuck Jimmy Buffett"

THEY BUILT A MARGARITAVILLE ON HOLLYWOOD BEACH WHICH WAS ONCE MY FAVORITE PLACE IN THE WORLD AND NOW I CAN'T GO BACK BECAUSE IT'S UNRECOGNIZABLE SO FUCK JIMMY BUFFETT

For my friends and my youth

Shell-less lobster lookin' ass, you are
Florida personified—that is shallow
and hollow, filled by a slowly consuming
darkness that anyone with a soul fears, you
tacky, cheap piece of shit, I hope every
crab in the world marches into your home
in the dead of night like an unending wave
of hard, furious zombies and pinch you
to death. Margaritas aren't even good.
Fuck you fuck you fuck you fuck you.

JENNINE CAPÓ CRUCET was born in Miami to Cuban parents and grew up there. She is the author of three books. Her novel *Make Your Home among Strangers* (Picador, 2016) was a *New York Times Book Review* Editor's Choice book, the winner of the 2016 International Latino Book Award, and cited as a best book of the year by NBC Latino, the *Guardian*, and the *Miami Herald*. Her story collection *How to Leave Hialeah* (University of Iowa Press, 2009) won the Iowa Short Fiction Prize, the John Gardner Book Award, and the Devil's Kitchen Reading Award. In her third book, a collection of essays titled *My Time among the Whites* (Picador, 2019), Crucet investigates through a personal lens concepts of race, gender, immigration, and the American dream after the 2016 presidential election. Her work has been featured on the *PBS NewsHour* and published in the *New York Times*, *Los Angeles Review*, *Guernica*, and elsewhere. A former contributing opinion writer for the *New York Times*, she is also the recipient of a PEN/O. Henry Prize, a Picador Fellowship, and the Hillsdale Award for the Short Story awarded by the Fellowship of Southern Writers. Her fourth book, a novel tentatively titled *Say Hello to My Little Friend*, is forthcoming from Little, Brown.

"Feliz Año Nuevo, Connor" is fiction.

> Do I actually need to walk you through all the things my abuela said in her busted English—a language she never needed in Miami—and then all the things he said back in his Taco Bell Spanish, how we were all, over those five days, basically reenacting a much more fraught and depressing episode of *¿Qué Pasa, USA?*
>
> From "Feliz Año Nuevo, Connor"

FELIZ AÑO NUEVO, CONNOR

He was the first American white guy I'd ever dated, so it didn't occur to me that inviting him to spend New Year's in Miami would turn into such ridiculousness. This was in college—where else would I have found a white guy?—and the little city the college dominated was the opposite of Miami—cold, lonely, quiet. I was a sophomore when I met Connor, so that's two years into that cycle of desperation where I swung back and forth between wanting to get away from Hialeah's swelter and my family's particular brand of chusmería and wanting to come back and eat the food my body actually recognized as food and brush my lips against people's cheeks daily in greeting. Two years in, so maybe I should've known better, but I was (and am) in love with my hometown, couldn't yet see it the way an outsider would, despite all the training I was getting at doing just that.

It's that very training that makes me want to ask, before really getting started: How many times do I have to tell this story? If I tell it here, once and for all, can I retire it? Will clearing it out like smoke through an open window make room for something else, some new thing that I've been waiting and waiting for, swirling through the air instead?

There is only one way to find out.

Let's start with the obvious. Yes, of course I should've broken up with Connor long before the chance to extend this invitation ever came up. Dude was not cute, not to me at least. Dude was not even close to my type. Dude was named Connor. One night a couple weeks into us hooking up, he stayed the night in my dorm room, and the next morning he slipped on my jeans instead of his own by accident, and when he was able to button them and have room to spare in the waist—tell me if there isn't a clearer sign from God that me and this guy were anything but doomed. I tried to deny it, yelled at him to take them off, but instead he spun around as if this was something to show off. I pictured him among my beefy primos and could not imagine him holding a cigar to his mouth without my cousins stifling their laughter behind their giant, hairy fists. He checked out his own ass in my jeans in the closet mirror and I knew then it was over; we were together another five months.

And those five months happened to span our school's winter break, and that's when some evil spirit possessed me and invited him to visit me in Miami. I thought it might help him understand me somehow. Also, he'd never been, which I found unbelievable. He was from some New York suburb—his father was a Lockheed Martin engineer who'd, like, invented the Black Hawk helicopter or something, which, seriously, fuck me for not seeing that as a red flag immediately. I'd met his parents once, when I'd gone home with him for fall break a month or so after we got together. Our second night there, his mother—who probably had a real name but who everyone (even Connor) called Bunny (red flag!)—had tugged him by the wrist across their kitchen (but not really out of earshot) and referred to me as a phase. I was Connor's first Cubana, his first not-white anything, and I would also be his last, but Bunny's comment probably did more to keep us together than anything Connor could've done, literal scroll of red flags be damned. We both thought we had something to prove.

I can't even remember now how we found ourselves hooking up, aside from the fact that he often made me angry with his theories about how the world should work (he called himself a libertarian, like so many twenty-year-old white guys who claimed to be liberal and refused to admit they were rich, instead calling themselves upper middle class), and I was in that part of my life—which lasted way too long—where I conflated rage with passion, where I thought disliking someone was a prerequisite to getting married someday, something to get over and live with.

Connor's parents had no problem flying their son down south for five days to celebrate New Year's Eve with me in Miami, but their upper middle class sensibilities drew the line at getting him a hotel room on the beach, which basically ruined my secret plan to have a real New Year's. I had talked a lot of shit about my experience with Miami's nightlife, but the reality was that I had no idea how to get us on any kind of list; I'd always relied on friends from high school who actually lived the kinds of lives I purported to live to hook me up whenever I was home. But New Year's was a big ask, borderline out of the question, and way out of my budget even if I'd had the balls to ask Mikey or Ruben or Raul or any of the dudes with whom I traded flirtation and dance-floor making-out for a pre-arranged easy entrance into a Miami Beach nightclub.

So that's where things got bad right away; Connor needed a place to stay, and my parents weren't about to let my Americano boyfriend stay in the same house as their presumably still-a-virgin (false) daughter. Which meant he was staying down the street with Abuela, who spoke as much English as he spoke Spanish, which is to say: nada.

Over the phone in the days leading up to his flight, he had a lot to say about the housing arrangement, about how different our cultures were, about how his parents had not hesitated to let me stay in their house, etc., etc. I let him talk. I'd thought it strange when, over fall break, his parents didn't insist I stay in his brother's old room—I had been the one to ask—and they'd smiled sweetly at me in a way that made me think the word *peasant*. Bunny made a big show of having to wash a second set of sheets, of handing them over to me in a basket to put on his brother's bed myself. I remain unconvinced that she knew how to operate her own washing machine.

Anyway, Connor complained about staying with Abuela—who, granted, smoked a pack of cigarettes a day, but Connor didn't know that yet—but it wasn't enough to make him rethink the trip, and when I picked him up at Miami International, my younger sister with me (she was a freshman at UF, also home for the break, though for her, coming home was an almost-weekly occurrence), she hid her laugh behind her hand after I said That's him and nodded toward the whitest white guy walking in our direction, his hard-sided roller bag skimming along at his heels.

Jacqui, she said to me, What the fuck are you doing with that gringo?

Anything I want, pretty much, I said.

She let her hand fall from her mouth and said, I cannot.

Connor, still too far from us, raised one arm in anticipation of a hug and yelled, I made it! I made it to Miami! Jacquelin! Carla! Mucho gusto! Bienvenido a Miami!

Make him stop, Carla said.

Okay Connor, relax, I said, trying to laugh into the space still between us, but he was already channeling Will Smith's version of the city. It was already too late.

Do I really need to recap that drive home, his face against the window, my heart and hometown up for dissection, his spectacle? Do I really have to play-by-play that first night's dinner and all the dinners to come; don't you already know the questions he asked and that were asked of him, the obvious and inevitable indigestion? Do I actually need to walk you through all the things my abuela said in her busted English—a language she never needed in Miami—and then all the things he said back in his Taco Bell Spanish, how we were all, over those five days, basically reenacting a much more fraught and depressing episode of *¿Qué Pasa, USA?* with Connor playing the part of Sharon, saying her signature line—You crazy Cubans!—even though she was usually saying it while standing in a Spanish-speaking household, outnumbered and no longer on her own turf?

You've gotten all this before—from me even. You already know how it all went down. How on earth I thought for even a second that it would go any differently is not what this story is about. Whatever foolish hope I had, whatever expectation I thought we'd all rise to—that's not what it's about either. What it's really about—what it's always been about and what I've never been able to fully capture in English and in all the various tellings—is this: how on New Year's Eve, having found an 18 and over club up in Fort Lauderdale that would let us in without costing us fifty bucks a person (it was in a strip mall; Carla and I were cool with it once we realized Connor had nothing to gauge its crappiness against, as he'd never been to a real club anyway), Carla and I stood in the mirror of my abuela's bathroom, choosing to get ready there instead of in our own house as a way to make Connor more comfortable— because everything has always been about making them more comfortable, hasn't it? I learned that in college too. As we shellacked our lashes with a second coat of mascara, he came in behind us wearing—no joke—a long-sleeved button-down white shirt and fucking khaki pants. And I swear Carla and I both had the same thought: that white, white shirt glowing like a beacon in the club's inevitable blacklights, how much he would stand out, how much he didn't belong there.

And his skin—his skin in the light of Abuela's bathroom looked green, sallow. Disgusting even. His blond hair green, too, an alien invading the sacred space around Abuela's sink. Carla looked at me, her cheeks and the bones of her brows glowing gold.

She said to me, Jacqui, please. He cannot go dressed like that.

And because of everything not written here, everything I didn't need to tell you because we've already told it in so many different ways, so many stories and poems and essays about this place we've learned to call home and have made ours, I said: Let him. He'll be fine. If we're lucky, they won't let him past the door.

And then we laughed together at his face in the mirror. We laughed and laughed. We knew the power of it, because we'd been laughing like that our whole lives, long before we knew people like him, before we learned enough of their language to be understood. We would laugh again later, as we entered that strip-mall club holding hands, our slick shoulders touching, him trapped outside and still fumbling with his wallet to pay the cover the bouncer refused to collect from us—two girls he recognized without knowing us—but not from him. We laughed in Abuela's bathroom and let the sound, like the music later, drown him out, the forceful ja ja ja floating in front of all our faces, bouncing back at us from the tile. We acted as if he weren't standing right there, Abuela's cigarette smell clinging to his hair, him demanding with that ugly skin to know what our problem was this time—quejándose, como si mereciera algún tipo de explicación.

Acting as if he didn't even exist, in the end.

MICHAEL GARCÍA-JUELLE is a Cuban American writer and teacher from Miami, Florida, and a graduate of the MFA program at Florida International University. His work has been published in *Shotgun Honey*, *Typehouse Magazine*, and *Ghost City Review*, with more forthcoming.

"The Miami Underground and Nico" is fiction.

Halfway through the five-minute track, there was movement at the house. The door had swung open, and Nico had spilled out onto the porch, swinging his arms—was he yelling? It was a woman at the door, just beyond the threshold. She was maybe thirty, with curlers in her hair and a scowl on her face and a baby in her arm. She flicked Nico off, one of the most brutal and final middle-finger fuck yous I've ever witnessed, and slammed the door shut.

From "The Miami Underground and Nico"

THE MIAMI UNDERGROUND AND NICO

The last time I "hung out" with Nico Lopez I was trying to cop from him.

It should have been a simple one-minute exchange: him leaning his lanky frame against the driver's side of my car, reaching in to pass the baggie discreetly via handshake; what you been up to? and how's the family? and all right bro, be easy. That's how it went with good dealers, anyway. With Nico, shit—you'd be lucky if it went that easy half the time. More likely he'd have you sitting in some strip mall parking lot—fifteen minutes, thirty, forty-five. You'd call and he'd insist he was on his way, then you'd call again and he was somewhere else, but don't worry, it's just around the corner, and if you could just make it over to him . . .

Or, if he counted you as a friend, he'd have you wait outside in the driveway of his father's house, come out to the passenger side rather than the driver side, and wait for you to unlock the door, pointing at the lock mechanism through the window. Then, once he was inside, he'd look at you through those big Steve Urkel spectacles, put a pleading face on, like he was fucking Oliver Twist or some shit, and say that your stuff was somewhere else, just around the corner, and if you could just give him a ride . . .

You'd never know, of course, how far you had to go until you got where you were going.

You learned to anticipate this sort of thing if you'd known Nico as long as I had. I'd met him five years before this last incident, when we were both freshmen at Miami Lakes High, class of '08. He was this pasty-white, toothpick-shaped Cuban kid wearing a T-shirt that hung to his knees, saying nigga this and nigga that like he was auditioning for a Tarantino movie. It wasn't until sophomore year that I felt like I knew him enough to ask him why he talked that way.

"It's part of the culture," he said. "Don't come at me with that soft-ass shit just cos you and your niggas talk like white boys."

I didn't really get it at the time, but now I see that what we were talking about was one of those weird Miami things: you could live on the same middle-class suburban street as somebody, be born the same year, go to the same school, and be descendants of immigrants from the same country, but the way you'd walk, talk, and act would be totally different based on which vein of American culture the people around you tapped into—whether your big brother got you into Tupac and Biggie, for instance, or your mom turned you on to the Bee Gees and Michael Jackson.

Despite my "soft-ass" ways, Nico took to me and we stayed friends for most of high school. He called me "Stevie-Steve," which I hated at first, but when some time passed and nobody else but Nico did it, it started to kind of grow on me.

We were never each other's closest friend, though. We each had a clique, as teenagers do, that didn't overlap very much. We hung out enough, though, that I helped broaden his taste in music—showed him stuff like the Stones or Sam Cooke or the Velvet Underground—and he introduced me to smoking pot behind the Walgreens on 183rd Street and getting C's and D's on my report cards.

We were fifteen, maybe sixteen years old when Nico started "trappin'," as he called it: buying as much weed as he could afford, usually a few grams, wrapping it in three or four layers of foil and polyethylene and putting it in special odor-blocking jars and tin boxes so he could bring it to school and sell it off, half a gram at a time. He soon became infamous for leaving his clients sitting in a bathroom stall for half an hour, or waiting behind the dumpsters by the cafeteria through all of lunch period, trying to dodge the security guards.

That's what annoys me the most about this final ordeal with Nico: I knew the score when it came to him, knew the kind of person he'd turned out to be. And I went to him anyway.

To be fair to nineteen-year-old me, I had known well enough to keep away from Nico by that point, and I only turned to him out of what I perceived to be necessity.

In fact, pulling away from my friendship with Nico was an integral part of Mission: Steve Gets His Shit Together. See, the year after high school was one big party for me, a drug and alcohol-fueled gap year of which Nico had very much been a part. The comedown was brutal, though: summer '09, Mom got laid off, Dad went down for fraud, and we lost the house. This served up the motivation I needed to try and do some growing up, an impetus that walking across the stage to shake my school principal's hand had somehow failed to provide.

I sold the only decent guitar I owned to help my mom put a deposit on a new apartment, putting my musical aspirations on hold. I swore off the drinking and partying and got a job loading trucks at the local UPS warehouse. The work set fire to my muscles, and the hours made a good night's sleep a rare luxury, but the pay was decent for what it was, and the tuition benefits allowed me to enroll in classes at Miami Dade College.

About halfway through that first semester, my mom found herself a decent job and bounced back enough that she didn't need such a big cut of my paycheck anymore. I started saving up for my dream guitar: an icy blue Fender Telecaster, the one that seemed to float just off the wall at Guitar Center like a holy artifact. I finished the first semester with straight A's and commenced my second in January 2010. I was successful, I think, largely because I distanced myself from Nico, who seemed to go further and further into the "Miami life," as we called it, the more I pulled away. Whenever calls came in from Nico, I silenced them. I'd read his texts but leave them unanswered.

This went on until the day came when I found myself in a bind and thought—no, hoped—that maybe Nico could get me out of it. Look, I know how that sounds, but hey, I was young, dumb, and in a dilemma that could well have precluded me from the opportunity of having sex.

Okay, so there was this girl in my Intro to Philosophy class that I'd had my eye on, real cute: hourglass figure, hazel eyes, dimple on just one cheek . . . I thought she was a little out of my league, if I'm being honest. But one day she came to class wearing a Floyd shirt, and not the usual kind, so I took my shot while we spilled out into the hallway after class.

"Wish You Were Here," I said.

Even confusion looked good on her. "What?"

Aw shit, I thought, was she one of those people that wore band T-shirts for their aesthetic qualities but had a tangential at best knowledge of the music? It was too late to back out now, so I gestured at the image of the flaming man on her shirt. "Interesting choice. Most people go with Dark Side of the Moon."

"Oh!" She glanced down. "I forgot what I was wearing." Yep, mild embarrassment looked good, too. "No, Wish You Were Here *is* my favorite of theirs. 'Shine On' is better than anything on Dark Side."

Something came over me then. I don't know what I'd call it now, but to a horny nineteen-year-old it felt like love.

The rest of that first conversation went well. I got Tali's number—yeah, I think that was her name, short for Thalía or something—and over the next forty-eight hours we texted almost nonstop. By the time class met again, we'd gotten on well enough that we had a coffee date scheduled after. That was going well too until she took a phone call from her mom, which I took as an invitation to check my phone, as is customary. That's when I saw that I'd received what I thought might be a conversation piece, a new opportunity to keep her giggling: an image text from Nico.

Nico wasn't just a drug dealer. That was how he made most of his money, sure, but he also tended to cycle through all of the typical aspirational Miami jobs—club promoter, rapper, DJ, photographer—gigs that might (but likely wouldn't) make him rich beyond his most depraved dreams and didn't require deferral to authority. Kind of like selling drugs. Around this time, Nico circled back to club promotion, and every few days I would receive a text with a heinously garish e-flyer attached—eight fonts, at least five colors, and a Photoshop-enhanced model with her ass turned to the camera—promising free drinks and beautiful women at nightclubs I'd never heard of, with addresses in neighborhoods on par with Afghanistan in terms of survivability.

Still, I had a soft spot for Nico, so I didn't block his texts from coming in. They were postcards from another of the seemingly inexhaustible variety of lifestyles woven into the fabric of South Florida, one I had no real contact with otherwise. I found them fascinating, actually, funny in a sad way—exactly the kind of quality content I was expecting when I saw that I had received an image from Nico.

When I opened the text at that coffee date with Tali, though, I found fortune so serendipitous that it made me feel like the center of the known universe (not that I needed much to convince me of that back then, mind you).

"Sorry about that," Tali said, then started to explain why she'd taken a call.

"It's fine," I said. "It's fine. Hey, you ever been to the laser light shows at the planetarium?"

One Friday a month, the planetarium at the Miami Science Museum hosted a laser light show themed around the work of a specific music artist. People would lie down on blankets or sit on beach towels and gawk at explosions of psychedelic flowers set to the sounds of Sergeant Pepper, or bursts of purple galaxies blinking in time with Jimi Hendrix's blistering guitar. As you can probably imagine, it was primetime for young druggies, hipsters, and fiends of every variety. It was maybe the only place in Miami where you could see a smiling family of four and a group of twenty-year-olds hopped up on methamphetamines at the same ticket counter. I found it exhilarating.

I can't remember what Tali said about whether she'd gone to the light shows before, but I remember saying, "You won't believe it, but this Friday they're doing Pink Floyd."

"No way!" She's giggling a lot in this memory, now that I think of it. Maybe more than she really was.

"Would you want to go?"

"Sure," she said. And then a moment later—just long enough to make it seem as if it was an absurd notion that had come out of nowhere, she said, "Hey, you know what—I mean, tell me if this is crazy or whatever, or if you're not into it—but . . . wouldn't it be cool to get some molly for it?"

You're probably thinking that I was pretty conflicted about this, seeing as I was on an upward trajectory away from being a fuck-up and a teenage drug abuser. However, I was not conflicted at all.

"Yeah," I said, thrilled at the possibilities that taking ecstasy with Tali presented. "Yeah, that might be cool."

"I don't have a connect, though," she said, frowning.

"Don't worry," I said, grinning like an idiot. "I can definitely get."

Yeah, sure you can, buddy. Sure you can.

*

I texted every number on my phone that I thought might sell molly or know someone who did. Some of them I'd only met once and could barely put a face to. Half the texts were undeliverable, bouncing back from long-since-burned burner phones. A few said, "I'll see what I can do" or "let me text my boy," then dropped off the grid. More than one said, "Who's this?"

After a couple hours of trying, I was down to one option: Nico López.

Normally, if I needed a favor from an old friend, somebody I hadn't spoken to in a while, I might do some work to conceal what I wanted. I might ask them to hang out, get coffee or something, and wait for an opening to casually mention something that might compel them to help. But it was Thursday afternoon, the date was Friday night, and I had told Tali not to worry, that I already had the pills. I had no choice but to be direct.

Hey Nico, the text went. It's been a long time! Hope you're well. Looking for Molly. Lmk.

I spent several minutes sitting at my desk, staring at the phone, my leg bouncing up and down with nervous energy. When I couldn't take it anymore, I got up and started pacing the room, occasionally checking the phone to see if I'd somehow missed the ping of a new text.

But the ping never came. Instead, my phone started blaring the organ solo from "Light My Fire," my ringtone at the time, and the screen lit up: NICO IS CALLING.

Ah fuck, I thought. Here we go. I answered the call.

Nico was laughing breathlessly. "Come on Stevie-Steve," he said. "How you gon' text me some Leave it to Beaver-ass shit out of nowhere like that?"

"What?"

He put on a mocking voice. "'Hope you are well.' How you gon' do me like that Stevie?"

"Hey, man," I said, unable to stifle a chuckle at his gleeful laughter. "I know, I know. I've just been so busy. You know about my old man, right?"

"It's no pressure, playa," Nico said. "You good man, I know how it is."

"Right. Yeah. How you been?"

"You know what it is, Stevie," he said. "Out here grindin', makin' my paper."

"Yeah," I said. "I might be able to help you with that."

Nico laughed. "That's right, that's right. Listen, I gotchu fam. How much you need?"

I felt embarrassed asking for only two, considering how I'd come out of nowhere on an old friend. Also, drugs on a Friday night were kind of similar to nonperishables in a hurricane: better to have too much than too little. "Can you do four?"

"Four? Yeah, let me see. I can do four. I got, uh . . . green diamonds, blue dolphins, pink teardrops . . ."

Designer pills were all the rage then. It was said that the color and logo of each pill was like a brand, a signature—a stamp of quality, almost, so if you had one blue teardrop and liked it, you could count on blue teardrops being fire from then on. I thought that was all bullshit.

"What do you recommend?"

"These blue dolphins are trippy man—crazy visuals. Perfect for the planetarium. That's what you coppin' for, right?"

"Yeah," I said. "That sounds good."

"Aight, four blue supermans. That's gonna be $40, g."

"Blue dolphins, you mean?"

"Yeah," Nico said. "Blue dolphins. Din't I say that?"

*

Nico was too busy to meet that night, but he said I could swing by "around one or two" tomorrow and my pills would be waiting for me. I doubted that would be the case, but since I didn't have to be at work until four p.m., I felt prepared for anything.

I was at Nico's by one-thirty. His father's house was immaculate—beautifully painted, spotless, and with a lawn so perfectly evergreen I might have suspected it was turf if I hadn't seen him tending to it myself. I remember thinking it was a little unusual how much Nico's father tended to the house, but then I had never seen or heard of Nico's mother and had never asked him about her. But his dad had done well for himself; I remember looking at the house, waiting for Nico to bring me my drugs and thinking, He has no excuse, he's had every advantage.

The exchange began with promise. I waited only ten minutes—just ten minutes!—for Nico to come outside, and when he did, he approached my side of the car. I knew it was rude not to get out to greet him after so long, but I figured staying put might be the best signal that I didn't have time to fuck around. I rolled down the window.

Here we go. He'd reach through the window to clap me up, and I'd have my pills in hand.

"Wassup Stevie-Steve," he said, reaching through the window.

"Hey bud," I said, grinning, and meeting his hand with mine.

It was empty.

In the memory, I see myself frowning and looking at my hand, puzzled, like a cartoon—like Tom when Jerry successfully closed a mousetrap on his fingers.

"Listen," Nico said. "I need you to give me a ride to go pick up your shit."

I wanted to say, Why did you tell me you'd have my shit here if you were going to make me go who-knows-where to pick it up, asshole? But I wanted the pills way more. "What happened to your whip, man?"

"My whip's in the shop," Nico said. It was always in the fucking shop. "Fucked it up a lil bit coming home from Shadow Lounge the other night. Remind me to tell you about that shit."

"Nico," I said, trying to keep my cool, lest he blow the deal up on the spot. "I gotta be at work in a little bit man. How far we gotta go?"

"Just down the street," he said. It was always just down the street.

"You know New York City is just down the street, right? If I-95 is the street."

Nico backed away from the car. "Come on, nigga, you know I ain't gonna make you drive to no fucking New York City, man. Fuck you talkin about?"

Shit, I thought, maybe I'd pushed him too much. "All right," I said. "I got you, but Nico, I gotta go to work."

But Nico was already out of earshot, coming around the car to the passenger side. "Aw yeah," he said, as he got in. "Riding 'round with my boy Stevie-Steve."

I managed, I think, something approximating a smile.

"Just like old times, huh?"

"Just like old times," I said.

*

One thing I've never gotten used to about Miami is the savage contrast from one block the next, and the next, and the next; it was a tale of thirty cities, with some basking in varying degrees of tropical pleasure while others wilted in the hot white heat of poverty. Palatial houses and evergreen lawns, Targets and Starbucks one minute, cross a major intersection and the coffee houses and chain restaurants give way to adult video stores and pawn shops with barbed wire lining the roofs and rows of dilapidated houses with stripped cars almost swallowed by the overgrowth in their front yards. The apartment building Nico guided me to was in Carol City, a fifteen-minute car ride from one end of the spectrum to the other.

I don't remember what we talked about for a whole car ride. I remember Nico fiddling with my iPod, which was plugged into the car radio, and saying, "I'm gonna play some of this retro shit. Some that whatcha call it . . . Lou Weed?" He laughed, despite this being the third time he made the same joke. He laughed so hard he snorted. "I'm just fuckin' with ya, Stevie."

I remember him asking if I was still in a band. "Nah," I said. "Had to sell my guitar to pay some bills."

"Damn," Nico said, looking out the window. "It be that way out here."

"Yeah. I'm saving up for another one though. I got a job at UPS. And I'm going to Dade, too. Already finished a semester."

"Shit," Nico said. "I need to get on that. What you studyin'? Music?"

"I don't know. I don't have to pick yet. I'm leaning toward English, I think."

"English?" He chuckled. "Fuck you gonna do with that?"

"I guess I'll see," I said, feeling like I didn't need to explain my academic aspirations to fucking Nico of all people.

"Stevie, oh Stevie, where are thou Stevie," he said, speaking in mock melodrama.

"That's not even how it—"

"I guess I got a guy to do my papers, at least," he said. "You know, for bread, of course."

Typical Nico, I thought: How's it going to benefit me? Oh yeah, now I'll have a Homework Guy to go along with my Weed Guy, and my Used Tires Guy, and my Free Entrance on Ladies Night Guy.

"Of course," I said. "How 'bout you, Nico? How'd the Subway gig go?"

"Man, fuck Subway," he said. "Manager showed me how to do it, like, maybe once or twice, then put me to work on the custies. He said he didn't like how

I's doin' it. I said, yo—take yo got damn sandwich then fuckboy." Nico made a throwing motion. "Then I walked out. I kept the apron though." He chuckled. "Fuck that nigga."

This dude's a mess, I thought, but I said, "Yeah, fuck that guy."

Next thing I remember is pulling up to the apartment building, which I would have guessed was condemned if not for the half-full parking lot. It had a six-foot-tall black metal gate; I figured Nico would have to call somebody to get it open.

"Wait here," he said. He hopped out and started pulling at the gate himself. It creaked and whined but gave.

I drove in and parked in the spot he was gesturing at. I watched him disappear into the depths of the apartment complex. It was two p.m. Plenty of time.

*

I saw it from the moment he came into view from around the truck parked to my left. Nico's face had turned white—an unnatural, absent white, like a pustule—and he walked with his mouth agape, as in dumb shock. He was in trouble—big trouble.

If the terror on his face hadn't given it away, the look of the guy that shadowed him would have: shaved, tattooed head; scowling face, covered from the nose down by a blue bandana; a wife-beater tank top, pants clinging precariously to his boxer shorts; but worst of all, a hoodie draped over his right arm, which from my angle he seemed to be pressing against Nico's back.

Shit, I thought. He had a gun. It wasn't even the concealed right arm that did it—a guy walks different when he's packing heat, even more if he's looking for a reason to use it. I thought about throwing the car into reverse and letting Nico deal with his own mess, but I just sat there, watching them walk toward the car, the way they say some people freeze in front of an oncoming car when the only smart thing to do is jump out of the way.

Nico got in the car without saying anything. It was already running, of course, it being a February day in South Florida. Nico's friend got in the backseat behind us but didn't say anything either. I figured the best move was to play it cool, like nothing was amiss. I almost turned around to look at him, but then I pictured my brains getting blown out onto the windshield, looking like so many chunks of spilled grapefruit in the sunlight, and thought better of it.

"Sup," I said, to no one and everyone.

"Wa—" Nico was trembling. "Wassup."

"Buddy need a ride?"

"I don't need shit," the mystery man in the back spoke up. "It's ya homie here said you'd give him a ride to pick up my money."

I snuck a peek in the rearview. The smattering of wrinkles around his brow revealed that the mystery man was at least ten, fifteen years older than we were.

I waited for the usual it's just around the corner jig, but Nico just stared out the window, finicking with the end of his shirt.

"Ain't that right, McLovin?"

I remember thinking, yeah, he does look like McLovin, doesn't he? If it were anyone else saying it, at any other time, I might have laughed.

"Yeah." Nico's voice cracked a little.

I started backing out of the space. "Where am I headed?"

"Just go down Red Road," he said, still looking away, still giving me directions piecemeal, as if guarding against the possibility that I might say, Nah man, that's too far, you and the gun-toting masked maniac are going to have to take the bus.

"This motherfucka," mystery man said. "Gonna come on my block like it's all good, like he don't owe me two stacks. I hate niggas that play dumb."

Jesus, I thought. How do you borrow two thousand dollars from a guy like this and not pay him back?

Nico whipped around—his face was flush, had he been holding back tears?—and snapped. "I told you, Che, I was trying to re-up so I could get you your—"

"Turn the fuck around."

I thought I heard the rattle of gun metal. Nico obliged. I shot him a What the fuck stare.

"Dumb ass nigga," Che said. "Thought you was just gonna fuckin' waltz into my building—bet you didn't think you'd find me sitting on Willy's couch, playing Madden? Shoulda seen the look on yo face." He chuckled.

"Why do they call you Che?" I was trying to be chill, be cool, play dumb, even—show him I'm not a threat.

"Cos I'm the only Argentine in the hood," he said. "It's Che like 'Che Guevara,' except this Che is all about the paper, naw'm sayin?"

"Yeah." I tried a smile. "Che—that's cool. I'm Steven."

"Hey Steven," he said. "Why they call you nosy? Oh wait, never mind." The joke was awful, but at least he was laughing.

We drove on with just the low hum and occasional honk of afternoon traffic. When the silence became too much to bear and we were stopped at a red light, I turned on the radio, keeping the volume low, and picked a playlist of popular hip-hop songs—just something to have in the background, but nothing that would work this guy up too much.

We'd been driving down Red Road for twenty minutes when Nico had me turn onto 57th Street, a residential block in Hialeah, and ordered me to stop in front of a small house with a chain-link fence.

"I'll be right back," he said. I glanced at the time; it was three p.m.

"Hurry up Nico," I said. "I gotta—"

But the door had slammed shut.

I anticipated that Che might accompany him, but when he didn't, I felt my gut wind itself into a tight knot. I guess Che was more worried about me driving off and leaving them there than anything Nico might do inside the house.

Almost as soon as Nico disappeared inside the house, Che spoke. "Man," he said. "If this nigga ain't back in five minutes . . ."

"Sorry about this," I said, and felt disgusted with myself almost as soon as the words left my lips. What kind of a man apologizes to a dude holding him at gunpoint?

"That's funny," he said. Maybe he was thinking the same thing.

"Light My Fire" started playing again. It was my mother. Shit, my mom. What if I didn't get out of this? What if Che was the real deal? I imagined a cop knocking on her door, breaking the news of my untimely demise—death by drug-dealing idiot—pictured her collapsing, crying in heaving bursts so strong she'd suffocate.

"You gon' get that?"

I silenced the call. "It's my mom," I said. "Don't want to worry her."

He let out a mocking aww. "You got a momma? How nice."

"Don't we all?"

"You serious? Shit—that's the dumbest shit I ever heard. You Miami Lakes niggas are something else."

"I guess." I was growing weary of Che. I felt myself getting dumber every second we breathed the same air. But then, I remember thinking, if I was really too smart to be sitting in the same car as a guy like Che, I wouldn't have been, would I? Yeah, Steve, I thought: if you were so god damned smart you'd at least try to find a way out of this.

The best I could hope for, I figured, was to get on Che's good side. I picked up my iPod discreetly, the way you might if you were shoplifting, and thinking of the way Che had introduced himself, looked for a playlist I'd made of classic Spanish folk tracks. Kanye was playing. I glanced in the rearview at Che; he was scrolling through something on his phone, chuckling to himself. I turned my eye back down to my iPod until I found what I was looking for and queued it up. The iPod went back in the cupholder on the center console, and I went back to staring at the house, waiting for Nico to emerge.

A short while later, Kanye's auto-tune faded out, and an angelic female voice began to sing in Spanish, accompanied by the soft arpeggios of an acoustic guitar.

"Oh shit," Che said. "Turn that up!"

"What?" By now I was almost an expert at playing dumb.

"Turn that shit up!"

So I did. I turned the dial to raise the voice of Mercedes Sosa, folk singer and mother of the Nuevo Cancionero movement.

"My abuela used to play this shit all the time man," Che said. "Like, all the time. How did you know?"

"I didn't," I said. "It was just on my iPod. I had it on shuffle."

"Nah, seriously," he said. "Don't fuck with me." Did I hear a cracking in his voice? "Who has this old ass shit on their iPod?"

"I'm a musician," I said. "I listen to everything, man. Everything and anything."

"Damn," he said. "Whatever, man. Turn it up."

I did. I glanced in the rearview, watched Che look out the window, adjust his makeshift bandana-mask, heard him mumble something I couldn't discern.

Halfway through the five-minute track, there was movement at the house. The door had swung open, and Nico had spilled out onto the porch, swinging his arms—was he yelling? It was a woman at the door, just beyond the threshold. She was maybe thirty, with curlers in her hair and a scowl on her face and a baby in her arm. She flicked Nico off, one of the most brutal and final middle-finger fuck yous I've ever witnessed, and slammed the door shut.

Che missed all of it. He was leaning back in the seat, mumbling along to the song, looking up as if he might somehow see the sky through the car ceiling.

Nico opened the door but didn't get in, as if Argentinian folk music carried a stench he could not abide. "Fuck is this shit?" He was shouting, still fired up from the fight he'd just survived.

This snapped Che out of his trance, who shouted longer. "Fuck wrong wi'chu bruh, you tryna spook a nigga?"

This was the first time I saw the gun.

Fuck, Nico, I thought. I had it. *I had it.*

"You tryna cause an accident?" Che was practically waving the gun behind my ear. "Sit the fuck down."

Nico got in the car and closed the door.

"Turn the music off—uh, what was your name again, boss?"

Boss? "Uh, Steven," I said. "Steve. My friends call me Steve."

"Aight," he said, leaning back in his seat again. "Turn the music off, Steve. I don't want this dumbass to ruin it for me, ya feel me?"

"I feel you," I said, and turned the radio off.

"So," Che said. "What you got for me?"

He hadn't seen what I'd seen. It was a genuine question, not a taunt. I knew he'd be disappointed. I braced myself and placed my left hand on the door handle, getting ready to run. Maybe if I ran in a zigzag pattern . . .

Nico fished some cash out of his pocket. "I got—" he started, stopped, swallowed, tried again. "I got you two hundred dollars, Che. That's all I can get right now. Like, a down payment, naw'm sayin'?"

Che laughed. Oh fuck, I thought.

"All right, listen, Steve," he said. "You don't need this nigga to drag you down anymore than he already has. I got a friend—a real good friend—that lives not five minutes from here, on 52nd Street. Why don't you drive us there and be on your way."

Nico protested. "Listen, Che, you don't need to—"

"Shut the fuck up, McLovin. I'm tired of your shit."

I started to drive. "52nd Street, right?"

"Steve," Nico said. Tears were forming in his eyes. "You can't . . . Bro, listen. You don't know what this guy is—"

"Don't worry, Nico," Che said, savoring the sarcasm on his lips. "I'm gonna get you home safe and sound."

This was going to be tough. I felt for Nico, I really did. But I was so tired of him, too, so tired of his shit. He didn't think about anybody but himself and his stupid schemes, schemes that never worked and just fucked people over and made him look bad. Nobody told him to live like this, always robbing Peter to not even pay Paul. Nobody made him do it—he just did. And me? I just wanted to be done with it, all of it.

"It's gonna be all right, Nico," I said.

"No, you don't get it—" Nico's cheeks were wet now.

"Listen to your boy," Che said. "It's gonna be just fine."

"Steve," he kept saying. "You can't. You can't."

I drove down Red Road, and when I passed 52nd Street and turned on 49th, Che protested. "You blind, Steve? That was the turn, bruh."

"Give me a second," I said. "I'm gonna—"

Before I could finish, Che raised the gun again. "You betta not be tryna play me, fool. I fucks with you, but you betta not—"

"I'm getting your money," I said. I pulled into the parking lot of the bank near the corner of Red Road and 49th Street. "Wait here."

"You don't come back," Che said. "Or you come back with anybody but yo damn self, yo boy's done."

It was after lunchtime, so there was no line to see the teller. I cleaned out the savings account I'd named GUITAR, leaving just over forty dollars. I remember the teller smiling and saying, "Guess you're going shopping!" I did my best, but I don't think I managed to smile back.

"Here you go," I said, handing a thick envelope to Che when I got back in the car. "Here's your money."

"Wow," Che said, taking the money. "You serious? This nigga don't deserve this shit from you."

I shrugged.

Nico was wiping his eyes. "Back that up, Steve," he said, the closest he could come to thank you. "I got you, fam. I got you right back with that."

"Sure, Nico," I said.

Nobody spoke the rest of the way back to Che's apartment complex. Nico looked out the window, and Che played around on his cell phone.

I left the Argentinian folk music lilting along softly in the background, just in case.

*

Before Che disembarked my car, he asked me to hit him up if I ever needed anything. "I got work [weed], I got white [cocaine], I got beans [ecstasy]. Nico has my number."

"Sure," I said. "Yeah, no problem." The guy was fucking nuts.

I didn't check my phone until then. There were three missed calls from my supervisor and a few unread texts. *Where are you?* at four o'clock and *See me when you get here* at fifteen after. One from Tali said, *I'm so excited for tonight! ;).* Another from my mom read, *Hey mijo, you OK?* I sent very different replies to each of them, but only my mom got back to me.

I sat in the car. I let out a sigh—a long, deep sigh—almost as if I'd been holding fear of death in my lungs for the last two hours.

"I'm sorry, man," Nico said. "I didn't—I mean, I knew he lived around here, but I didn't think—"

"Nico, man." I wasn't looking at him. I couldn't. I looked ahead at the steering wheel, at the windshield, at the chipped paint on the wall of the apartment building, at nothing. "Why does everything have to be a shitshow with you, man?"

It took Nico a long time to answer. "I don't know," he said. "I've tried to do it the other way, ya feel me? I tried that minimum wage shit. I tried the classroom, the cubicle. I couldn't do it, Steve. I just—it felt like dying, man. Nah, it felt like—like I was already dead."

I looked at him but could only bear a glance. His eyes were pools of dread—wide and black and afraid.

"I understand," I said and put the car in reverse.

Even then I knew I was lying. I didn't understand Nico at all. And I understood him less when, just two weeks later, after I'd ignored every phone call, text, and email from him, he sent me a message directing me to check my mailbox, where I found an envelope packed with cash. Twenty-two hundred dollars. I counted twice to make sure.

I didn't understand Nico when I saw him six years later in the men's bathroom of a South Beach nightclub. "Stevie-Steve," he said, as if we'd just seen each other yesterday. "How are you man? Still doing the music thing?"

"Nah," I said. "Nah, it's just a hobby now. I'm a teacher now, if you can believe it. How about you?" I felt a flutter in my chest—hope, I think—waiting for his answer.

"You know what it is," he said. "Out here grindin', tryin' to make my paper. You wanna take a bump with me right quick?"

I didn't understand Nico López. But I didn't need to.

"Just one," I said. It had been years. "For old times' sake."

We took the bump, went back out to the bar. I bought him a rum and Coke, and we chatted some more. He still lived in his father's house, he said, but he was dropping a new single on SoundCloud next weekend, and it was gonna be huge.

"I'm gonna make it, Stevie," he said. "I can feel it, man."

That's the last thing I remember about Nico Lopez. I don't remember how I met back up with the people I'd come with or when I left the club or how I got home. I don't even remember saying bye to Nico.

A couple years later, when I heard he'd gone down in a drive-by in Miami Gardens, one that wasn't even intended for him, I tried to dig through the refuse of my memory, tried to pry something out that I felt had to be there, hidden in the muck shoveled in by time. What was the last thing I said to Nico López?

I closed my eyes and tried. The nightclub, the lights—purple, pink, blue—the drinks in our hands. I tried to remember if I'd shaken his hand, if I'd hugged him, if I had told him I was sorry, and if I even knew what I was sorry for.

But all I could remember was Nico smiling and saying, I'm gonna make it, Stevie. I can feel it. I'm gonna make it.

Poet, novelist, journalist, translator, and teacher **ACHY OBEJAS** was born in Havana, Cuba. When she was six years old, she and her family immigrated to the United States during the Cuban Revolution. She is the author of the short-story collection *The Tower of the Antilles* (Akashic, 2017), which was a finalist for the Pen/Faulkner Award for Fiction, and of the novels *Ruins* (Akashic, 2009), and *Days of Awe* (Ballantine, 2007), which was a *Los Angeles Times* Best Book of the Year, as well as of the poetry chapbook *This Is What Happened in Our Other Life* (A Midsummer Night's, 2007) and *Boomerang/ Bumerán*, a bilingual poetry collection published by Beacon Press in 2021. Her poetry and fiction have appeared in such publications as *Another Chicago Magazine* and *Conditions*. She has translated the work of Wendy Guerra, Rita Indiana, Junot Díaz, and Megan Maxwell, among others. Obejas is also an accomplished journalist; she worked at the *Chicago Tribune* for more than ten years, and her articles have been featured in a variety of publications, including the *Village Voice*, *Vogue*, and *The Nation*. She is the recipient of a USA Ford Fellowship for her writing and translation, a fellowship from the National Endowment for the Arts, and residencies at Yaddo and the Virginia Center for the Arts. She lives in the San Francisco Bay Area, where she works as a writer and editor for Netflix.

"The Many Deaths of Fidel" is fiction.

> The next time Fidel died, we said, Hasta cuándo, coño? Some of us had moved to Indiana and Wisconsin, but the retired Watergate burglars kept inviting us to the Miami Book Fair to hear them read from their memoirs, described as "the definitive phantasmagorical history of Cuban influence in the United States from 1492 to the present," according to the blurb by Zoé Valdés.
>
> From "The Many Deaths of Fidel"

THE MANY DEATHS OF FIDEL

The first time Fidel died, we banged pots outside Versailles, like a chorus of cowbells, a wild herd galloping down Calle Ocho porque, por qué no? Our soundtrack was Pitbull, loud, very loud: *It's going down, I'm yelling timber.* The story was crazy, how one of the Watergate burglars had come out of retirement to disguise himself as a presidential bodyguard and quickly switched Fidel's usual cigar brand for a Wile E. Coyote stick of dynamite and then BANG—dead, his nose hanging off the ceiling—we saw it there at Versailles, all slimy, its slight hook pointing down at us accusingly as we waited to catch it in our pots, smash it against the wall, maybe toss it at each other like a bridal bouquet or the ball in a game of jai-alai. The next time Fidel died, he was coming down Ocean Drive in Miami Beach in a pink Cadillac convertible, leading a big parade, a big UMAP Pride or maybe el día de San Lázaro parade (hard to say, there were people crawling on the sidewalks, rolled in neon-colored beach towels, begging to be healed or at least taken to the SIDAtorium at the Fountainbleu). That's when another Watergate burglar came out of retirement and shot him cold with a mail-order rifle from a sixth-floor window at the Beacon Hotel. Sitting next to Fidel in the open car, Celia Sánchez got her butch drag splattered with a little scrambled egg from his open skull, but she just brushed it away like nothing and made eyes at Ingrid Casares, partying in the crowds. *You better move, you better dance,* and Ingrid shook her little tits and Celia drank a Key Lime Martini just for fun. The next time Fidel died, he was watching a Spanish-language slapstick comedy starring Mama Cusa that featured two women in blackface and an ongoing English-language discussion about racism and colorism led by two second-generation Cuban-American professors from FIU (both U.S.-born), when one of the actors turned out to be a retired Watergate burglar who leaned over the floodlights (so he could get a better look), yanked the popcorn and the Malta Hatuey from Fidel's lap, and promptly pumped him full of lead. If only he'd been watching something at Miami Light Project instead, algo más serio, asere, pero no. The next time Fidel died, we were swimming in a pool of cocaine at the Clevelander and we heard the shots ricochet down the street. Fidel had been standing at the railing of the Beach Patrol Headquarters when a retired Watergate burglar poked a Remington 760 Gamemaster between the blinds of the bathroom window in a room across the street rented by a Colombian warlord (not a narco leader, in spite of what the papers said) who was in town for peace talks, or bribery, either was okay, or maybe just to sing backup with the Miami Sound Machine (it was the soundtrack of our lives). We watched when a resurrected Che leaned down to cradle Fidel's body and got a big bloody Rorschach on his shirt (we tried to get him to strip it off, to lie down bare-chested, to roll his eyes, face up, booty down, and look ethereal but no, no, stubborn bastard wouldn't go for the shot, too pure for Instagram). The next time Fidel died, we were at Publix loading up on frozen croquetas, frozen plátanos, frozen deditos de queso, and frozen ropa vieja when we heard over the loudspeaker that Fidel had been minding his own business when a mysterious figure initially mis-identified as Liván Hernández threw an explosive that missed and bounced off Fidel's steel-trap head and blew apart the guy behind him, a flamboyant Texan Canadian named Rafa, and it was only then, when Fidel and Celia went to visit him in the hospital that a retired Watergate burglar who'd been posing as Rafa's surgeon pulled a pistol from his medical bag and shot them both point blank (only later admitting he hadn't meant to hit Celia but was too excited to know what he was doing). It took so long to hear the story, like one of Fidel's own New Year's Day speeches, or the wait for his New Year's Day speeches, or the *wait*—the eternal wait with all things Fidel and Fideli-fied—*you know exactly what we mean*—that the croquetas and plátanos, de-ditos de queso and ropa vieja melted into sludge. Somebody said, "Todo e' una mierda, ve'?" And the cashier made us pay for everything anyway, which was una injusticia. The next time Fidel died, at first all we heard was that the assassin greeted him and bowed as he crossed Manatee Bend Park escorting four Venezuelan beauty queens to see—what else?—the manatees. Later, we heard the killer was a retired Watergate burglar who'd dressed up as a mana-tee and bit Fidel's head off. His ten-year-old granddaughter had tried to tell him, "Abuelo, manatees are docile creatures, their snouts so fat they can't use their teeth to attack," but he was already zipped up in the manatee suit, fangs filed to a killer *Vampiros-en-La-Habana* point and much too committed to the cause. The next time Fidel died, we were at the secret gay nude beach in Biscayne Bay that everyone knows about and there was a guy holding a white handkerchief to conceal his family jewels and he just stared at Fidel when he showed up, laughing with Celia and Che and Marco Rubio, Fidel unbutton-ing his shirt to show everybody he wasn't wearing a bulletproof vest, that his tender pink skin was just as exposed as everybody else's—and that's when the guy with his nuts in the white handkerchief—yet another retired Watergate burglar—pulled the trigger and everyone ran for cover. The next time Fidel died, it was a false alarm. He just fell, broke an arm, chipped a tooth too, but the news didn't report that, though we heard about it on a secret Alpha 66 frequency run by the wives and ex-wives of the retired Watergate burglars. We would have cried, to be honest, but we were busy down in Little Haiti, driving through the Grove, buying a linen guayabera for a quinces in Hialeah that would feature a twenty-one-piece orchestra that played only electric cha-cha-chás that turned into a bachata-reggaeton-tango mix. The next time Fidel died, we said, Hasta cuándo, coño? Some of us had moved to Indiana and Wisconsin, but the retired Watergate burglars kept inviting us to the Miami Book Fair to hear them read from their memoirs, described as "the definitive phantamasgorical history of Cuban influence in the United States from 1492 to the present," according to the blurb by Zoé Valdés. The next time Fidel died, that Cuban guy who murdered his girlfriend and posted it on Facebook tweeted: "Q fokin grande somos, bro," and a columnist from the *Miami Herald* got on his case about the poor lighting in the crime scene photo and how it did not meet Facebook's community standards. The next time Fidel died, somebody left a flan and a dead raccoon by the ceiba tree behind the Bay of Pigs memorial with a little note that said "Gracias Fidel," and went on their way. By then the retired Watergate burglars had really retired, given up dominos and coups, and were now sponsoring a tournament at the Varadero Golf Club, the former Xanadu, winnings in dollars.

DAINERYS MACHADO VENTO is a Cuban journalist, writer, and literary researcher. She is the author of *Las noventa Habanas,* a collection of short stories published by Katakana in 2019. Dainerys is a PhD candidate in literary, cultural, and linguistic studies in the Department of Modern Languages and Literatures at the University of Miami. In 2016 she completed her master's degree in Hispanic American literature at El Colegio de San Luis, Mexico. Her articles have appeared in magazines including *Emisférica, Cuadernos Americanos*, and *Decimonónica.* Her short stories are part of the compilations *Proyecto Arraigo/Desarraigo: Antología de literatura americana* (Se Hacen Libros y Distintas Latitudes, 2017) and *Ellas cuentan: Antología de crime fiction por latinoamericanas en EEUU* (Sudaquia, 2019).

"Floridaness" is nonfiction.

I returned to Miami several times. But I never went to see Benita again. Never felt strong enough to face so much loneliness. And yet, in my mind, Miami itself had become synonymous with Florida, and Florida, synonymous with the United States, and the United States was, for my family, a place of isolation and estrangement, a place you could visit but not live in, a place with too many sad stories behind its sunny days and happy colors.

From "Floridaness"

FLORIDANESS

Port of Mariel, Cuba, 1980.

It was then or never y punto. The entire family would leave Cuba on the Mariel Boatlift. The port would open for departures in a few days. There was not a moment to waste.

Once the decision was made, the entire family set about quietly selling or giving away all they had, from furniture to milk cans, from clothes to the heavy black-and-white TV set that was their most treasured luxury.

They decided to keep the pictures, but entrusted Han Solo, their dirt-colored mutt, to a neighbor with several mutts of her own, who, old, white-haired, and stick-thin, nevertheless seemed to love her dogs enough to feed them better than she fed herself. Han Solo would be fine.

Over a decade before, one of my grandmother's brothers, Uncle Angelito, had managed to leave the island and settle in Miami. Now he set out to travel the ninety or so miles between Miami Beach and Mariel on a small motorboat that was nevertheless big enough for at least ten people and more than enough to bring his entire family—those people he loved but hadn't seen, or touched, or hugged, in years—back to Miami with him.

But once at the port of Mariel, Angelito was immediately forced to fill his boat with strangers, state-sanctioned ransom in exchange for the possibility of taking two of his own with him, one last payback for having left.

On land, my family quickly realized the government had no intention of allowing anyone to leave together, as a family. It meant that they would have to be willing to accept separation, to leave the only land they'd ever known with no assurance that the others would make it out safely. Or at all. One last payback for having stayed.

My mother just stood there in silence, her gaze lost at sea while holding my sister, then only three years old, determined to stay and wait however long for another boat, or for a new miracle.

But Mima (my grandmother) and Pipo (my grandpa) wouldn't hear of it. *¿Cómo iba a quedarse allí sola, una niña con otra niña?* My mother was nineteen.

In the end, the four of them ended up walking down streets they had already said goodbye to and back to an empty house that was no longer their home. Back to no furniture, no food, no dirt-colored mutt with a movie name to call to.

Still. They were together and it was all that mattered, even if it meant they'd have to continue to stand on the side of those who would think nothing of throwing eggs at gusanos like themselves, at the escoria who had dared to think it could decide to leave la "Patria o Muerte, ¡Venceremos!" just like that.

By the time I am born in 1986, the story of the day all my family's dreams were dashed at the Port of Mariel was an old story, one shared by many Cubans, so, not even unique, except for this:

When the people of El Cerro, my family's neighbors, saw them coming back with vacant stares and empty hands, their feet slow and their bodies heavy, they began, one by one, to return every milk can, every piece of furniture, each item of clothing, the weighty television, and even a cranky, barking Han Solo.

Let the government tell others they had to throw eggs at friends they loved, just for trying to escape the regime's criminally failed cause. Let them tell others, because the people who lived on our street wouldn't do it. Instead, those neighbors, themselves having little or nothing, found ways to restore, to console and give love to a family that had lost their migration plans as quickly as they had conceived of them, the new life they had only just begun to glimpse, lost forever as well.

Years later, much later, some of those same neighbors were able to leave the country.

But not my granddad, who died in that house that had once been emptied and refilled in the span of one day, with physical things, and acts of solidarity, but also with hopelessness and the sound of Radio Martí at its lowest volume.

And not the rest of my family, still there to this day, never again so much as attempting to leave Cuba, each one of them broken by that day in Mariel, and yet also strangely strengthened by their decision, the one reaffirmed by fate, to stay together, to remain a family.

La Habana, Cuba, 2012.

Later, much later, my research on the censorship suffered by Cuban writer Virgilio Piñera would become my first ticket out.

I had already done extensive research on his work and life when a friend introduced me to a visiting University of Miami professor putting together a congress about Piñera's theater. Would I be interested in attending their events in Miami just a few months later?

Before leaving Cuba, I went to Pipo's grave in the Colon Cemetery and promised him that I would enjoy the voyage he had been denied. That I would look with grateful eyes at the places he had always wanted to know and would try to reconstruct the story that had been lost when my uncle's motorboat set sail toward Miami without them. I said those words out loud, never suspecting all the ways in which I would be able to honor them.

That day, lying on his grave, I also promised him that I would go to Miami and return, that I would guard the notion of family unity that he'd inherited, and passed on, instilling it in all of us even before I was born.

Miami, Florida, 2012

I was in Miami at last, for the first time in my life, and that first week, I went to visit my tía Benita, in an attempt to envision, to reconstruct, the life my family could have had, the one that existed only in their minds.

Benita was the widow of my uncle Rogelio. All their life they had tried to have children to no avail, and it had been precisely this: their childlessness, their category, "couple, no children," that allowed them to board my uncle Angelito's boat back in 1980 and be the only two family members he was able to take with him on the very motorboat my grandparents had refused to set foot on if it meant leaving my mother behind.

When I met her, Benita was living in what in Spanish we call a Plan Ocho building. She was alone, without the children she never had and without the dogs that had been a comfort to her for years because that particular Plan Ocho building did not allow dogs.

She told me how happy she had been while Rogelio was alive, told me all about the business they had started and grown "always here, in Florida, in the same place."

She also told me about a strong storm they had encountered on their way from Mariel to Florida in Angelito's boat:

"A bigger ship had to rescue us at some point. All I remember is the sky was black, and the sea was black too."

She told me her story in Spanish because she had never *had* to learn English. "It is because of Spanish that this place feels like home," she said.

Before I left, Benita made me the best "cafecito cubano" I have ever had and gave me a twenty-dollar bill, a gift to take back to Mima, a small treasure. "Si vas a regresar a Cuba, al menos vuelve pronto," she said. "Come back soon."

I looked at her then, so vulnerable, lonelier than ever after the death of my uncle Rogelio, and could not help thinking about all the lonesomeness my grandparents had avoided by not getting on that boat.

I returned to Miami several times. But I never went to see Benita again. Never felt strong enough to face so much loneliness. And yet, in my mind, Miami itself had become synonymous with Florida, and Florida, synonymous with the United States, and the United States was, for my family, a place of isolation and estrangement, a place you could visit but not live in, a place with too many sad stories behind its sunny days and happy colors.

Look at Benita, I would tell myself every time I had doubts about whether or not I should come and stay, try to live in the United States. *Look at Gabriel, that other uncle you knew so well, who went to live in the states in 2006 and died alone in his apartment just a couple of years later. Remember how people told you he'd been dead a week before they found him, lying on his bed, lifeless, his body smell the only thing alerting the neighbors that within the small apartment was a man alone, a dead man.* My uncle Gabriel. I grapple even now with how hard it is to even write his name, much less say it out loud.

San Luis Potosí, México, and Miami, Florida, 2014–2017. An epilogue.

The irony of this story, of this history, is that I write this memoir, these memories, armed only with the English I learned in Florida after I moved there for my thirtieth birthday.

Yes, I did it. It was a long process that started in 2014 when I moved from Cuba to Mexico to work on a master's degree in literature.

In Mexico I fell in love with the country and with a man. We married, and two years into my degree, I received a fellowship to continue my studies, now toward a PhD, at the University of Miami, the same institution that had brought me to Miami in the first place.

By then, Florida was no longer a symbol of loneliness or even solitude for me. I would go there with my love, my partner in life, and a promising career. I would never die alone like Gabriel. The smell of my body would not have to let my neighbors know I was gone forever. Eventually, I would have some American kids to hold my hand in the end, or at least to find me a Plan Ocho building in which dogs would be allowed.

Seven months after moving into a small apartment on Calle Siete, my husband had had enough, told me this country was crap, and he couldn't bear the pace at which people lived here. Not if he had to spend another month in the little apartment that was all my scholarship could pay for us.

Then, for close to three agonizing years after that heart-blowing conversation, we tried to sustain a long-distance relationship. He, back in México, me in Miami, studying for my doctorate and trying not to resent having the great opportunity of a five-year teaching assistantship to keep me here without him. Of course, divorce was inevitable.

Once again a single entity, my image of Florida as a place of loneliness returned full force. I thought Florida was my Macondo and that I was suffering my own Floridaness.

I thought that it didn't matter that my grandparents had been able to avoid a life of loneliness in this land. And that perhaps, when I promised Pipo that I would see life with his eyes, what I really assumed was a promise to live all the loneliness that he and my grandmother had avoided for so many years.

And yet, I am still here, the last few years, learning new lessons.

I have learned, for example, that the suffix "-ness" in English is used to form nouns from adjectives, nouns that usually denote a state or condition, like aloneness, lonesomeness, loneliness. That is why I often tell people that I suffer from Floridaness, my own personal state (and destiny?) of isolation.

But what I have more recently realized is that the suffix "-ness" also applies to kindness, and loveliness, and togetherness. That my neighbors and friends from El Cerro, like so many other immigrants, had already made their trip to Floridaness before me and understood that it is the process by which we learn to bring home with us, set it down in a new place.

Those people who returned milk cans, furniture, and even our dog in 1980, they were the true inheritance my grandparents left for me in this land. They are, and some were, here to remind me that being in a state of Floridaness does not have to mean a permanent state of loneliness and that even when destiny seems inevitable, we are the only ones entitled to write the conjunctures, the circumstances, and the details of our personal story and make them true.

ANA MENÉNDEZ has published four books of fiction: *Adios, Happy Homeland!* (Black Cat, 2011), *The Last War* (Harper, 2009), *Loving Che* (Grove, 2004), and *In Cuba I Was a German Shepherd* (Grove, 2001), whose title story won a Pushcart Prize. She has worked as a journalist in the United States and abroad and as a prize-winning columnist for the *Miami Herald*. As a reporter, she wrote about Cuba, Haiti, Kashmir, Afghanistan, and India. Her work has appeared in *Vogue*, *Bomb Magazine*, the *New York Times*, *Tin House*, and several anthologies, including *The Norton Anthology of Latino Literature*. Born in Los Angeles to Cuban parents, she has a BA in English from Florida International University and an MFA from New York University. A former Fulbright Scholar in Egypt, she has also lived in India, Turkey, and the Netherlands, where she designed a creative writing minor at Maastricht University. She is an associate professor at FIU with joint appointments in English and the Wolfsonian Public Humanities Lab.

"The Apartment" is fiction.

> Anna, the property manager, sent a two-word email: "Call me."
> That's how I knew it was going to be bad news. When I reached
> her by Skype the next day, she gave me the short version: My
> tenant had taken the pills while in the bathtub of my South
> Beach apartment. My first reaction was harsh. I'd spent the last
> five years living in Cairo as a highly paid witness to all the ways
> heroic struggle can slither into bloody farce faster than you can
> say "The revolution eats its . . . ," well, you know. I guess I took it
> personally, the first mistake.
>
> From "The Apartment"

THE APARTMENT

We Run

from Ithaca, Rome, Prague, Florence, Al-Andalus, Corollos, Menjez, Tripoli, Skye, Mull, Valverde, Damascus, Beirut, Burgos, Minsk, Kiev Bethlehem, Kumzar, Kailahun, Gijon, Buenos Aires, Dara, Havana, Mir Adina, Toronto, Bangui, Coral Gables, Jerusalem, Beirut, Amman, Tampa, Kalmar, Imatra, Liverpool, Dover, Lelystad, Little Havana, Brugge, Berlin, Bialystok, Rzeszow, Silesia, Toulon, Granada, Cadiz, Napoli, Zadar, Constanta, Les Anglais, Chambellan, Vladivostok, Guilin, Patan, Karachi, Edo, Tangier, Kumasi, Dar Es Salaam, Rumdo, Port-au-Prince, Oaxaca, Puebla, Piura, Lahore, Mesaieed, Cairo, Tehran, Palmyra, Alexandria, Bazgir, Jíbaro, Varadero, Cardenas, Güines, Sagua la Grande . . .

We run from deserts and swamps, grand houses covered in green, and wooden shacks guarded by skinny chickens. We run from boys with guns, from despots and lovers, run from curdled pasts, from home to here and here.

Looking, still, for a place to belong.

The Death of Lenin García

Anna, the property manager, sent a two-word email: "Call me." That's how I knew it was going to be bad news. When I reached her by Skype the next day, she gave me the short version: My tenant had taken the pills while in the bathtub of my South Beach apartment. My first reaction was harsh. I'd spent the last five years living in Cairo as a highly paid witness to all the ways heroic struggle can slither into bloody farce faster than you can say "The revolution eats its . . . ," well, you know. I guess I took it personally, the first mistake. Hard, though, not to safeguard hope, even if everything in our training seeks to rid us of that luxury item. By the time Sisi came to power, my dispatches had become increasingly emotive—my supervisor's word. I was spending less space analyzing the political situation and more time detailing the shape of the violence, the disfiguring Rorschach of spilled blood. So please forgive my initial reaction to the news that a young man in the poshest, most placid paradise had slit open his life and let it drain down the sewer.

"Christ," I said. "What a mess."

"You don't have to come, the police—" Anna said before her face pixilated and then melted into silver.

"I'm sorry, the police what?" I said. "I lost you for a moment."

Her face magically rearranged itself on the screen. "I was saying that the police finished their investigation and I'll take care of . . . the apartment."

It took me a moment to figure out she meant that she'd hire someone to scour the place. I knew businesses existed that dedicated themselves to this task: biohazard cleaners, a species of human vulture, and I mean that with utmost gratitude and respect. They're the people you call when an old person dies and no one finds the body for weeks. They arrive after the murder, after the police have photographed and annotated the scene, taken their samples, documented each bullet. After the death, the crime, the impulsive lunge into the abyss, the human vultures descend in space suits with their industrial-strength vacuum cleaners, their gallons of bleach. It's work with an extra measure of dignity: Let us praise these men and women who emerge from our oldest fairy tales to restore order to a disordered world.

"Thank you," I said. "I'll see you in a few weeks."

The timing worked. I'd been ordered to take leave through the holidays anyway. Burnout, the medic said. Granted, I hadn't planned to be "home" for the holidays. After my parents died, I'd put up my South Beach condo for rent and stopped going to Miami. For my parents I could endure the species of angry nostalgia so many of their generation had perfected. But I could not bear Christmas Eve at my brother's house. The guy was only six years older than me, but he'd taken it upon himself to reprise all the greatest hits of el Exilio histórico. I'd even heard him tell an American colleague that he had been born in Havana, which was a lie unless one accepted Hialeah as an alternate spelling of Guanabacoa. The last party I attended at his house, in 2008, started off well enough, given the recent election. But then my brother raised his glass in a toast—on Christmas Eve!—and said, "To the death of communism." I should have just stayed quiet, but I'd had a few, and my work was stressful enough. So I raised my own glass and added, "And eternal damnation to the Huguenots." No one laughed. But, really, communism? Who talks about communism anymore? In Miami, that's where. Miami: Where it's warm year-round, and always 1961.

. . .

I take an Uber straight from the airport to my building. Anna is waiting for me downstairs in the lobby.

She kisses me on both cheeks and hands me my keys.

"Good trip?"

"Boring."

"Yeah, well, boring is preferable." She nods at my backpack: "That all you have?"

"I'm shipping the rest of my stuff."

"Well, then you can take this." She hands me a small yellow cardboard suitcase.

"I found it in the bedroom closet," she says. "It was his. The police said to give it to you."

The Helena

Of my neighbors, I know the Cubans best: Ernesto the elderly piano player, Milagros with her illegal garden, and Teresa the militant. There was also a recent arrival, a woman, who moved in just before I left for Cairo; I didn't know her very well. The rest of my neighbors I confess I barely knew. I couldn't even tell you how many lived in the building. Ten or fifteen at least. There was Anna, of course, the realtor who managed my apartment. The others I knew by face: Susan and her daughter Emily; Robert who was blind, the older man who used to be in tech, or so they say, and the hateful former New Yorker who lived below me. The building where we live is named after a woman, Helena. It was built in 1939, the same year as The Webster, with which it shared an architect, Henry Hohauser. In Europe, these were the years of advancing despotism. But in Miami Beach, the thirties and the forties seemed to be lived outside of time. Most of what we now know as the Art Deco district emerged during those two bloody decades, a show of irrational optimism in the face of war and other disasters. The 1926 hurricane, the jack boots in middle Europe, even the Great Depression, were met with cheery oblivion in this sunny sliver of barrier island. In the relieved aftermath of wind and fire rose these incandescent buildings constructed in the new Parisian style. What war, what sorrow? said the chevrons and ziggurats. What dark star? asked the round Vitrolite. The straight white walls that blazed in sunshine, the open grillwork, the decorative flourishes all enclosed a space apart, where alternate lives could dream themselves new. The immigrants never stopped coming.

It occurs to me now that the confidence of the facades might have operated as a kind of feint, a chameleon's coat displayed to the world. Maybe all of South Beach was this: a relentless frivolous party sheltering a sacred idea. The Helena's happy shell enclosed a remarkably egalitarian framework, for every apartment was identical to every other one, laid out back to back in mirror images on either side of the supporting beams. Each two-bedroom, one-bath leaning on its neighbor—dining room to dining room, kitchen to kitchen. If you peeled away the walls and peered inside, you'd find us resting, bed to bed, foreheads touching.

The Mysterious Roadwork

I'm forty-two years old, have lived everywhere, and don't spook easily. I shove the yellow suitcase into the hall closet, shower, and fall asleep immediately, undisturbed.

I wake at midnight. Jet lag—I've learned not to fight it. I lie in bed for a moment enjoying the silence, the first in years, a cashmere silence, sumptuous luxury. Then the sound of tiny feet above me, beyond the ceiling. I turn on the light and it stops. But now comes an unfolding rumbling, like an ache in the building's foundation. I cross the living room on my tiptoes. Lights and crew in the street below. I pull on my travel clothes and step outside. After Cairo, the late September evening feels almost cool though the breeze carries something putrid. Workers have blocked off a corner with orange cones and police tape. A group stands inside this makeshift pen surrounding what looks like a miniature digger with its own miniature driver and next to it, a rectangular machine (motor?) the size of a van. I've never seen anything like it before. When it starts up again with a shudder, I realize it must have been the source of the rumbling. A tangle of gray tubes sweat on the pavement, and as I come closer, I realize that the other end of the largest tube is buried in a hole two men seem to be guiding it down. They work by floodlights that cast batlike shadows but don't reach into the black hole where the farthest end of the tube is sunk. I stop a few feet from the spectacle trying to understand what I'm seeing. A sewer break? The workers don't talk to one another, and even the clubgoers pass by in silence, not glancing at the great soup-making operation before them. The ground trembles. When at last the machine stops, one of the workers shouts, Está bien! and breaks the spell.

When I pass the same space in the morning, everything will be gone, not so much as the trace of a scar remaining in the ground.

Why I Draw

These days, it's mostly faces. It started as a way to force myself to see. One of the problems with a self-referential culture is that it creates self-referential beings. I was smart enough to join the service but not wise enough to see beyond the cardboard-and-sticks story I grew up inside of. I made mistakes, incorrect assumptions. A mentor listened and then—bizarrely, I thought—suggested I sign up for a drawing class. The first thing I learned was that the reason so many of us can't draw is because we presume knowledge we don't have. We think we know what a face looks like, so we don't ever really see it. The mind is like the patriarch who knows what he knows and can't be persuaded otherwise. Yes, that's another problem of the culture that raised me.

Some Principles
In a drawing, each line exists in relation to another line. A face is built up from a web of context, the sum of hundreds of small decisions. You don't need to imagine the whole face. All you have to do is see that the eyes are halfway down the skull. Calculate the distance to the nose. Place the nostrils in relation to the pupils. Line by line. If you have faith in the small gesture, the face emerges, as if by magic. But if you make a mistake early on, the entire face will be distorted. Sometimes you can correct these, and sometimes the errors become part— maybe the most human and charming part—of the finished work. I'm not making any grand claims. This is just one of the things that drawing taught me.

Teresa's Theories
I'm not a week back when Teresa stops me on the stairs.
"You're not afraid to be living there?"
The question confuses me at first—it's what people always asked about Cairo.
"You mean, in my apartment?"
"With everything that happened?"
I tell her what I've already told others: I'm not afraid of phantoms. I smile to end the conversation, but she doesn't go away.
"Stop by later," she says and puts a hard, cool hand on my wrist. "I have some theories about what happened."
I remember Teresa mostly from her feuds with Milagros. "Cultist," Milagros called her, her favorite name for anyone who expressed loyalty, in her view, to rigid ideologies. I'm curious about what Teresa would have to say about Lenin. But not curious enough to pay her a visit, so I ignore the invitation. Two days later, I'm heading for a run when she opens the door to her apartment.
"Ven acá, ven acá," she says, jerking her hand. "Un momentico na'más."
She looks forlorn. Milagros says not one of her four children ever visits.
Inside, Teresa points to a rocking chair and orders me to sit.
"A gift from my son," she says, nodding at the chair. "It makes me car sick."
It's always strange to visit one of my neighbors' apartments. The layout is the same, though sometimes in mirror image, which can induce a kind of vertigo.

When I was a little girl, maybe five or six, I woke from a dream to find that everything in my room had been rearranged: the bookcases normally to the right of my bed had been moved to the left. The dresser had migrated to the opposite wall. And my nightstand was in front of the door, nearly blocking my exit as I ran to my parents' room. In between sobs I tried to explain to my father that my furniture was on the run. *For heaven's sake, it's three in the morning,* my mother mumbled. But I would not relent, begging my father to come take a look. *Okay, okay,* he said. *You'll see that it was just a dream.* It's been almost forty years and I still haven't forgotten my shock and disappointment when we returned to my room to find that all the furniture had scrambled back to its original spot. *You see,* my father said. *A dream.*

"You mentioned phantoms," Teresa says. "And I'm here to tell you that I've seen him."

"Seen who?" I felt dazed.

"Him," Teresa says. "Your tenant."

"I'm not following."

"I think he faked it."

"His death?"

Teresa nods. Her bathroom and bedroom have swapped places, and the living room where I now sit should be the kitchen. But I'm surprised to spot a chair just like one Anna bought for my apartment in almost the same spot that it sits in my own place.

"You've seen him around?" I say.

"Yes," she says. I hadn't noticed that her hands were moving, and now I see that she is crocheting something as she speaks, the nervous source of the doilies and blankets that cover the side table, the back of the blue sofa, the top of the boxy old television set.

"You've seen him since, you mean?" I say.

Chocheando? I figure Teresa must be the age my mother would be now, and that realization gets caught in my throat, as if sadness could acquire form and choke you.

"Que?" Teresa says, watching my face. "You knew him? He was family?" She says this last with a hint of suspicion.

"Lenin?"

"Ay! Don't say that name. Demonios!"

"Maybe we can talk another time," I say and stand.

"He always had a girl in there, maybe a wife, do you know about that?"

"I don't see what that would have to do with—"

"Life insurance. I know he had it because his mail was sometimes delivered here. These new Cubans, they know all the tricks."

"Okay, Señora Teresa, I'm going to be going. We can talk another time."

"They come here already knowing; they know more than those of us who've lived here for years. All the scams. You are naïve—these people don't belong here."

She has begun to raise her voice, and her needle moves faster and faster. She seems to be crocheting a sweater for a baby.

"Lenin! Who names a child Lenin these days!" she says, almost shouting now. "What idiot kind of mother gives her innocent little baby a name like . . . Demonios! And this in, what? He was born after the fall of the wall! What a moron. Can you think of a more moronic thing to do? But what can you expect from these people? That generation is ruined, ruined. I read in a book how damaged they all are . . . zombies the writer called them, and that is exactly what they are. Every last one of them. They have spent the last fifty years scamming and scrambling. They don't respect anything. How could they? A lifetime of the government lying to you, your neighbor lying to you. Your own mother . . . Lenin! . . . lying to you. What is there left to believe in? The walking dead is what they are. They've stopped thinking. History will not absolve them! Not one bit. History will condemn them. No, no, I have no sympathy for any of them. Envious parasites. These are the people who shouted gusanos at us. These are the people who could not wait to get their hands on our property."

I'm halfway out the building but I can still hear her shouting: "Do you know what kind of people became communists? The lazy, the stupid, the petty criminal. The envious!"

Margot Bianchi Remembers Her First Home

"This young man—he wasn't the first one in this building. They say a woman killed herself here in the 1940s, right after it was built . . . something to do with the war. She was just twenty years old, threw herself down the stairwell from the third floor . . . some nights, the people say, you can hear a thump and then the cries of her mother. I've heard it myself. Though I don't believe in any of that. There's always an explanation for things."

Margot Bianchi was born in Argentina, and I've come to see her on the insistence of Milagros, who, I now suspect, simply wanted someone to pay a visit to her lonely friend on the third floor. There used to be many more old people on the beach. Before this building went condo in the early nineties, I think most of the tenants here were retired. Now there are just a handful left, and, I suppose, they all know each other, banding together like exiles from a distant Miami Beach.

Of all of them Margot is certainly the most glamorous. She wears her blond hair up and swept back high, like a spun sugar crown, and she moves her hands delicately as she talks, wanting me to notice her glossy red manicure.

"I was twenty-six years old in 1976 and newly married to a man who was nine years older than me," she is saying. "Am I boring you?"

"Of course not."

"Would you like some coffee?"

"Thank you, I'm okay."

"Nowadays, twenty-six-year-olds are wise and experienced. But in my time, in my circles, girls were naïve. Even girls in their twenties. I knew almost nothing about the world, nothing about my parents' role in society, and certainly nothing about my new husband's place in the terror that was slowly engulfing us. This is not to excuse myself. Of course I have studied that painful history. Steeped myself in it. But I'm telling you this because you are a woman too, and you, excuse my saying this, are not so young anymore. And, anyway, even at twenty-six you were probably never naïve. You want to understand the mind of this boy who took his life, but I'm telling you that is impossible. We women cannot understand the minds of men . . . I read somewhere, a long time ago, that a female human has more in common with a female chimpanzee than she does with a male of her own species. And vice versa. It sounds funny, but I know this to be true."

I laugh.

"Are you sure you don't want coffee."

"I'm absolutely sure."

"We lived in Núñez, my husband and I, not far from the school for mechanics. My in-laws had bought us the apartment as a wedding gift, already furnished. A high floor. I think maybe it was the sixth. It's funny that I can't remember the floor precisely. And yet I can remember other details as if I had lived there only yesterday. It was a mysterious place, even spooky, and I had trouble sleeping in it. There was a room off the kitchen. Maybe it had been a dining room in the past. But now it contained a collection of mismatched chairs, arranged in a kind of semicircle beneath long windows framed by heavy red curtains. I hated those red curtains at once, and the following year, they were the first thing I changed. They were the color of blood, though I didn't dare complain about it to Martin. We were in love. We were happy. But the curtains seemed to promise no good. And all those empty chairs . . . I never walked past the room without feeling chilled.

"The thing is, in another house, it might have been beautiful. The dark floors were glossy; someone had obviously looked after them with care. The walls, where they met the high ceiling, were finished in elaborate molding, probably original. And all of it seemed arranged in such a way as to highlight the three paneled windows, which were the first thing one saw on entering. It was the kind of haughty room that might have benefited from a set of comfortable couches, a book-covered coffee table, neat shelves along the wall. But instead the last owners, or my in-laws, had decorated it with only a single painting. A hideous dark painting illustrating some forgotten war. And those chairs. More than a dozen all together, some high-backed and straight, some that barely seemed stable on their insect-like legs. Only one chair was upholstered, its high, wide seat covered in a deep green velvet that at night seemed almost black.

"The first thing I did—we hadn't even unpacked yet—was upset the arrangement. I arranged the chairs in groups, reserving the two plainest ones for a small table I brought in from the living room. I thought we could eat breakfast there, tame the room that way. The deep green chair I placed near a corner. We never used it. Even after all that arranging, we only used the room for breakfast. We ended up spending most of the time that autumn in a kind of long hallway, which held the apartment's only couch, a small love seat.

"I can't remember what morning it was. A couple of months into our marriage. Martin was still in bed. I was setting out the breakfast things when I had the feeling I was being watched. I turned slowly. My gaze met that infernal painting of war. But it wasn't that. It was something else. Something about the chairs. One of the chairs had moved. The green chair. Just a bit, but moved just the same. And its deep cushion held a slight imprint. I'm a rational person; I was raised in that same neighborhood with some religion, it's true, but my father was scrupulously lacking in superstition, and he had imparted me with the same. It was clear to me—at least I wanted it to be clear to me—that I had simply missed this detail when I'd first arranged the chairs. So I fluffed the seat, moved it back into place and forgot about it. A few mornings later, the chair had moved again. And there was no mistake anymore: a body had recently sat in it. The imprint was fresh and deep. Do you believe in ghosts, my child?"

I shook my head.

"Well, I didn't either. Maybe you are too young to remember, but 1976 was the year of the military coup. It was the beginning of the national reorganization. My husband left for work in the late mornings—what glorious mornings those were in Buenos Aires, in the 1970s, when I was young. He returned later and later in the evenings. I thought perhaps he was already having an affair. This is the way my set was used to thinking about things . . . I didn't have the vocabulary for all the possibilities. We were afraid of the communists, afraid of your Fidel, understand. Everyone I knew was afraid . . . I understood that my husband was engaged in that fight, against the ERP. We didn't want violence . . .

"One night, already near the end of the year, I woke alone and frightened. My dreams were haunted by all the things I refused to see. Martin was not in our bed. Outside, the city shouted, but our bed was still and cold. I rose carefully, trying to keep the floor from giving me away. I walked slowly in my bare feet. Shadows everywhere. I stopped in front of the room with the red curtains. A figure there, outlined against the light. I took an involuntary step back. But in the next moment I understood what I was seeing."

She stops and looks at me, throwing her beautiful hands in the air: "What do you think it was? It was my husband! It was Martin. He was sitting in the green chair, this husband I didn't know and would never know, half facing the window. The street's glow caught him in a faint spotlight. His eyes were open but fixed on something beyond. Some darkness that rested at the end of his field of vision. There is darkness at the end of everything we gaze upon . . ."

"I'm sorry," I say, but Margot doesn't seem to hear me.

"Martin sat perfectly still and straight that night. I watched him for a long time, waiting for him to turn and find me there. But he didn't move. And after a while, I turned quietly and returned to bed . . ."

Teresa Is Sorry

I am sketching by the window. Soft knock at the door. I consider ignoring it. But the person is not going away. On the other side of the peephole: Teresa. I freeze.

"Please, querida, I know you're there. I heard the boards creaking."

I sigh and open the door. She's holding a plate of pastelitos.

"Homemade," she says, shoving the plate at me. "Please accept them as a form of apology. We Cubans speak with food, you know."

That's what she says, this woman who probably made poor Lenin's life a "yogur.'"

I hesitate and she pushes inside to set the pastries on my dining room table. "The triangles are guava and the rolled ones are cream cheese."

"I know," I say.

She's not moving and stands staring at me. "Did I interrupt something?"

"Well, actually, I usually use the morning to do some drawing."

"So you're an artist! Ernesto told me you were a spy!"

I can't hide my shock. "Ernesto told you that?"

She makes air quotes: "State Department."

"I'm not a spy. I'm a program officer; it's not the same thing."

"Lo siento," she says. And I can't figure out if she means she's sorry for me or is apologizing for her mistake.

Her lower lip trembles for a moment and then the tears come. Good lord.

"Please," I say, "take a seat. I'll make us some coffee."

When I return with the two small cups of espresso, I find Teresa half curled on the sofa, eyes closed. I watch her for a moment. At rest, she seems smaller, more frail. I set the cups carefully on the coffee table, but she wakes. She takes a sip of coffee and the tears start again, a slow trail down the side of her face.

"Is everything okay. Do you need to see a doctor?"

She shakes her head.

"I'm ashamed of myself," she says. "All that shouting the other day. You were right to flee."

I raise my eyebrows but don't say anything.

"I hope you'll forgive me. But, see, you didn't live through what we lived."

"It's really okay. No offense taken."

"No, no, me pasé. But I hope you can try to understand me. Imagine now someone awful comes to power in this country, begins to change everything, begins to divide the country, to shut down the press, to co-opt the courts. Begins to wreck your institutions one by one. Installs his family members into positions of power. All for his own glory and profit. Those who disagree can leave. Or go to jail. Or be on the wrong end of a firing squad. How would you like that?"

I sip my coffee, quiet.

"And then, when your parents finally decide that the country has abandoned them and they apply for permission to leave, the neighbors gather outside your house—your house! The house that your father built, your own immigrant father who didn't make his money from bolita or prostitution or gun-running, who was a hard-working Gallego whose stores sold good products and who was so frugal that he was able to put together another store and then another and build a decent house for his family. For your mother and your brother and yourself, your sixteen-year-old self, who now stands inside the house your father built with honest sweat while a mob gathers outside shouting *Worms, Worms, Worms!* What would that be like for you? Would you be able to forgive? Would you be able to forget the sight of your father? The way his hands shook when he moved to lower the blinds? Tell me!"

"Señora . . ."

"It has not left me. Almost sixty years and the bitterness has not left me. Not everyone understands . . . My father lost his first country to poverty and his second to thieves. My parents never regained their status here. Some exiles, you look at them, it's like they picked up where they left off. Houses in Cocoplum, servants, good cars. My parents were not like that. They emerged from exile . . . broken. My mother went to work at a shoe factory. Can you imagine! Gluing soles. And after that it was a plastics factory. And finally as a cashier at Sedanos . . . My father died in 2007, of colon cancer. In the end, he and Fidel wore colonoscopy bags at the same time. Fate has a sick sense of humor. That son of a bitch is still alive and my father is dead. Do you know . . . two days before my father died . . . he died at Mercy Hospital—the name never struck me until my father was dying there, facing the sea—two days before he died, he summoned me. Not my brother. He told me to come alone. Imagine. I did not want a bedside confession. I didn't know what to expect. He was . . . forgive me . . . one moment . . . he was . . . so small in the hospital bed. Wrists so thin. He told me to listen to him, that in the second drawer of his nightstand, in a green folder wrapped in string, was the deed to his burial plot. There in Woodlawn Cemetery on Eighth Street, where Machado and Somoza and Mas Canosa are buried. That's where we buried, my father, on March 13, 2007. He'd reserved the plot in 1976! He knew this was where he was going to die. Miami, Miami is where we will all die. Even Lenin. Even Lenin dies and is resurrected . . . in Miami!"

I spend the rest of the day erasing what I drew.

Speak to Us of Houses

Kahlil Gibran says, *Then a mason came forth and said, Speak to us of Houses.*

And he answered and said:

Build of your imaginings a bower in the wilderness ere you build a house within the city walls.

For even as you have home-comings in your twilight, so has the wanderer in you, the ever distant and alone.

Your house is your larger body.

It grows in the sun and sleeps in the stillness of the night; and it is not dream-

less. *Does not your house dream? and dreaming, leave the city for a grove or hill-top?*

I, Too, Thought the Doorman Was Cuban

Or, more accurately, assumed it, a mistake I'm usually careful not to make in my professional life. It's not just the Americans who make assumptions based on the cut of a face or color of the hair. Accents are easy to fake; I know that from my own work. Names give you away, but those can be changed.

He's our part-time doorman. Addresses everyone in Spanish, even the Americans. Tremendo calor está haciendo. Miami es un verano sin fin. That sort of thing. Once, I swear I heard him say on the phone, "Asere, que boláááá." I never talked to him much before, but one quiet afternoon in October, he stops me to say welcome back and how am I doing. He has kind eyes. And maybe that's why I decide to ask him about Lenin. Though it's true that I'm doing that a lot—asking my neighbors about Lenin.

"This unfortunate person . . . Yes, I saw him often. He had many visitors," he says. "Lenin—do you think this was his real name? Perhaps, perhaps . . . This Lenin . . . just a boy with such a heavy name! He didn't wait long enough. This is what I think. The first year is the most difficult. He gave up too soon. He was missing the gift of patience. Do you know Rumi? The wound is the place where the light enters you. Rumi said that. He was Afghan."

Armando is searching my eyes as he says this. "Yes! Afghan like me. Did I fool you?"

"You're not Cuban?" I was suspicious. I didn't think I could be fooled. Armando spoke Spanish like a Cuban and English with a Spanish accent.

"Not Cuban!" he says and laughs. "Look at me. I am smiling like a Cuban, though! And if you had seen my life!"

The front door opens.

"Buenas tardes, Señora Teresa."

"Buenas tardes, Armando." Teresa's smile is sweet. The eyes don't age, my grandmother used to say.

She gives me a quick nod.

When the elevator doors shut, Armando turns to me, still smiling.

"Very good people live here. I greet everyone by name. Every single person. I don't live here myself—I live near Wynwood—you know it? My building is not so nice as this one, but we also have people from everywhere in the world. This is what I like about Miami. Russians, French, Haitians, Venezuelans. Even one Persian lady, can you believe it? She's an electrologist in Aventura. I can talk to her also, a little bit. But most of the people I meet are Cubans, I think. The older ones, they want to talk about the island. First, I thought I would tell them I was born there. But that would have been difficult. I would have had to study, and someone would have known it was just a story. I don't have anything to hide. I've had an honorable life. It's simply easier to be Cuban here, don't you think? But not everyone understands that. If they found out I was not what I said I was, they would assume bad things. It could be unpleasant for them and me. So I realized I could say I was born there but left when I was a baby. This is true of many people in Miami, no?"

"You got that right!" I said.

"So I looked at a map and picked the smallest most lonely village. That will be funny, the day I meet someone from Jíbaro . . . Do you think I should have just said 'la Habana' like everyone else? Then maybe it would not be so strange if no one knew my parents there. I imagine Jíbaro is some place like Bazgir, everyone is related in some way. So now I hope I don't meet anyone from Jíbaro . . . you are not from there, are you?" He laughed again. "I can tell you this, and you can tell anyone you want. I am not a criminal. I am not hiding under a new identity. I am an American hero. This is a funny title, no? Haha! I laugh to myself also. American hero . . . but it's true. That is how I am here, with all the papers . . . Tell me, you do not think this casino man will be a problem for us, do you? Everyone is telling me, don't worry Armando, he'll never be elected. And even if he is, he won't do the things he is saying, that can never happen here. But I am not so sure. Americans, I think, are a little bit . . . what is the word? . . . like children. Yes, naïve, that is it. You are not American are you? My true apologies . . . I did not mean to insult."

I assure him I take no insult and consider telling him I have traveled through Afghanistan but then think better of it. For all I know, this, too, could be another identity.

"What is it like, your country?"

"I was born right after the Soviet invasion. Whole life war. No men left in the villages. Can you imagine this? War made us a country of orphans and cripples. And still we continued! Me too, no mother, no father. But at least I did not see them murdered in front of me, as so many did. Only one brother left, he stays now in Pakistan but I am trying to bring him. Inshallah, next year. We are Tajik, not Pashtun. I know Americans don't know the difference. But we hate the Taliban; I am always trying to explain this. The great leader Massoud, who would have finished the Taliban, he was murdered the day before September 11 happened in New York. That is why nobody remembers him . . . he was just one death. You don't remember him either, do you? But we mourned Ahmad Shah Massoud the way we mourned family. For a long time people said he had not died . . . that he was playing a trick to ambush the Pashtun. Maybe this is true. Maybe Massoud is not dead. My brother, he worked as an interpreter for the United States also, but his English was not as good as mine. Do you know, I did not go to school for my English? No, I learned from BBC radio. And then when I met my first American, he had no idea what I was saying! But American English is easier. I learned it very quickly. I travel everywhere. I saw my country for the first time. I am not sure how much I can say . . . Maybe this is not allowed. I saw bodies . . . baby's bodies. I saw so many things. So many many ugly things. For that whole first year I could not sleep, remembering. Once we were in a convoy through the Desert of Death, this is a true name, and there is nothing, nothing, nothing until we come to a small village and a little boy comes running . . . Maybe four years old . . . maybe a refugee thinking big noisy trucks are for candy, not killing. This boy he is running and behind, his mother screaming and everyone on the truck screaming. I am screaming stop, Ist! Wadrega! Ruken! in every language I know, but the little boy, he keeps coming and after the first explosion, I look away. I am covering my face with my scarf and crying . . . But my country . . . My country is beautiful. Not beautiful like here. Here is a place of blues and greens. There, everything is brown, but the mountains, when the sun is rising, there is no vision like that. It is a vision of God."

He stops to look up to the ceiling, and we are both quiet for a moment. Then he turns to me again with those soft eyes.

"I have lived in Miami four years. The first time I realized I will have hot water every day, whatever time I want, that was like a festival! But then soon I forget about the hot water, like everyone else. My grandfather, who raised us, often said that no one needs time to get used to good things . . . But I did need time. The first year alone was very difficult. No friends. The people here . . . they are not very neighborly . . . not like where I come from, where everyone is invited inside for tea and pistachios. So I invited some of the neighbors. And they said no thank you. I am lonely for a long time, thinking I am alone in all the world now . . . but my religion does not allow despair. Hope is holy. Only hope is holy. Now I am making friends everywhere. The Cubans love me very much and I love them like brothers. Some of them know I am not Cuban from Jíbaro, but they don't care. They say I am clever and a good man. This makes me full of a good kind of pride. I think I will have a very good life here. I feel this is my home. If only I could have talked to this young man, this Lenin, before . . . maybe I could have helped. It is a pity that I did not help. I could have explained to him that hope is holy."

Miriam Nader Tells Me about Beirut
"Lenin García . . . You were the landlady . . . Please, come in. Take a seat there on that armchair. Be careful! It's softer than it looks. I'll be right back."

Miriam's apartment is directly above mine, so the layout is the same: living room and dining room; kitchen over the back alley. I can't see them from where I sit, but I know the hallway divides two bedrooms, with a bath in between. The armchair I've been directed to is made of wicker, with a soft blue cushion. When she returns, Miriam sets some things on the wooden coffee table and takes a seat on the white bench sofa opposite. A painting of mountains hangs over her.

"Some tea," she says. "And I hope you are not allergic to walnuts. I made these yesterday. They were a favorite of Lenin's . . . no, it's okay, I'm sorry . . . I called him Lele. I took him something at least once a week—Easter cookies, salad, stuffed grape leaves. The poor boy didn't cook much."

"How often did you see him?"

"Every week. I met him in the elevator and immediately addressed him in Arabic. He laughed and shook his head. But he was so much like my Daoud. Same tall, slender build, same face, right down to the eyes, the way they turned down at the corners . . . forgive me, I grieve again . . .

"The next day, I took him cookies, just so I could look at him again. He was always smiling, that Lele . . . this is why I can't understand why he would do this . . . do this act that is against God . . . Every Thursday afternoon I knocked on his door. That was his one day off, Thursdays. He worked two jobs. One of them at a cafe, the other I don't know. But he was proud of working like this, proud of the money he was sending back to his mama. Such a good boy he was. I would take him a bit of food . . . he was so skinny, you see, I was worried that he didn't have enough to eat . . . I would take him a bit of food and then I would sit with him, just for a little while, a few minutes at most. He was a young man and young men do not like to spend time with old women . . . No, no, those are just pretty words, I am old. I have mirrors! I see for myself. But my dear one, if you could have seen me at eighteen . . . At eighteen before the troubles began and life was sweet and every man at the St. George wanted my hand in marriage. Beirut still shimmers like that in my dreams, the harbor that holds the entire sea in its embrace . . . I would sit with Lele in the apartment . . . your apartment. He didn't have a lot of furniture, the poor boy. But he always gave me the soft chair, brought me strong dark coffee served in doll cups decorated with roses. Sometimes I told him stories, but mostly he talked. I loved to watch his eyes when he talked, and those full lips so much like my Daoud's when he was a little boy and would pout when something displeased him, when some request from mother touched that independence that was growing, growing wild in him . . . Lele told me stories of being a boy in Havana. His father also died when he was very young, he had only fleeting memories of him. In one of them—this is a story I will never forget—the boy was perhaps four or five and they had gone to a beach for the weekend. It was an indistinct memory, though Lele didn't tell it that way. Lele told it as if it happened the week before. Maybe he invented the details, all of us do that sometimes, don't we? He was walking with both his parents along the shore, in between them, as the happy small children of this world are allowed. Lele was the first to notice the sand moving. At first his father thought they were crabs. But they were baby sea turtles, hundreds and hundreds of them, all heading in the wrong direction, toward the big Spanish hotels that had just then started to come up. Lele's father watched for a moment, and then suddenly, he shouted to pick them up and move them to the water. Lele remembered how his mother had gathered her full skirt and in this way was able to transport more turtles than anyone. But when they dropped the sea turtles at the shore's edge, many just came back up and started pulling back again toward the dunes. Tourists at the hotels came at the sound of shouting, and then they too tried to rescue the turtles. But again and again the babies fled the sea for the bright hotels. Those turtles, forever following the wrong light . . . And, you see, now I am grown old in a foreign country . . .

"I tell Daoud about Lele. He visits me, Daoud. He sits there in the chair where you are sitting now and he looks exactly the same as he did that night, the night I saw him off with a kiss to the forehead. He was fifteen, already so tall that he had to bend down to receive my blessing. And his smile . . . his smile is still the same smile he wore that eighteenth day of February in 1981, our season of ruins."

Miriam takes a deep breath and a sip of her tea before continuing.

"After my Daoud was killed, I was left alone in a city at war. I think back now and it is all like a dream, a terrible dream. How did we survive it all? My building was three blocks from the Green line. Two of the north-facing windows had blown out in a blast and I'd cut up a shower curtain to cover them. They expanded and contracted in the wind, like lungs. But you couldn't stay indoors forever. You had to go out for water, for food. I was a woman, all alone. My brothers were all in the north. I had not heard from them for months. Those of us left in the building, we helped one another, warily, protecting the little bit that we had, but helping . . . sharing, when we could. There were times of the day when the snipers were worse. You didn't go out then. In my neighborhood, they were most active in the mornings, when the children were supposed to be going to school . . . and in the afternoon. Do you know that human beings can be like this? Normal human beings, the boys that you took care of, the friends of your son, nice boys. Did you know this could happen? That some malignant blood would rise in them and set them on rooftops like dark angels, deciding who would live and who would die? After war, it is so hard to believe . . . so hard."

We are quiet. I eat one walnut cookie and then another.

"You went out at dusk," she continues after what seems a long while. "Thinking that's when their aim wouldn't be as good. And you scurried like a rat, hugging the ruins, keeping your back to the pockmarked concrete. Skittering back and forth across the city like this, like the lowest animal, just to buy a bit of bread, a small bag of garbanzos. And when an old man was shot just behind you, you kept running, you did not turn around, you ran past the ruins, and you did not stop. You never turned around, you understand?"

She begins to cry. And I reach across the tea and cookies to take her hand and hold it.

"Who of us really knows what happens when we die? You said just now that you don't believe in ghosts. Why not? What do we know of this world and its ten thousand forms? Why could this boy not be Daoud come back to me? But of course, you say, that is madness. Even I knew that. He rescued sea turtles with his father the way Daoud and I saved that nest of serins, fallen to the pavement on a cold, blue spring day before the war, when Daoud was still the little boy who took our hands, between me and his father, still alive, then, both of them, still alive."

She turns to me with pale eyes.

"Birth and death are perched on a precipice, my dear one; the years in between, we cling to love."

PEDRO MEDINA LEÓN was born in Peru, studied literature at Florida International University, and is an award-winning writer, speaker, and editor. He is the author of the short-story collection *La chica más pop de South Beach* (Sudaquia, 2020) and of the acclaimed novels *Varsovia* (Sudaquia, 2017), which won the Florida Book Award in 2017; *Mañana no te veré en Miami* (Oblicua, 2013); *Americana* (Sudaquia, 2019); and *Marginal* (Sudaquia, 2018). He is also the author of *Tour: A Journey through Miami's Culture* (Jitney, 2019) and co-editor of the anthologies *Viaje One Way* (SED, 2014) and *Miami (Un)plugged* (SED, 2016). Medina León is a speaker member of the Florida Humanities Council and co-creator of the Escribe Aquí Festival for the Betsy Hotel, which was awarded a grant from the Knight Foundation. In 2008 he created the cultural portal Suburbano Ediciones; today its affiliated portal, suburbano.net, is the leading Spanish-language cultural network in the United States.

Please see translator ANDREÍNA FERNÁNDEZ's bio on page 38.

"Those Days I Spent with Mar" is fiction, translated from the Spanish by Andreína Fernández.

> She was seated at the small table next to mine, Mar, immersed in a book. She held her chin in one hand and drummed her fingers on the table with the other. Her drumming distracted me. She turned the pages of her book slowly and between each turn she'd take a moment to raise her head, stretch out the sleeves of her blue Gap sweater until they covered her hands, and gaze out the window at Biscayne Bay.
>
> From "Those Days I Spent with Mar"

THOSE DAYS I SPENT WITH MAR

I saw Mar for the first time at the Starbucks on West Avenue. It was my day off at the Pegasus shipping agency, and after lunch at By the Slice, I stopped by the café to read a bit. I'd just begun reading *Going to Miami* by David Rieff and hoped to have enough time for it there. I struggled with readings in English; they soon began to feel convoluted and it took me a long time to become invested in the story.

She was seated at the small table next to mine, Mar, immersed in a book. She held her chin in one hand and drummed her fingers on the table with the other. Her drumming distracted me. She turned the pages of her book slowly and between each turn she'd take a moment to raise her head, stretch out the sleeves of her blue Gap sweater until they covered her hands, and gaze out the window at Biscayne Bay. She'd stop drumming her fingers for a few minutes, during which I tried to focus on my reading, but soon she'd start drumming again. Finally, I closed my book, placed it over my legs, and stared at her: immersed still in those pages. It was futile. I was not going to be able to read. It was turning out to be a slow season at Pegasus. I'd just have to read there instead.

They had transferred me from the warehouse to the front desk. The work was simpler: receive orders and input them into the database. There was plenty of free time. They had replaced me in my previous role with Machito, a Cuban a few years older than me who spent all of most days playing cards with a deck he kept in his pocket.

A few days had passed since that afternoon at Starbucks when a white BMW parked at the front door of the agency and a woman stepped out, talking on the phone. It was her, the one who would not let me read, I recognized her. Without finishing her call, she approached the front desk and pulled an iPhone out of her purse. She told the person on the other line that she was here now, about to ship a package to her brother in Caracas, and would be studying at Starbucks all day tomorrow. The person on the other line asked something else, but she said she was already standing in front of the "pana" from the agency, was keeping him waiting, she'd call a little later.

"Amigo, I need to send this package to Caracas."

While I thought about it, Mar browsed my copy of *Going to Miami*, which was sitting on the counter.

"Interesting. The book, I mean," she said.

And I responded yes, it was good so far.

I needed some details from her to complete the order: Her name was Marianella Figuera, she lived in the El Mirador building on West Avenue, and her phone number was 7863538887.

"The package will arrive in two days."

I walked into the warehouse to drop off the iPhone, and Machito was playing solitary, business already dead for the day. I told him he could go if he wanted and reminded him that I was off the next day so he would need to open the agency and staff the front desk. Tranquilo, socio. Relax. Tomorrow I'm in charge of the ship.

I spent the next morning organizing the piles of clothing that had been accumulating around my bed and then went to Publix. Then I had lunch, as had become my habit by this point, at the By the Slice. Then I went to buy my coffee at the Starbucks on West. On the way there, I remembered Mar. The day before, at Pegasus, she had said to someone on the phone that she'd be holed up in there all day studying, and, surely enough, Mar was again immersed in her book, legs crossed over the chair, drumming her fingers. After buying my coffee, I passed by her table and we exchanged glances. Although it took her a bit to recognize me, she waved and smiled.

"Lots to study?" I asked.

"Mid-terms, yes."

"Good luck with that," I said and took a sip of my coffee.

"Look, I keep thinking about that book you were reading. I study sociology. For one of my courses I have to submit a final essay, and I want to write something about Miami, but I am not yet sure what."

I suggested she write something about the Miami riots of 1982 in Overtown. She had no idea what I was talking about. So, I told her that a conflict had erupted between Black people, gringos, and Latinos in Miami, that it had poured out into the streets, and that there were a lot of culture clashes between those groups back then. Severe ones, with deaths. Between the late '70s and the '80s there was a lot of this kind of turmoil in Miami. She could write about that, and if she was going to be at the café a bit longer, I could go to my house and bring back some books for her to take a look.

"Seriously?" she asked, pushing aside her book and crossing her arms over the table.

"Yes, of course. No problem."

"Chévere, I'll be here. I have to study all afternoon. What's your name?"

"Martín." I extended my hand.

"Ah, I'm Mar, pleasure to meet you."

It took me about forty minutes to make it back, and by then she was nowhere to be found. At her table, an elderly couple drank tea and ate muffins.

Mar turned up at Pegasus the next day, around two in the afternoon. She apologized for having left. Her landlord had called her, and she'd had to go deal with something related to the contract for her apartment. I told her no worries, and she asked me what we could do about the books, she was really interested in taking a look at them. I'd be done at the agency around seven, and if okay with her, we could figure out a time then. Mar said she'd be at Starbucks that afternoon, no matter what, they'd have to kick her out for her to get up from her table and leave. It's settled then, I said, I'll leave here, stop and get the books, and meet you at the café. She thanked me and apologized again, and we said goodbye.

There wasn't much movement at the agency the rest of the afternoon, and I spent almost the entire time playing blackjack with Machito. He mentioned he was putting together a few sets of good poker players for some championship rounds playing at Zeke's bar, asked if I'd be interested in playing. I was busy that night since I was meeting up with Mar, but next time for sure.

I arrived at the Starbucks with the books around eight thirty and there she was, at one of the tables. I set down *Going to Miami* and *Miami, City of the Future* next to the book she was reading, and she looked up.

"Épale, Martín, thanks so much," Mar said enthusiastically. "Let me buy you a coffee."

The books I had brought were for a course on dysfunctional collective behavior, she said, interested in what I had told her about the Miami riots. She had been Googling information, the topic would be perfect. As we talked about Miami, it became ten thirty and they told us they were closing.

Mar drove me to my efficiency in her BMW. In the background, at low volume, Patti Smith sang "Frederick." We live close to each other, she said when she started the engine, and then we spent the rest of the ride in silence, listening to the song. At the door, Mar asked me to give her a few days to look through the books. I had already read them so I had no rush to get them back, she could take her time. We exchanged phone numbers; we'd talk soon. As I was leaving, I said "Frederick" was a really great song.

Before bed, I received a text from Mar: *Martín, a million thanks* ☺.

Let me know if you need anything else, saludos, I responded.

Machito insisted on inviting me to poker. The championship was really no such thing. It was just Machito, Kimbombo (a friend of his who sometimes picked him up from the agency), a guy named Carmona, one named Cabalito, and I, sitting at one of the tables in the back of Zeke's, betting on rounds of beer. The poker was also not very much like poker either: it consisted of putting together trios and pairs, and those who had hands of nothing or made the lowest trios and pairs had to buy a round of beer for everyone. I don't know how many trios I made or how many rounds I lost. The only thing I remember is that one of the times I went to the bathroom and checked my phone, I had a text from Mar saying she had just finished reading Rieff's book and thought it brilliant.

I went back to the table. Machito had already put away his deck, and Carmona and Cabalito had left. Kimbombo was hugging Machito, saying that he was his brother, his brothersazo. Machito made a gesture that meant Kimbombo was already drunk and it was time to go.

I stayed a while longer and ordered a Heineken at the bar. The television on top of the refrigerator was playing music videos from the '70s and '80s. I drank a few beers waiting for "Frederick" to play, but they only played videos from The Cure, Hendrix, The Clash; Patti Smith never came on. I left a ten-dollar bill next to the empty bottle and left.

I walked with "Frederick" stuck in my head, with Patti Smith, with Mar driving her BMW, with Mar engrossed in her books. I pulled out my cellphone and opened my text messages app. Instead of going home, I walked a few blocks down to El Mirador. Almost all of the apartment lights were off. In which one did Mar live? Was one of the few lit-up apartments hers? I pulled out my phone and opened text messages again, clicked compose, but no, I didn't write, I put it away. At home I played "Frederick" on YouTube and left it on repeat. I opened a Heineken. I drank the beer in two gulps. I opened another. I had barely begun drinking it when I felt a volcano overflow from my stomach and up and out of my mouth. The night ended with me hugging the toilet, in front of a viscous, yellow liquid with bits of ham and noodle in it.

It could not have been later than ten in the morning when my phone rang. Half-asleep and without looking to see who was calling, I answered. Mar was at the door. She had come to drop off the books, had already ordered copies for herself. I apologized for looking so disheveled, I had been at a bar until late last night. She laughed and said that if I were ever to see her right after waking up I would surely stop speaking to her. She asked what bar I had been to. A little bar here on Lincoln, Zeke's, "Do you know it?" She didn't. In fact, she didn't know anyone in the area. Her few friends were her classmates at FIU. She had gone out with them a few times but only to sports bars. So, I invited her to a bar on Saturday, and she thought it was a great idea.

I was unable to do a thing the rest of the day; the hangover had wiped me out. I spent the day lying in bed; when I got hungry, I called the taquería La Chismosa and ordered the two-for-one burrito special: one was my lunch and the other was dinner. At night I wrote a text to Mar asking how her exam had gone. She responded saying she thought it went well and was at Starbucks studying for the exam she had the next day.

On Saturday night, I arrived at El Mirador at nine. Mar came out dressed in jeans, a white Lacoste shirt, Converse shoes, also white, everything matching perfectly. I asked if she liked '80s Spanish-language rock music and she said she did. Then I told her we'd go to Al Capone, a bar on Washington where they played that music and sometimes had live bands. On the way, Mar told me that, a couple years earlier, her dad had decided to send her to Miami because with Chávez in power, things back in her country were impossible. Her dad worked at the Mercantil Bank, and the government had it out for bankers. Mar's plans were to finish studying, find work in Miami, and not return to Venezuela. She'd graduate in a few months and look for work. She had already started but hadn't found anything yet.

No band played that night at the bar, which was a shame. I would have loved to hear the Pistolas Rosadas, but the music they did have was a tribute to Soda Stereo, which you can never go wrong with. We sat at the bar; she ordered a Corona from the gringo wearing a Red Sox cap, and I ordered a Heineken. I saw Cabalito at the other end of the bar, one of the poker players from Zeke's; we greeted each other from afar. After opening the beers, the gringo at the bar went to talk to him. Mar kept staring at the wall behind the stage where a set of drums, a guitar, and a microphone were resting along with an enormous caricature of Al Capone. He was another one of our notorious residents, I said, supposedly loved to place his illicit bets at the Clay Hotel on Española Way, at least that's how the urban legend goes. Mar asked me what I had studied; she was surprised by how well read I was. I told her that at the moment I was just working at Pegasus, saving up money to resolve the issue of my papers. I was planning to marry a Cuban woman next year, get my residency, and study sociology, like her.

I was on my fifth beer and she was on her third when she said that if she had one more, she'd vomit, that too much beer did not sit well with her, so we left.

A few blocks away from the Al Capone the rain became intense and we picked up the pace. By the time we were saying goodbye at El Mirador, the rain had become a thick mass of water that bathed the fences, palm trees, and tops of cars. "Call me when you arrive," I heard from behind me after I had already run a few meters.

Mar was already in bed when I called, had been just waiting for my call to go to sleep. She wanted to be sure I had made it home okay.

"Okay, sure, but really wet," I said, and she laughed.

She said she'd had a good time. And I said she was excellent company.

"What are your plans for tomorrow?" I asked.

"Nothing—I mean—I don't have any."

"We should see each other for a bit, what do you think?"

"Vale, sounds good. Want to come to my place for lunch?"

"Around what time?"

"At noon. I'm going to cook. I cook every Sunday."

We agreed and said goodbye, and before brushing my teeth and getting ready for bed, I played "Frederick" on YouTube.

El Mirador was one of those aquamarine-colored buildings that surrounded the smooth ocean of Biscayne Bay and that you could see from the MacArthur Bridge when entering Miami Beach. On the other side, the enormous houses of Star Island were being built, shielded by palm trees and yachts. Mar lived on the ninth floor in a one-bedroom with white floors, walls, and ceiling. The only furniture—centered in what would perhaps have been the living room or the dining room if it weren't also the only room—she had a table, also white, where her books lay, disorganized. Beyond that were scattered blue cushions. Mar had cooked ravioli, and within a few minutes our plates were empty.

"Coffee, Martín?"

"Alright."

I got up from the table, grabbing the plates to take them to the dishwasher, and in the kitchen, next to the coffee pot, before she turned it on, I searched for her lips and found them. We let ourselves be guided by impulse, by our hands, giving in to one another. Without breaking our kiss, we made it to the cushions.

A little while later, I collapsed on top of her and stayed there while she gently caressed my head, until our breathing had begun to regain its rhythm.

We spent the rest of the afternoon among cushions, all over the place, eating vanilla Haagen Dazs ice cream, talking about her end-of-semester project, listening to the entirety of *Patti Smith Live at Montreaux*.

"She doesn't sing 'Frederick' in this," I complained.

"Good, so you don't get bored of it."

At six I told her I had to go. I wanted to go to sleep early. I had to open Pegasus; we expected UPS on Mondays.

From then on, I would go to El Mirador each afternoon after leaving Pegasus. Mar researched and wrote her project; she was in the last few weeks of class. I would arrive, she'd take a break, we'd make coffee. On the weekends we'd go to Al Capone or Zeke's or some bar on Lincoln, Washington, or Española. Mar loved discovering South Beach. She said each time she'd understood more why I was so fascinated by the city. On Sundays we cooked pasta. According to Machito, I had fallen in love. I was no longer a regular for poker. He said they were playing incredible championships and I didn't know what I was missing.

Mar did well on her Miami riot essay. A different topic from the usual ones, very interesting, said Professor Cruz, and he gave her an A. I suggested we celebrate by drinking a mojito in each bar we passed as we walked down Española, Washington, and Lincoln. She thought it was a brilliant idea; it was the least we could do to celebrate her graduation and an A on her essay. We went to nine or ten bars; I don't quite remember. The last one was on Española. She could not drink any more, Mar said, she couldn't even walk, and if we could please take a taxi home. At her apartment I put on "Frederick" and we fell asleep.

On one of my days off, as we sat on the rocks overlooking the water at Smith and Wollensky Park, Mar said she was thinking about returning to Venezuela. It was not what she wanted, but she had graduated two months earlier and still had not found work. Her student visa would expire soon, and she did not want to become undocumented. Her dad had told her to return, that he'd find something for her there. Moreover, her lease at El Mirador was about to end, and under these circumstances, she couldn't even think about renewing it.

"Understood," I said, averting my gaze toward the Carnival cruise headed to the Bahamas, filled with hundreds of happy passengers waving goodbye. Before long, we were each back in our respective homes.

Several days passed without hearing from each other. Machito provided encouraging words, That's what women are like, compadre, you have to look on the bright side, we have you as another regular for poker again. In addition to him, Cabalito, Kimbombo, and Carmona, there were a few people now who got together at Zeke's. Tuesdays and Thursdays at ten had become the established playing nights. There were two tables; players were eliminated until there was just one table left.

Mar and I broke the ice with a call from her to the agency. She wanted to see me after work, at the Starbucks. I arrived at the coffee shop at seven and she was there, waiting for me. She asked how I was, and I responded saying I was well, missing her. She grabbed my hand, saying that there had not been a single day that she did not think of me. I looked at her but said nothing.

She was leaving for Venezuela now, and she meant now as in that day. The taxi would come for her at El Mirador in a few hours to take her to the airport. Her eyes were shiny with held-back tears. She pulled Patti Smith's CD out of her bag, gave it to me, and then kissed me on the forehead.

"Never forget number nine," she said. "Take care of yourself."

I searched for her lips but did not find them; she had turned away.

I stared at her through the window of the Starbucks as she walked out and merged confusedly with the people coming and going on West, until she entered El Mirador.

I asked the time: it was just past eight. I ordered a tall blond and collapsed onto the same chair I had sat in the first time I saw her. I looked at the song order on the CD. Number nine was "Frederick." I pulled my phone out of my pocket and had a text from Mar that said to take care and another from Machito wanting to confirm that I would be at poker at ten, asking if I'd still be a regular or if they'd lost me again.

I responded to Mar, told her to take care of herself as well, and to Machito I wrote yes, I was still a regular.

JAVIER LENTINO is an Argentine writer whose work has appeared in *Vogue Hombre* and *El Mundo Américas*, among other publications. *Los Onetti* (Galerna, 2021) is his first novel. More of his short stories as well as his chronicles, essays, and other nonfiction are on his website, https://www.javierlentino.com. Florida has been Lentino's home since 2002.

Please see translator ANDREÍNA FERNÁNDEZ's bio on page 38.

"38 Hours" is nonfiction, translated from the Spanish by Andreína Fernández.

> The guy starts off in Spanish, doesn't realize he's going back
> and forth between languages. I just sign forms I don't bother to
> read. There are so many instructions and too many questions
> for my English, which understands everything but has no soul
> and knows nothing of feelings.
>
> From "38 Hours"

38 HOURS

The stretcher rolls down hospital hallways on its way to the operating room. Its large wheels glide silently over polished rubber floors, shiny from being so clean, from reflecting so much LED light.

I go covered in wires, reclined in reverse, which is to say leaning forward, almost seated like in those commercials for smart mattresses that seem to air every few minutes on television. I pull on the sheet a bit in order to cover my legs and use both hands to arrange my hospital gown as if it were a blazer, a futile attempt to look less sick than I am.

My stretcher glides, swift, through hospital bowels, toward its destination, corridor after corridor a repeat of forced smiles and thumbs-up gestures. My wife walks alongside me, smiles now and then. Her hands are cold.

It has been thirty-six hours since they told me, in English, that I have a tumor and that they have to operate. Believe it or not, I am calm.

It is a curious calm, this calm of mine, poised just so between chaos and stillness like a sunny, windless day, hours before a hurricane. If I were a bit more of a snob, I'd say my calm is the peace that comes with being present. I'm okay, if barely so.

Do you cease to be a foreigner when you are able to feel safe in a hospital? Even if you can't recall the name of the doctor doing your surgery? I still have fuzzy memories of the hospitals in Buenos Aires. I am suffused to this day with the smell of sickness that seeped from their hallways, with my memories of childhood ghosts and the moments before other surgeries, the bed sheets that didn't belong to me, and my mother's "quedate tranquilo." I have not told her any of this. What for? So she can anguish over it from four thousand miles away?

"Has anyone called?" I ask my wife, unable to tolerate the silence any longer. I don't get an answer. She walks wrapped in her own thoughts.

The stretcher rolls and rolls down more corridors, all identical, traced clones, unending. Healthy people, sick people, wheelchairs, crutches, families visiting, a doctor holding a cold can of Diet Coke. LABORATORY. X-RAYS.

ORTHOPEDICS. DIAGNOSTICS. ONCOLOGY. ONCOLOGY. ONCOL-
OGY. ONCOLOGY.

Children's art fills the walls. I think of my kids, about all the things they still have to live through. Will they make it without me?

Doors continue to open, automatically, to the rhythm of my attendant's access card swipe.

"I will not wish you good luck because you don't need it," he tells me in his thick Miami accent as we wait for an elevator. He rearranges the disposable cap that contains his hair and continues to verify the information on my bracelet. "Luck is for those who aren't being treated by the best . . ." he goes on reciting his script, but I don't want to hear any more of it.

Usually, I'm prone to small talk. I chat with Uber drivers, in waiting rooms, and even with strangers in line at the supermarket, but today I just wring my fingers, instinctively trying to fend off bad energy. My Latino fetish for super-stition waylays me: the ritual of lighting candles, the triple signing of the cross, the Virgin. I search for the cross on my naked chest now, but all my amulets stayed back in the room, along with my clothes and my wedding ring. I am go-ing in alone and without protection, with only those good-luck charms etched in my DNA, like an airplane shaking through turbulence, like when I took the citizenship test, or when my brother-in-law (at the time) gave me flowers minutes before my daughter was born.

At last, the elevator arrives and the attendant maneuvers the stretcher back-ward, sharply dinging one of the metal walls. "Good thing he's not the one doing my surgery," I think and laugh like an idiot.

"Do you know why we enter backward? Why I stand beside you?" he says walking over to stand at my side. "If there were an emergency or a fire in here, I'd have to push in order to get us out. If someone were between the stretcher and the door, they could be crushed and killed. Everything here is thought through with security in mind."

"Are you from here?" I ask because I can't bear hearing of yet another death scenario. My wife rolls her eyes and twists her mouth like she does every time I say something just to hear myself talk. "Born and raised, but my parents are Cuban." When I tell him I'm Argentine, he makes a comment about asado, says he went to Buenos Aires as a kid, but then the doors open and I turn into a pa-tient once again. More hallways, the same rubber floor. I no longer know where we are until a sign reads, SURGERY—AUTHORIZED ACCESS ONLY.

"Name and date of birth," demands a woman while I am parked yet again in a room without doors or windows, and the cast of health care workers renews itself as if it were time for a change of shift. The last person in closes the curtain. He is a short, muscular guy with a Peanuts surgical cap and an iPad covered in stickers. "English? *Español?* I am the anesthesiologist," he says with a customer-service smile. "How are you feeling?"

The guy starts off in Spanish, doesn't realize he's going back and forth between languages. I just sign forms I don't bother to read. There are so many instructions and too many questions for my English, which understands everything but has no soul and knows nothing of feelings.

"We're ready," a nurse says finally, and everyone steps back a bit. Then the thumbs up, the smiles, it all repeats. They give my wife a buzzer like the ones you get at restaurants and speak into her ear. She asks something. "No more than two hours," they tell her. The stretcher rolls on again. I say goodbye without looking at her. If I look, she'll cry.

The operating room has so many screens it looks like a television studio set, or perhaps it's like all operating rooms in this country. There are voices speaking in Spanish, and a slow reggaeton plays in the background. I know this because a small, involuntary smile appears on my face, and I am not even drugged yet. I look for the doctor I just met but can't pick him out amid all the masked faces and monochrome gowns.

"Tranquilo bud, we'll take care of you. A bit of a warm feeling . . . no te preocupes que es normal. Now relax, deep breath, will see you in no time."

Down with superstitions, buried are the good-luck charms. I want to speak but I can't, not even in Spanish. I do not pray, I don't want to, I no longer believe. I do not think. What for? The screens move away. The noise, the people, the lights dim slowly. They're in no hurry. There is nothing left to do but close my eyes and wait, comfortable, warm. I don't know if it will be death or life. It shouldn't all be the same to me. But I can't seem to figure out which of the two is the easiest option.

CARLOS HARRISON is a Pulitzer Prize–winning journalist, an editor, and a writer of more than a dozen books in English and Spanish. A former national and international network television correspondent, Harrison has also written two award-winning TV documentaries and seven feature-length screenplays as well as hundreds of newspaper articles and magazine pieces for publications including the *Miami Herald*, *New York Times*, *Washington Post*, *People*, and *Southern Living*. Born in Panama to a Panamanian mother and an American father, he has worked as a newspaper reporter and editor; as a magazine writer for numerous national travel, celebrity, and business publications; and as deputy managing editor of *People en Español*. He was also an on-air correspondent for the NBC and Fox affiliates in Miami.

"Other" is nonfiction.

That year, I saw my first hurricane. My dad took me out and into its eye to marvel at the calm amid the destruction. The sky gleamed clear and radiant blue, a transient tranquility before the storm struck again. A metaphor, it turned out, for my life.

From "Other"

OTHER

I don't remember when the first one arrived. I remember when I did.

We drove down through the Appalachians. Me, squeezed against the passenger door next to my mother. She, in the middle of the pickup's bench seat, between me and my dad. I looked out my window as he navigated us through the turns of a narrow mountain road, and I looked down, down, down—and saw clouds. White puffs drifting between the mountain peaks far, far below. I gulped. I'd never been so high. Nor on a road carved so precariously along a cliff's face, with an edge that dropped away so sharply. Like a slice of cake or a line on one of my childish drawings where I imagined the world ended.

I came from a flat place and had gone to another. Now I was here, pressed against the door, on my way to yet another, the flattest of all. I was four. And I was afraid.

Dad was proud of the dusky blue '49 Ford pickup he painstakingly maintained, wouldn't dream of leaving behind. He piled it high with sticks of furniture and boxed bundles of clothes. My tiny child's rocking chair rode high on top, like Granny's in *The Beverly Hillbillies,* an ornament perched on the bulging mound beneath it, roped firmly, I hoped, to the pickup's bed. I could feel the tug of our huge black Buick hitched to the bumper behind us, or thought I could, and felt sure we would plunge off the steep mountain on some too-sharp curve.

I came, originally, from Panama. It's a place of mountains, too, but not for me. For me they existed only in the distance. It was, where I was born, at the edge of the famed canal at the edge of the capital city, mostly a place of lowland and beaches curving around a broad bay. We moved to Michigan when I was too young to feel loss or longing, before words in Spanish formed on my tongue. Before the sounds and songs and ways of my birthplace seared themselves into my soul. In my mind, Michigan was home.

Time wipes away some memories, like wind scouring sand from the shore. Others rise up unbidden, like faded Kodachromes.

I remember a white German Shepherd at a house down the street, and a yard that stretched for what seemed like miles. The year the snow drifted so high it reached the roof was the year my dad said we had to go. I remember my confusion that morning when I got up, seeing the picture window in the living room blacked out. I'd just asked Mom where Dad had gone off to when he pulled open the front door and stood there huffing and sweating with a snow shovel in his hand, saying, "Start packing. We're leaving."

He'd lived in Michigan as a boy growing up, before he'd gone off to war. He met my mom in Panama, still wearing his uniform, got married, and I was born. The snow reminded him of why he'd left in the first place. So he loaded us up in his precious pickup, lashed my rocking chair on top, and drove south as far as the road would go. We arrived in Florida as 1959 edged into 1960, when mine wasn't the only world changing.

That year, I saw my first hurricane. My dad took me out and into its eye to marvel at the calm amid the destruction. The sky gleamed clear and radiant blue, a transient tranquility before the storm struck again. A metaphor, it turned out, for my life.

We settled in a place called Riverside, a Miami neighborhood I didn't realize was poor, a place for outcasts clawing their way to new and better. It was then, largely, "the Jewish neighborhood." A place that accepted strangers shunned in other parts of town. Billie Holiday, it's said, stayed in a hotel a few blocks from the building where I lived because "coloreds" couldn't stay at "white" hotels. In Riverside they could because in Riverside they knew that money was green no matter the color of the hand it came from. The new arrivals regularly mistook the open door for a welcome.

Castro had seized power in Cuba less than a year before. The exodus had begun. The refugees came empty-handed and forlorn. Broke but not broken. They couldn't take stuff with them when they left. Fidel wouldn't permit it. Some resourceful souls, though, found a way. They swallowed their engagement rings and wedding bands before they boarded the planes, then picked through their shit when they landed. Not for sentimental reasons. This was pure commerce, ante for their new lives. The pawn shops, of course, took advantage. But something was better than nothing, enough for some food and cheap rent in a poor neighborhood called Riverside.

My dad was Donald Harrison, Don to his family and friends. Barely educated but sharp. Hardworking and resourceful. He'd run away from home and the Michigan winters when he was fifteen, while the world was at war. Small enough and wild enough to squeeze into the rear of an Army Air Corps bomber, he manned a tail gun against enemy fighters in the sky. Got caught at seventeen and kicked out for being underage. Went back on his next birthday.

That time, he went to Korea. Then, when peace finally came back for a while, he got sent down to Panama, met my mom, and learned to speak Spanish like a native.

Mom and Dad spoke English to me. Spanish was their private language. Easier than spelling things out. Sometimes, at dinner, my dad would give Mom *that look,* you know, and mutter a few soft words I didn't understand. She'd giggle or blush. Then they'd tell me it was time for bed.

I don't recall the details, can't be sure I ever really knew, but somehow Dad finagled a job as manager of the apartment building we now called home, across the river from downtown. Not that he'd ever done that kind of thing before. Dad, though, was a natural. Good with his hands, quick with a joke, possessed of an easy smile.

And since he spoke Spanish, easy for the new, non-English-speaking arrivals from Cuba to talk to. And about. Word spread. The building became a magnet for exiles. To them he was *Don* Harrison, pronounced the Spanish way—an honorific for the lord of the manor. Instead of just "Don," some guy from a hardscrabble patch near Detroit.

First came an old couple with a cocker spaniel they treated like their child. They carried toilet paper with them when they took him for a walk, wiped him carefully after he did his business.

Then came a kid close to my age. I don't remember his name. I do remember the dark-haired girl I fell madly in love with who lived at the end of the hall. Iliana. Her dad was a doctor, or had been in Cuba. Now he loaded freight by day and studied English at night. He was the one who cleaned and closed the ragged gash on my knee when I slashed it open on a hunk of metal, diving for something shiny in the grass. We couldn't afford a "real" doctor. Neither, I suppose, could he.

The building seemed to explode into Spanish that summer. The Corripios moved into the apartment next door. Then came Armando, an older bully I didn't like, and plenty of kids I did. The neighborhood filled up with new playmates who all spoke only my parents' private language, while I spoke only the language of TV.

I soon picked up the obvious words—"Yes." "No." "Run." "Come here." I knew our tiny green toy army men were *soldados* and that the *niños* and *niñas* I played with were my friends. In any language.

Soon, too, I was eating Cuban bread from the *panadería,* and the flavor of Latin life filled both my belly and my head. Salsa spilled from open doors and windows, Celia and Benny Moré.

There were many words I didn't understand—*miércoles* and *primo, familia,* and *trabajar*. But I'd store them up and ask my mom when I came home for lunch or dinner. "Mom, what does *viernes* mean?" And busy and distracted as all moms are, she answered without thinking of why I was asking or what I would do with what she said.

Little by little, as the summer went by, words became sentences. It all became easier to understand.

Then one day, after school had restarted, my parents had one of their "private" conversations in Spanish. And I, without thinking, chimed in. In Spanish. Their mouths dropped open.

Dad died four years later, the year the next big hurricane came.

A year after that, Mom met a man, a Cuban who'd come on a raft. Soon after, they were married and he moved in. He spoke hardly any English. I struggled to understand.

Riverside, by then, had a different name. Now it was "Little Havana." The Jews were mostly gone, replaced by the influx of Cubans. The world had changed around me. Now it changed at home.

I had been a gringo who spoke Spanish, just like my old man. Yeah, Mom hailed from Panama. But to me, that was just a word. Overnight, I became a refugee, the same as my little friends. Plucked from a world I recognized, forced into someplace strange.

With Dad we'd been of modest means. Now we were poor. The ornate spire of the Freedom Tower became a regular feature of life. Mom and I sweated in line with the wide-eyed Cuban women and their hollow-eyed kids, just two more among the faces full of hope and fear. We were exiles too, by marriage, waiting for handouts of welfare food: bricks of Velveeta and tins of Spam. Powdered milk in boxes and peanut butter in cans, the oil floating on top, slick and thick. You had to mix it like batter before you spread it on your bread. Like stirring cement.

The refugees had lost their homeland. I had lost my place. They had traditions and customs I had never learned. I suddenly had none of my own. Dinner had been meat and potatoes. Now it was black beans and rice. There were no more yams and baked ham at Christmas. We ate roast pork the night before. Thanksgiving became just another day off, as likely to bring turkey as *bacalao*.

They had landed on a new shore. I had been swallowed by a rising tide. Like them, I straddled two worlds. But it wasn't quite the same. I wasn't just from someplace different. *I* was different. A half-breed. I not only lived in two worlds; two worlds lived in me. I wish I could say that's a good thing, but that's not always the case. It doesn't make you part of both worlds. It makes you part of none. Back then, it made me an outsider no matter where I stood.

Among my Cuban friends, it conferred a special passage. They invited me into their houses for their families to marvel at, like some exotic mutt off the street. The *abuelas* and *tías* treated me like an odd and distant cousin from some strange and far-off land. Someone from a branch of the tree they'd never really seen, but still related by blood. That accounted for my paltry dancing skills and why I didn't know the words of "*Mi burrito sabanero.*"

The difference they saw wasn't as obvious to me. I was like someone surrounded by fog, never clear about where I stood.

Then, suddenly, I saw.

We moved from the *barrio* to a place at the west edge of town where homes were cheap and people like us were rare. My new friends' families came from Georgia and 'Bama. They ate hominy and grits. They spoke only English. And they complained about the "Cubes" who didn't. But "not you, Carlos. You're OK. You talk just like the rest of us."

So, once again I was welcomed. But only just. An odd interloper with a visitor's pass. Someone expected, one day, to go home.

Instead, I went off to the Army. I was seventeen, unsure and confused about who I was. I'd been gringo. And not. Then gringo, sort of, again. I went from one side to the other and found both ends blocked. Half-breed, I'd learned, means living in halves, with no place to feel whole.

But that very first day in the Army, while we were still filling out forms, a sergeant leaned in with a menacing sneer and gave me an unintended gift.

The form I was working on asked for my race. I checked off the box next to "Caucasian." That's when the sergeant squeezed close by my side and hissed in my ear, "You're not Caucasian. You're 'Other.'"

He probably expected me to be offended. Instead, a giant smile burst across my face. I'd had a flash of realization. He was right. So much more than he knew. *An Other!* Of course. *That's what I am.*

I thanked him. His words had filled me with pride. I was no longer "not this" or "not that." I was no longer amorphous. I found, in that moment, what I'd been missing—identity, clarity, definition. And a place to call my own. A place I recognized: once again, navigating a narrow road, looking down, down, down the edge of a cliff, knowing some folks want you there, because they like nothing better than to push you off.

ALEX SEGURA is an acclaimed writer of novels, comic books, and podcasts. He is the author of *Star Wars Poe Dameron: Free Fall* (Disney LucasFilm, 2020); the Pete Fernández mystery series, which includes the Anthony Award–nominated crime novels *Dangerous Ends* (Polis, 2017), *Blackout* (Polis, 2018), and *Miami Midnight* (Polis, 2019); and *Secret Identity* (Flatiron, 2022). His comic books include most notably the superhero noir series *The Black Ghost* (New Wave Comics, 2020). He also created the YA music series "The Archies" and the "Archie Meets" collection of crossovers featuring real-life cameos from the Ramones, B-52s, and more. Segura is also a co-creator and co-writer (with Monica Gallagher) of the *Lethal Lit* crime/YA podcast on iHeart Radio, named one of the best podcasts of 2018 by the *New York Times*. By day, Alex is senior vice-president of sales and marketing at Oni Press, with previous stints at Archie Comics and DC Comics. A Miami native born to Cuban parents, he lives in New York with his wife and children.

"Star Power" is fiction.

> "Fuck Ricky," Mariela said, checking herself on her phone. The
> flicker of the phone's camera let me know she was mid-selfie. I
> tried not to roll my eyes. I'd be doing the same shit if I was her.
> But I'd never be her.
>
> From "Star Power"

STAR POWER

Mariela came into the dressing room, her bare skin covered in glitter and sweat, her swimsuit-tight dress reflective even in the dim light. Her mouth hung half-open, as if she were sleepwalking. My hand finished the G7 chord on my acoustic guitar as her eyes registered my presence. The expression on her face went from hypnotized to a knowing smirk, her green eyes almost glimmering behind her long, curved lashes.

"How'd you get in here, girl?"

I start to sputter, but she moves in fast, her hand on my bare shoulder. I get a shock, followed by a long, tingling sensation when our bodies touch.

"Relax, girl," she says, her voice a husky whisper, her lips near my face. I can almost feel her mouth form a wide grin. "Just giving you shit."

I let out a quick, nervous laugh.

"Ricky let me in," I said, still feeling the urge to explain myself, in my ratty Gap tank and jeans, holding my beat-up, cheap-ass Yamaha acoustic. Always desperate to understand why I belonged anywhere. "He said he wanted us to talk."

Mariela shrugged as she let her body flop down onto the ratty couch behind the makeup table. The room was cramped and moldy and seemed to be on the brink of falling apart. So, overall, pretty good for a backstage setup in Wynwood. Mariela had just finished a quick set at Grand Central, a venue that screamed history, having played host to acts like Dinosaur Jr. and Diplo. The crowd had been into her act, which worked even on a small, cluttered stage: the smoke, lights, tight backing band, all in support of Mariela, guaranteed star-to-be. Everyone in the audience felt it, too. Tolerated the covers because they loved the flair and delivery. This girl had "It," or would very soon. Everyone wants to be in on the ground floor of something great. I knew that. Hell, I was here, too. Waiting for great to arrive.

"Fuck Ricky," Mariela said, checking herself on her phone. The flicker of the phone's camera let me know she was mid-selfie. I tried not to roll my eyes. I'd be doing the same shit if I was her. But I'd never be her.

She put her phone down and looked at me for what felt like the first time since she'd sauntered into the closet-like room. Looked at me like I was the only person on the planet. It felt so good. I felt alive.

"How was it?"

"What?" I asked.

"The set, stupid," she said, the insult rolling off her tongue with ease, as if she were ordering a latte. "The songs. The crowd. You were out there, right?"

"Yeah, yeah," I said, nodding to myself, still processing the snub but eager to keep this going. "I loved it. You were great. I loved that cover, the Elton John number? I never thought that song could be sexy, but you—shit, I think everyone in the crowd was thirsty for more. I mean, you know your way up there. You don't just go through the motions. It feels, I dunno, natural. Like you've been doing it all your life. I'm jealous, honestly."

Mariela tilted her head, as if trying to spot a sleeping tiger cub at a zoo exhibit. Clinical.

"You have to feel it," she said, her voice flat and distant. "You have to want it."

I didn't know how to respond to that, so I didn't. Mariela seemed to be on another planet, like a kid rolling out of bed half-asleep. She was leaning back on the couch now, trying to absorb everything—still buzzing from the show, still wondering if she'd done okay, still looking for that validation that might let her sleep tonight.

"What were you doing in here?"

Mariela doesn't even look at me as she asks. I'm on my own, trying to figure out what the hell she means.

"Ricky said I—"

"C'mon, Gem, not that," Mariela said, scooting up, straightening in the seat. "We're past that. You think Ricky just let you in here to drool all over me about my set? You're not the Strong Island thick-headed thugette you pretend to be, okay? What were you doing on that—" she motions toward my guitar. "It sounded good."

"Oh, nothing, it's just something I'm working on," I said, repositioning my guitar and strumming the opening chords to the song; C, E, G7. "It's nothing, really—"

"You have to stop doing that."

"What?"

"Cutting yourself down before anyone else can. It's a shitty defense mechanism," Mariela said, leaning forward now, her eyes locked on mine, her pink lips slightly parted, as if waiting to say something else but eager to see if I had a response. "Own what you do. Only you can do it."

"Alright, yeah, you're right," I said. "It's called 'Gimme That.' I wrote it a few nights ago. I just have a melody, some words, but it's not—"

"Stop that."

We both laugh. Our voices blending together naturally, two birds chirping on the same branch. We stop at the same time and look at each other. She smiles softly, then motions toward the guitar with her chin.

"Play it."

I took in a deep breath, tried to play it casual.

"Alright," I said, then started the introductory chords again—a somber blend but also poppy and powerful, major notes blending together. I could see Mariela nodding her head from the couch, her hands tapping her knees, creating a backbeat only she could hear.

"Gimme that body, gimme that heat," I started to sing, my voice rough but feeling good, loosening up as I hit the rest of the verse. "Gimme that motion, gimme that beat . . ."

Now Mariela was closer, her ass barely on the couch, her eyes watching my fingers move from chord to chord, my pick strumming the worn-out strings of the guitar to make out the bare sounds of the song as I hit the chorus.

"Is it too much to want, something more," I sang, my voice cracking for a second. I didn't stop. "Is it too hard, to get off this floor . . . Gimme that rhythm, gimme that touch . . . gimme that freedom, give it to me rough . . ."

The chords were chugging along now, the stop-strum motion on cruise control, my hands moving around the guitar as if it were an extension of me, my voice curving back toward the verse, the only one I'd written.

That's when I heard it. Like a silk scarf wrapping itself around my neck, smooth, deceptive, and slithering. Mariela's voice joining mine, hesitant at first, then front and center, as if the song had been hers from the beginning. Would be hers forever.

Our voices blended together, as if we'd been doing this a long time. But it was the first time. I'd watched Mariela from the crowd many times—I'd never tell her that, but it was true. I never thought I'd be here, playing her one of my songs, singing it to her, with her.

My vocals, lower, less mannered, hold down the bottom. I let them, naturally step back, let her voice walk to the front of the stage, into the spotlight. Even after singing for an hour, her voice sounded polished and intentionally fragile, a woman who knows what's up but likes to pretend she's still a girl. She'd picked up the words on one listen and sang them now with a confidence that I'd never have. My heart ached and soared at the same time for the things I saw coming and the things I'd lose on the way.

After running through it twice, I started to tweak the chords, to pull us back—bring us in for a landing. Mariela understood, tweaking her delivery, the parts she sang loud and sexy at first were now hushed and desperate. We delivered the verse's final line together, two friends holding hands on a dark street, whispering to each other, confused about where to go next.

Mariela chuckled to herself and licked her lips, savoring the moment, her eyes wide and greedy, like she'd just stumbled on two twenties on her way to work. Pure luck. A good sign.

I rested the guitar on the table next to my seat and tried to mimic her comfortable laugh, but it just came out antsy and weird. The street kid having lunch with the cheerleaders. Waiting for reality to set in, waiting to be sent back to my bench.

The door swung open. I could hear Ricky's loud, gruff voice before I caught sight of him.

"That—now that, was fucking fantastic," he said, moving straight for Mariela, placing a sloppy kiss on her mouth, letting it linger, as if PDA were proof of some undying love and not just . . . kind of disgusting? "Baby, you were on fire. I could feel it. Everyone was grinding, moving. Trying to get close to you."

Mariela smiled, pulling back from Ricky, her eyes scanning his face—the stubble, bloodshot eyes, and sagging features. She looked like she'd accidentally kissed her uncle on the mouth.

"Thanks, babe," she managed to get out before repositioning herself on the couch to maximize the space between them. "It felt good up there."

"Good? Baby, it was electric," Ricky said, standing up straight, turning his attention to me for the first time. "Don't you agree, Gema? Tell her how great she was."

"She did," Mariela said, shaking her head at me, as if to say don't listen to this clown. "She was very nice. Thanks for telling her to meet me after."

Ricky smiled to himself, impressed by his own foresight.

"Yeah, yeah, thought you two could talk shop a bit, you know?" he said. "Gema has some songs, like, some good, good shit. And Mariela, you know you've been having troub—"

Mariela cut him off.

"Stop it," she said. "I'm fine."

"Oh, yeah, of course, baby, you know I didn't mean it that—"

"Shut the fuck up, Ricky," Mariela said. He'd hit a nerve. There wouldn't be a coming back from this right away. "Gema and I were working before you rolled in here like some kind of wild animal."

Ricky raised his hands in mock surrender. He knew Mariela well enough to see he'd set her off.

"Baby, baby, don't be like that," he said. "I'm just saying, you could help each other, okay?"

"Maybe I should go?" I said, starting to get up.

Mariela gripped my arm, her fingers wrapped around it tight. It felt nice. Nice to be wanted. By her.

"No, you stay," she said before shifting her narrowing gaze to Ricky. "You, leave. We can talk at home. I'll Uber."

"Uber? Baby, I've got the car outside, the bar's ready," he said. "I thought we'd hit some of the spots before calling it. I mean, we gotta celebrate? This is a sign of big things—"

"Did I stutter, Ricky?"

His body seemed to sag, folding into itself. His soft features melted away, and what was left was a petulant child trying to keep it together.

"Fine, whatever," he said with a shrug. He looked at me. "Gema, you need a ride home? I can drop you off."

I looked at Mariela and hated myself a little for even having to ask for permission. But dammit, I did need a ride home. Getting to West Kendall at this time of night was going to be a nightmare. If I could avoid that—and avoid spending money I didn't have on a Lyft—I knew I needed to.

"Go, it's fine," she said, a knowing look on her face. "Let's connect tomorrow. We can play."

Play? I wasn't sure what she meant. But I wanted to know more.

I stood up, my eyes still on her, waiting for more info, a morsel, anything that could help me know that this wasn't just a random one-off thing, a story I'd tell my kids as we watched the Mariela documentary ten years from now. A story they'd get tired of hearing.

"Yeah, totally, totally," Ricky said, sliding his hand onto my lower back, ushering me toward the door. "I'll set up some time in the studio. Afternoon good?"

Good? It was fantastic. I turned back to Mariela, wanting one last look at her, this angelic figure draped in silver and white, her features smudged and messy but still beautiful, her limbs splayed out on this dirty couch in this dirty place. Our eyes locked and she left me with a toothy grin, a genuine smile— something I'd never seen on her face before.

"Bye, baby," she said, her tongue resting on her top teeth. I wanted to believe she was talking to Ricky, but I knew she wasn't. Teeth and lips. Playful and sharp. "Don't do anything I wouldn't do."

I took one last glance at the room. She was looking at *me*.

JAQUIRA DÍAZ was born in Puerto Rico and raised in Miami. She is the author of *Ordinary Girls: A Memoir* (Algonquin, 2019), winner of a Whiting Award, a Florida Book Awards Gold Medal, and a Lambda Literary Awards finalist. *Ordinary Girls* was a summer/fall 2019 Indies Introduce Selection, a fall 2019 Barnes and Noble Discover Great New Writers Notable Selection, a November 2019 Indie Next Pick, and a Library Reads October pick. Díaz's work has been published in *The Guardian*, *Time Magazine*, *Conde Nast Traveler*, *T: The New York Times Style Magazine*, and *The Best American Essays 2016*, among other publications. Her second book, *I Am Deliberate: A Novel*, is forthcoming from Algonquin Books. She splits her time between Montreal and Miami Beach with her partner, the writer Lars Horn.

"Monster Story" is nonfiction.

> Sometimes we snuck out of the apartment on Bay Road, made a run for it, tried to make it to Papi's place before Mami caught up with us. But when our mother was high on coke, fast-talking and paranoid and enraged, she was like an Olympic runner. She'd take off after us in the night, barefoot and wide-eyed and angry, and she always caught us. Always.
>
> From "Monster Story"

MONSTER STORY

They buried Lázaro that December, after a funeral service at St. Patrick's Catholic Church on Miami Beach. The children from St. Patrick's school filled the pews, and the children's choir sang "On Eagle's Wings." Small memorials popped up all over Miami Beach: Teddy bears and prayers written on poster boards and crosses and images of baby Jesus. And lollipops. An entire city mourning the loss of a boy no one knew. We carried him with us. And even though he belonged to no one, he belonged to us all.

The spring after they found the body, Mami stashed us in a one bedroom in South Beach, a small place on Bay Road with a mattress on the floor and the stained rattan sectional Mami got in the divorce. We thought it was the same street that had been all over the news, North Bay Road, and for days it was all Alaina and I could talk about: how Mami had taken us against our will, how she'd brought us to live in a place where dead bodies were dumped.

It had happened one morning in early November. Two Florida Power & Light employees were working outside a house on 54th and North Bay Road when one of them discovered the body. It was the beginning of the dry season, and most of the Beach was still recovering from one of its legendary Lincoln Road Halloween street parties. the entire pedestrian mall transformed, every block between Alton Road and Washington Avenue overcrowded, stages with live music, haunted houses, floats with demons and vampires waving at us from the rafters. And everywhere we looked, Freddy Kruegers with their razor gloves, Jasons in their hockey masks, knife-wielding Michael Myerses. Serial killers were the most popular monsters that year.

When Craig Kriminger and Stewart Silver parked their FPL van in front of the house on North Bay Road to do some repair work on a utility pole, most of the neighborhood kids were already in school. The mourning doves sang as the two men worked, the smell of cat piss all around the block, and something else. Something stronger.

At around 8:30 a.m., Kriminger and Silver made the discovery: under the cherry hedge between the house's driveway and the garden wall, lying in a pile of grass and leaves, the dead body of the little boy.

In El Caserío Padre Rivera, parents summoned La Llorona, the mythical monster that kept kids from misbehaving. I was obsessed with monsters. I watched novelas about demons and exorcisms, movies about witches who came back from the dead to kill the townspeople who'd burned them at the stake. I loved zombies, werewolves, Frankenstein's monster, Dracula. I was fascinated by the possibility of killer alligators living in the sewers, a real-life Jaws stalking swimmers in la playa de Humacao, knife-wielding leprechauns running around town looking for their pots of gold.

La Llorona was a boogeywoman, sometimes a pumpkin-headed demon in a tattered wedding dress, sometimes a woman with a goat's head. She roamed the streets mostly unseen, unless you were so bad that La Llorona was hunting you.

Our titis always had La Llorona's phone number. Our fathers, if they came home from work to disobedient children, would be sure to get their hands on those digits. Our mothers sang us La Llorona lullabies, which were really horror stories about how she would come for you in the night. And when she finally found you, ripped you from the arms of your parents, or took you from your bed while you slept, what awaited you was a fate worse than death: La Llorona ate kids for breakfast.

If you were a troublemaker, if you got into fights, if you didn't eat what your abuela made for dinner, if you refused to sleep come bedtime, La Llorona rose from the darkness to make you hers.

That year, before Mami took us, we'd been living with Papi, Abuela, and Anthony in an apartment across from Flamingo Park, a small place with paint peeling off the walls, rusty hinges on the doors, a family of mice living in a hole behind our ancient refrigerator.

We'd find the mice in our shoes, in the kitchen cabinets, under the bathroom vanity, fast little fuckers that darted across the linoleum while Alaina and I screamed and ran for our lives, Anthony laughing his ass off.

Anthony was thirteen that November and thought he was our watchdog, so he beat us up when we didn't listen, or when we gave him lip, or when he was pissed at something we did or didn't do. He'd terrorize us with stories about mice building nests in our curly hair, chewing off the tips of our fingers while we slept, sucking the liquid out of our eyeballs. One day he got Abuela's cast iron skillet and whacked one, brain and blood and guts splattered on the kitchen floor, picked it up by the tail and flung it at us, me and Alaina ducking out of the way, screaming, *Oh my God, what is wrong with you?*

It would be months before a boy down the street threw a rock that sent Alaina to the hospital with a bloody eye, before I ran away from home, went joyriding in a stolen van, and took off for the Florida Keys with some older boys, before I swallowed my mother's pills, the first time, the second. Would be years before Anthony started using steroids, before he tried to strangle me, before I stabbed him with a steak knife. These were the days before juvie hall, before blunts laced with scutter and bottles of Cisco and quarts of Olde English, before school counselors and teachers and friends' parents and juvenile probation officers tried to save me, pulling me aside and looking into my eyes, saying, *Don't you know how dangerous this is? Don't you know?*

Before all that, there was a second mouse, a third, a fourth. And then it was the dead ones that started showing up in our shoes, our backpacks.

Once, while we waited for a hurricane to land on Miami Beach, the rain pelting our windows like pebbles, Anthony punched me so hard in the ear that he sent me tumbling across the bedroom we shared, my whole head ringing. Later, an audiologist would show me the results of my hearing test, look into my eyes, say, *It's pretty bad.*

Once, while running wild through the cañaverales behind El Caserío, Anthony pushed me face-first into the sugarcane, sliced a gash down my left thumb almost to the bone. Sometimes the scar itches. Sometimes, I can make out the sweet-brown burnt sugar smell of those summer mornings.

Once, that same summer, I watched my titi Tanisha take a sharp blade to the inside of her forearm. She was still a child herself—just four years older than me. Three years before, Anthony had slammed a door on her hand so hard it severed her pinky. They weren't able to reattach it.

In our family, the story of the severed pinky became the stuff of family legend, like a monster story. Told over drunken New Year's Eve parties and barbecues, each one of us claiming to remember it like it happened yesterday—the rush to the hospital, the severed pinky in a cup of ice. All that blood. All that screaming. All those years of resentment.

Even after they buried him, people in Miami Beach still told the story. The diaper wrapped in packing tape, the lollipop T-shirt. The severed limb of an entire community.

As the years passed, we could all remember where we'd been when we heard the news, how old we were when they found him. How we watched it all unfold, how we waited each day for developments, how we speculated about the parents, passed strangers in the park and wondered, *Is it her? Is it him or him or him?* And then later, how we learned his name, his mother's, that he did belong to someone. That he had not been, as we'd come to think of him, ours.

Anthony didn't go with us to the apartment on Bay Road. He simply refused, and Mami didn't bother trying to make him. He stayed behind with Papi and Abuela. Alaina and I had to survive living with Mami on our own. She'd just been diagnosed with paranoid schizophrenia and was on a cocktail of antipsychotics, anxiety pills, sleeping pills. Sometimes she snorted lines of scutter off our kitchen counter, off a hand mirror on her nightstand, off the cover of a Cosmopolitan. Other times she smoked crack from makeshift pipes made from tinfoil, a soda can. Sometimes she used an actual pipe. She'd be passed out on the couch for sixteen hours one day, and the next, she'd be manic, running around the apartment talking to herself, throwing things, laughing at nothing, at everything.

Papi came by a couple times a week, gave us a couple dollars apiece, and we'd stash it away for days when there was no food, keeping it a secret from Mami so she wouldn't steal it. When we were hungry, we'd hoof it to 7-Eleven for ninety-nine-cent hotdogs.

Alaina and I spent most weekends plotting our escape, resenting Papi because he let Mami take us, resenting Anthony because he had it so good not having to deal with Mami and eating actual meals made by Abuela.

Living with Mami meant we could never have friends over, could never have birthday parties or sleepovers like all those normal, ordinary girls. We were afraid our friends would find out about her madness, her drug use, her violent outbursts. So we kept it to ourselves, our secret shame, hiding bruises from teachers and classmates.

Sometimes we snuck out of the apartment on Bay Road, made a run for it, tried to make it to Papi's place before Mami caught up with us. But when our mother was high on coke, fast-talking and paranoid and enraged, she was like an Olympic runner. She'd take off after us in the night, barefoot and wide-eyed and angry, and she always caught us. Always.

Alaina and I didn't believe in monsters, not really. We weren't scared of the dark, or Freddy Krueger, or Pennywise the clown in Stephen King's *It*. And even though she was the youngest, Alaina was always the bravest. Nothing scared her. But I was a different story. My greatest fear, the thing that scared me the most in the world, was my mother. It wasn't the drugs, or her threats that one day she'd take us so far away we'd never see Papi or Abuela again, or even her violent streaks. I was afraid that, eventually, I would turn out just like her.

The first mouse was the hardest: the chaos in the kitchen, Anthony shoving me out of the way. How he trapped it, garbage can on one side, Papi's toolbox on the other. How he closed it in with a cardboard box. How, out of nowhere, he handed me the skillet. How afterward, I would lie, say it wasn't me who did it, but my brother. How in a different apartment years later, my brother coming after me and all I can do is breathe, brace myself, chest rising, falling, I open a drawer, pull out a steak knife.

One Saturday at the beach, the summer after she took us to the apartment on Bay Road, Mami met a man. He was younger than her, maybe twenty, and looked like he couldn't care less, with dirt under his fingernails, his sun-bleached T-shirt sporting a quarter-sized hole on the shoulder. He'd walked up to her while Alaina and I were swimming, struck up a conversation.

When we got out of the water, I found him lying on my towel, smoking a joint and getting sand all over my sneakers.

We looked at him hard. "That's my towel," I said, my mouth a fist.

He smiled, ignoring me, and handed my mother the joint.

"Your kids are tough."

By then, Mami had already schooled us in the ways of men: what they wanted, what they needed, how they let you down, abandoned you, made promises they'd never keep, how they hurt you then made you think you deserved it. Men were not to be trusted, not even our father. And especially not men you'd just met. But she decided to take this guy home anyway.

When we were ready to leave, Alaina and I wrapped in our towels, our curls frizzy from the saltwater, Mami announced that he was coming home with us. Just for a little while, she said.

During our walk home, Alaina and I argued with her, told her that we didn't even know this guy who could turn out to be some monster, a murderer or rapist looking for single mothers with girls. We told the guy straight up that we didn't want him in our apartment and there was no way in hell he was going there and that we would call our father and then our uncles and then the cops. But we didn't have a phone, and our threats didn't bother Mami. "Just ignore them," she told the guy. And he did.

When we got to the apartment on Bay Road, Mami and the man locked us out of the bedroom, left us in the living room, waiting. I thought about taking Alaina to the payphone at the Chevron station two blocks away, or walking over to Papi's job, but I couldn't leave my mother alone with some guy who could still turn out to be a murderer.

We sat out there most of the night—Alaina on one side of the rattan sectional, me on the other, both of us still in our bathing suits. Alaina in her purple one-piece with a ruffle skirt, red hearts on the bodice, her skinny arms dark brown, her cheeks and nose a reddish copper-brown. My little sister looked like me, except she was smaller, browner, with darker hair. If I stayed out of the sun, I got pale. But Alaina always looked brown.

I knocked on the bedroom door several times, reminding Mami that we needed showers, that we needed dinner. We were anxious to wash the saltwater off our bodies, condition and detangle our hair. We wanted to get to our secret cash—we'd stashed enough for two hotdogs and a Slurpee, maybe a bag of chips. We fell asleep waiting.

Later, every time I told this story, I'd say I was not afraid, just angry. I was mad at my mother for locking herself in the bedroom and leaving us to fend for ourselves with no food, for bringing some stranger into our apartment, into our lives. I would say that this is when it happened, in the middle of the night, when I woke to the sound of my little sister's snoring, asleep on an empty stomach, and decided that we didn't need a mother, that we could take care of each other. I would not say that when I woke, wearing nothing but my pink and black bikini with the zipper on the front, handed down to me by Tanisha, the man my mother brought home was standing in front of me in the middle of the living room, naked, holding his dick. How when I opened my eyes and saw him standing there, I pretended I was not surprised, pretended I was not scared, and said something like, *Get away from me, you asshole,* even though what I really wanted was to scream for my mother. Or how he laughed at the sound of my voice. Or how afterward, when we were finally allowed back into our bedroom, Alaina and I found our secret stash of money gone, how Mami admitted that he hadn't stolen it, that she'd let him have it. Because, she said, he needed cab fare.

It was his mother who killed him. Or that's what everybody said, every news station broadcasting the story, every day her picture in the papers, even after the case had been closed.

Once, months later, eating cereal in front of the TV, I watched the news on Channel 10, turned up the volume when they showed how the two women were transferred from the Miami Beach Police Station to Dade County Jail. I balanced the cereal bowl on my lap as the two handcuffed women were escorted by Miami Beach Police detectives, a crowd of locals, reporters, photographers, and camera crews waiting.

I put down my spoon, my frosted flakes getting soggy as each woman was walked past the crowd toward the police cruiser, the onlookers erupting, spitting at them, calling them "asesinas," "baby killers," "monsters."

After we got kicked out of the apartment on Bay Road, one of the many times we got evicted, Mami took us to stay with Mercy. We showed up at her one-bedroom apartment on a Saturday afternoon, all our clothes and shoes spilling out of black garbage bags. Alaina and I hadn't had anything to eat since our school lunches the day before. I'd stopped talking to Mami since she'd gotten us evicted, and because she wouldn't let us go back home with Papi, Abuela, and Anthony, where Alaina and I wanted to be.

Mercy opened the door, and my mother explained that we needed a place to stay for a while.

"Why isn't their father taking care of you?" Mercy asked. "Doesn't he know that his children are in the streets like stray dogs?"

My mother dropped her bags on the floor. "He doesn't care if his kids starve," she said. "He spends all his money on women."

"That's a lie!" I blurted out. "Papi brings us money every week." Then, on purpose, I spilled all my mother's secrets: how my father paid child support, but Mami spent it all on cocaine and beer; how we never had food in the house unless my father bought us groceries; how Alaina and I had to hide money from Mami so we could buy hotdogs at 7-Eleven; how she lied and told Papi that someone broke into our apartment and stole the rent money, when she'd spent it on a three-day binge with some scutterhead from the neighborhood; how they'd locked themselves in the bedroom, and when the guy finally took off, he left behind *dozens* of empty cans of Budweiser.

My mother slapped me in the face, told me to shut up.

Alaina got between me and Mami, even if it meant that Mami would slap her, too. We spent most of our childhood that way, me and Alaina, dodging chancletas and belts, always feeling like all we had was each other.

Mercy didn't pay me or Alaina any mind. "You need to be out in a week," she said. "And I'm not taking care of any kids. I already raised my girls."

My face was on fire. I was on fire. I hated my mother, hated Mercy, and I wanted to punish them. I looked Mercy dead in the eye, recalling all the times she'd talked about Abuela, called her "negra," made up stories about how she was doing voodoo in her kitchen to ruin my mother's life. How she always blamed my father for my mother's illness, saying my father drove my mother crazy, my father made her do drugs, my father, ese negro, who ruined her life.

I took a breath, said, "You didn't even raise your kids. You gave them away."

And then Mercy slapped me, too.

In 1994, four years after they found Lázaro's body, a tearful South Carolina mother, Susan Smith, would get on TV with a fake story about an armed black man, a carjacking, a kidnapping. She would look into the cameras, beg the so-called carjacker to return her sons safely. Her two little boys, three-year-old Michael and one-year-old Alexander, would be found shortly after, inside their mother's car, still strapped to their car seats, drowned at the bottom of John D. Long Lake.

After Smith's confession, after she admitted she had made up the story, had made up the armed black man and the carjacking and the kidnapping, she gave police all the details about dressing her children, strapping them to their car seats, driving the car to the lake, and parking it on the boat ramp. How she released the emergency brake, stepped out of the car. How she let the car roll into the lake, let it take her children.

Two years after police pulled their bodies from the lake, seven people—four of them children—accidentally drowned while visiting the memorial erected there for Michael and Alexander. They had been driving one night, parked their SUV on the same ramp, letting their headlights shine on the two marble stone pieces.

They had been drawn there, people said, wanting to see the place where it had all happened.

The lake, they said, had become like a legend, attracting visitors from all over the world. A mythical place.

In El Caserío, I spent hours awake in bed, listening for the sounds of La Llorona. I waited for crying, wailing, a woman's voice in the distance calling for her children—one boy, one girl—whose names I didn't know.

The stories say that La Llorona killed her children after being rejected by a lover. She had taken her two babies from their beds one night, had walked with them through the woods down to the river, held their bodies underwater until they both drowned. Then, when she realized what she'd done, with their lifeless bodies in her arms, she walked into the river and let it take her, too.

And so, the legend says, La Llorona wails in the dead of night, haunting rivers and beaches and lakes where children swim, parks and playgrounds where they play, calling out for her ghost children.

Five years after they found Lázaro's body, when I was sixteen, I sat in a holding cell at the Miami Beach Police Station. It was my sixth or seventh arrest, this time for stabbing my brother. The fight had started weeks earlier, after Alaina and I moved back with Papi, me and Anthony screaming at each other like our parents used to.

"You ain't my father," I said. "You ain't shit!"

"Count your fucking blessings," my brother said. "I woulda sent your ass away a long time ago."

He'd snitched to Papi about how I'd walked in stumbling drunk at 3:00 a.m., and I'd snitched about how I'd found syringes and vials of Depo-Testosterone in his backpack, both of us desperate for our father's attention. Anthony was already eighteen, and by then Papi was too tired or too busy or too high to be bothered.

"What kind of girl . . ." my brother often said, pulling out pages he'd read and then ripped out of my diary, holding them up for scrutiny, hard evidence of the monster I was, definitely not the girl I was supposed to be, the girl Abuela had tried to raise. "What kind of girl *are* you?"

That afternoon, the fighting had escalated to us wanting to kill each other: during one of Anthony's 'roid rages, after I'd flung his T-shirts, sneakers, and duffel bag off our eighth-floor balcony, after he'd slapped me and I'd slapped him back, he landed a punch on the side of my head that knocked me face-down on the floor. When I got back up, he tried to strangle me. Somehow, Alaina got him off me.

Then I went to the kitchen for the knife.

And when they arrested me, the knife on the living room floor, someone on the phone, Alaina crying and crying, the cops asking, *Was it a stabbing motion or a slicing motion? How was she holding the knife?* How my father, his forehead beaded with sweat, his eyes red-rimmed and puffy, kept asking, *¿Qué hiciste? ¿Qué hiciste? What did you do?*

Once, when we still lived in El Caserío, the two of us running wild with the other street kids, I pushed Anthony off the front steps of our building. The night before he had pulled out my hair in handfuls.

The sound of his head cracking on the concrete steps was terrifying, exhilarating.

My brother and I, we were the same: part monster, part mouse.

At the police station, every cop stopped by my holding cell, wanting to get a look at the kid who'd tried to kill her own brother.

"Jesus, I *know* you," one of them said, then turned to the others, "I've picked her up before."

I looked him up and down and said nothing. I was a runaway, a high school dropout, a hoodlum. I had been picked up so many times, for aggravated battery, for assault, for battery on a police officer.

I was questioned by two detectives without a parent or lawyer in the room.

The cop who said he knew me sat across the table, asking again and again, *Why did you stab him? Were you angry? Did you want him dead?*

"Yes, I was angry," I said.

"Yes, I wanted him dead," I said.

I didn't ask, "Where is my father?" and I didn't ask, "How is my sister?" and I didn't tell them that for years, after every black eye, every bloody lip, every fistful of hair yanked from the roots, I had imagined the weight of that knife in my hand.

And after I was fingerprinted and photographed and handcuffed and escorted into and out of the elevator and past the lobby and out the back door and into a squad car, after I was dropped off at the juvenile detention center where I would be held overnight to await my hearing with other girls who maybe stabbed their brothers and maybe didn't, I imagined that these cops who thought they knew me talked about me, that they called me "juvenile" and "delinquent" and "offender"—words they thought were a good fit for a girl like me.

What does it mean to rupture an eardrum? To scrape a dead mouse off the floor, save it for later. To pick up a knife, point it, thrust it. To sever a finger.

What is a finger without a child's body attached?

What good is a pinky anyway?

It was almost midnight when we arrived at the juvenile detention center, me and two other girls, all the cells in the girls' wing closed, all the other inmates asleep on floor mats. The juvenile corrections officer walked us to the showers, where we undressed as she watched, a juvie strip search, the three of us lifting our breasts and spreading our legs and opening our mouths. How none of us said a word as the guard poured lice shampoo into our cupped hands. Not a word as she told us to lather up our heads, armpits, pubic hair, or when she said and kept saying, *Let me see, let me see, let me see.*

Once we were in our orange jumpsuits, we had to braid our hair, she told us, or they would cut it off. So I braided my hair in front of the mirror while avoiding the other girls' questions. *Where do you live? Where do you go to school? What did you do?*

What did you do? People would always ask that question. But I wouldn't say, not for years, not after I got out of juvie, or after I turned eighteen and my record was expunged, or after I got my GED, started taking classes at Miami Dade College, thinking that it would change me, that it would get me off the streets and I'd be able to look my father in the face again, finally know what it felt like to have someone be proud of me.

After I braided my hair, they took me into one of the cells, handed me a mat and blanket for the floor, locked the door behind me. The room was empty, freezing, and once I was on the floor, shivering through the night, I thought, I've finally been put in my place.

I woke up the next morning to a new roommate. She was lying on her mat, crying, wiping her nose on her sleeve.

"Don't eat the grits," she said. "They put something in them to make you shit."

. . .

The scariest part was not that La Llorona was a monster, or that she came when you called her name three times in the dark, or that she could come into your room at night and take you from your bed like she'd done with her own babies. It was that once she'd been a person, a woman, a mother. And then a moment, an instant, a split second later, she was a monster.

In a few years, after leaving my mother's house for the last time, after my brother has become a grown man with a wife and a baby and a house of his own, after Ana María Cardona has been tried and convicted and sentenced to death, I would write to her in prison:

Dear Ms. Cardona,
    I would like to hear your story. Not what the papers said or what people said or what was on the news, but the truth.

And she would write back:

Dear Ms. Jaquira Díaz,
    This is not a story. This is my life.

FRANCES NEGRÓN-MUNTANER is a Puerto Rican artist, writer, scholar, and professor at Columbia University, where she is also the founding curator of the Latino Arts and Activism Archive. Among her publications are *Boricua Pop: Puerto Ricans and the Latinization of American Culture* (NYU Press, 2004), which won the CHOICE Award; *The Latino Media Gap* (Center for the Study of Ethnicity and Race at Columbia University, 2014); and *Sovereign Acts: Contesting Colonialism in Native Nations and Latinx America* (University of Arizona Press, 2017). *The Essential Manuel Ramos Otero* is forthcoming from Columbia University Press in 2022. Her films include *Brincando el Charco: Portrait of a Puerto Rican* (1995), presented at the Whitney Biennial, winner of the Audience Award at the 1995 San Juan CinemaFest, and a Merit Selection at the 1995 Latin American Studies Association Film Festival; *Small City, Big Change* (2013); and *Life Outside* (2016). Negrón-Muntaner has received fellowships from the Ford, Truman, Scripps Howard, Rockefeller, Pew, and Chang-Chavkin Foundations. Major funders such as the Social Science Research Council, Andy Warhol Foundation, and Independent Television Service have also supported her work. Recognitions she has received include the United Nations' Rapid Response Media Mechanism designation as a global expert in the areas of mass media and Latin/o American studies (2008); the Lenfest Award, one of Columbia University's most prestigious recognitions for excellence in teaching and scholarship (2012); an inaugural OZY Educator Award (2017); the Latin American Studies Association's Frank Bonilla Public Intellectual Award (2019); and the Bigs and Littles Impact Award (2020) for her work as a mentor, artist, and scholar. Her latest project is Valor y Cambio (Value and Change), a storytelling and community currency project in Puerto Rico and New York.

This is one of several versions of "The Ugly Dyckling," first written in Spanish in 1998, and since published in English, Spanish, and bilingual graphic forms.

For the first time since her childhood, she longed for a hollow tree trunk, wishing she could hide there. But the dyckling overcame this desire and instead picked out her finest armored feathers for transvestite travel.

From "The Ugly Dyckling"

THE UGLY DYCKLING

In New York, a heat-filled autumn night is approaching.
It seems the birds have fled to the islands.

Manuel Ramos Otero, *Invitación al polvo* (1991)

From the sky above, the pond was barely visible. A murky substance produced by decades of industrialization and pharmaceutical waste covered most of its once crystalline surface. The pond's water lilies and birds co-existed among floating diapers, beer bottles, and other objects discarded by a society taken by consumption. It was then, in this swan-dominated pond, that a young swan named Dolores spawned a daughter who was very, very ugly.

Over the years, the community came up with various hypotheses to explain the origin of such ugliness. A few argued that Dolores's daughter was the product of a biological mutation caused by the environmental crisis plaguing the pond. Others supported a conspiracy theory that blamed all the pond's evils on foreign customs and lifestyles. Most residents, however, attributed her ugliness to the alarming rise of broken homes without strong father figures.

In any case, it all began on a hot summer day, when tempers often rise to a boiling point. The little one seemed in no hurry to break out of her eggshell, perhaps foreseeing the daily vicissitudes that would pervade her life. Dolores, although saddened by the inexplicable failure of all her other eggs to hatch and exhausted from the long wait, enthusiastically nibbled away at the shell to help her sluggish spawn come out. With her mother's encouragement, the cygnet took her first wobbly steps, falling flat on her rounder-than-normal behind. Despite the daughter's lack of grace, Dolores was so delighted at her daughter's affectionate disposition that she pecked her, fluffed up her fuzz, and gently pushed her forward so they could immediately meet the rest of the flock. Secure in her mother's devotion, the infant followed Dolores, who fully expected the warmest of welcomes upon their arrival.

As the newborn and her proud mama walked through discarded mufflers, Superman lunch boxes, and containers of Spic and Span disinfectant, the other animals could not contain their contempt. "Óyeme, that's the ugliest swan I've ever seen!" said a goose of Cuban origin named Gossy. "We never had any swans like that in Cuba." But Dolores was so blinded by her motherly love that she didn't hear the goose's insults. She carried on until she saw her neighbor Chiquita, an attractive young hen who became so mesmerized that she smacked into her new beau Cocky as he strutted by: "Sweetheart," she told Dolores, are you sure that thing is yours? I mean, I'm sorry, but . . . I've known of cases in which swans have sat on eggs of geese, hens . . . even ducks. I have a cousin on the other side of the pond who specializes in such cases. If you'd like, I'll get him first thing." And the chatter continued.

Seeing all the commotion that greeted them wherever they turned, the naturally cheerful baby became sad as night. The ugly dyckling thought that there must be something terribly wrong with her, and she asked, "Are they talking about me, Mami?" Before Dolores could assure her that she was as lovely as all the other swans, a loud cry came from across the pond. "But that's a monster!" declared Señora Sofía, the paternal grandmother, an old Galician swan sporting a blue bow. Having always objected to the indiscriminate philandering of her eldest son, the pond's incorrigible Puto, Señora Sofía was completely mortified. "I would have helped you prevent this egg myself. I swear to you, Dolores, we are a proud race, and we owe our stature to our extraordinary beauty. And what will she be called? I hope that you won't give it our regal name of Villaruz!"

Overwhelmed by all the slurs, the small mutant looked around with tears in her dark bright eyes. She asked a second question, this time as mother and daughter contemplated a burning sun that resembled the one in those old tourist postcards that the local government had long ago stopped printing out of sheer embarrassment. "Is this all the world there is?" Dolores, as stunned as her newborn over what had transpired back at the pond, replied, "No, my love, this is just a tiny piece of the world. Don't worry. You'll find your place." The little one turned to hug her mother's elegant black feet and stayed there. For the first time since laying this odd egg, Dolores stopped to contemplate her only daughter, who still looked beautiful to her, even after that fateful moment when they had entered the pond. But Dolores was a mother and she knew the deal: life would get harder for both of them. "In true swan fashion, my ex Puto hasn't been back here since my other eggs didn't hatch. And now that our only baby is ugly, I'm not even going to see his beak's shadow again! Nor get any child support!"

While the mother lost herself in feminist thoughts, several male swans circled the cygnet as she swam with difficulty around the pond. "Too many birds ruin the meal," commented Nico, a swan with big plans for himself despite his young age. "This pond is overpopulated. There aren't enough jobs for our impoverished swans, let alone for mutants like her. To these queer birds, I say, 'Get out!'" Hearing this, the usually mute snow-white swans were ready to put their money where their beaks were: "Let's go after the ugly one!" they yelled in unison. Dolores, distressed by the savagery of her fellow swans, blocked their way and begged, "Leave her alone, she hasn't hurt anyone!" The mother's devastated look only made them deride her with soprano guffaws. "No!" they said, their voices reaching an ear-piercing pitch. "She is queer and ugly. Doesn't even look like a normal duckling, she's more like a . . . dyckling. Ha!"

Before the mother had a chance to intercede, the swans' chaotic pecking came to a sudden halt. The birds saw a huge garbage truck approaching the pond at full speed, and they cowered behind the few remaining plants around the pool. They watched, in fear, as the humans dumped containers with labels of ominous-looking skeletons flashing toothy grins into the water. Although as frightened as the other fowl by the outbreak of humans in their midst, Dolores took advantage of all the commotion to grab her daughter by the neck and seek refuge in the community's only spiritual center.

From behind a broken and rusty window, the pastor Luis Arcadio had spent the last few minutes observing the riled-up pond without daring to intervene. While he meant to share his ministry with everyone, the pastor had to acknowledge that it was the whitest among the swans who had contributed most generously to the cause of the abandoned bus, which he had little by little transformed into a spiritual refuge. As for humans, he felt largely ambivalent toward them. They certainly had the power to enact much cruelty and destruction; their hearts were not always in the right place. But they were also the ones who had most closely reached the Creator with their exquisite style and sacred chants. Luis Arcadio had learned this well when he lived as the spoiled pet of a virtuous family. There, he had accepted that physical purification began from within, from the goodness of the soul, and that the putrefaction of the pond was in part a reflection of animal baseness, particularly among the most wanton of species, like ducks.

However, the opportunity to help this troubled mother and her terrified offspring was a great relief for his tortured conscience. He immediately welcomed them. "Please, come in," he said with that studied baritone he reserved for formal occasions. Dolores followed the pastor's gesture toward the artificial pool he used for baptisms and other rituals. Once they reached the circle, Luis Arcadio, the pastor without a true flock, washed the newborn's forehead with as much tenderness as he allowed himself in public. Afraid he would lose control

over his emotions, the pastor did not complete the ceremony. Before returning the little one to the mother, Luis Arcadio found just enough courage from
beneath his feathers to add a different message to his usual pronouncements:
"They call you the ugly dyckling, the queerest duck. But you have another
name unknown to them. Remember that they are white and understand each
other. Get out of their way." It would be the first but not the last time that the
ugly dyckling would feel her fear and sadness reflected on the face of another
duck traveling incognito.

While the mother hoped that time would be kind to her daughter, life only
got worse. Unlike other ugly swans who lose their resemblance to ducks as they
matured, the ugly dyckling got uglier and uglier. Her neck remained stuck in-
between species, too thick for a swan, too long for a duck. The way she waddled
was so queerly duckish that she provoked both desire and hatred in other birds.
The pond's overendowed rooster, Cocky, made it a habit to chase after her, his
claws thirsting for her fully formed behind. The dyckling's extended family resented her and prayed for her to be taken away by a butcher or a hungry beggar.
In response to so much contempt, her mother, who had fallen ill but had not
told anyone, began to worry about her ugly dyckling's future: "Now that you're
older, mi amor, you can't avoid your dycklingness. I can't protect you anymore.
Find your own."

That same night, saddened to leave her mother, the ugly dyckling flew to see
her long-lost father. After Dolores's inability to produce healthy eggs, Puto had
settled down with a new mate despite the rumor that he was also somewhat of
a queer bird because of the habit of waking up early every Thursday with green
makeup on his crest. Much to her disappointment, as she had hoped to par-
take in a dramatic reconciliation with her father, Puto acted as he always had
throughout his oh-so-comfortable life. He washed his feathers of her. "Don't
complicate your life, my girl. Take flight," he remarked with a frank, Solomon-
like attitude. He walked his daughter away from his lair so he could resume
the business he had left behind in the bushes. The dyckling said goodbye and
wandered for a few minutes in a daze. Her vision blurry as she looked up at the
starry sky, she could not help but ask once more: "Is this all the world there is?"
But this time, she would seek the answer on her own.

The ugly dyckling fled east, to the side of the pond where other queer ducks
and strange birds were rumored to live. There she found a crazy duck who
spoke out to whoever would listen. The dyckling discovered that she was part
of a controversial urban phenomenon: the queer duck community. She learned
that queer ducks are tolerated in some pond environments but not all of them.

Some are successful in entertainment and in the arts. Yet most swans and ducks prefer the company of straight birds to that of queer ducks, even if their scorn threatens the survival of all.

Although the dyckling could never manage to sleep, given the great gatherings that lasted through the night on the pond's queer side, she adapted immediately to her new environs. Between the drinks that waiters imaginatively concocted from discarded substances and the partygoers who joyously drank them, she first heard the stories necessary for her animal survival. "In the natural world," explained a very respected elder named Mildew, "seasonal migrations are defined by the movement from north to south, from cold to warm weather." But in the unusual pond where the ugly dyckling was born, this logic did not apply.

"Over the last four decades," Mildew continued, "queer birds have moved en masse in the reverse direction of natural migration: from warm to cold weather." It was then that the ugly dyckling heard about those residing far from the archipelago who preferred snow to their tropical environs and smog to the still green mountains that surrounded the pond's landscape. These old ducks told her about thousands of fellow birds who migrated annually to the north, particularly the northeast. They also informed her that although its waters contained all conceivable affection, her pond of birth was sometimes a dangerous place for many queers: "Don't fool yourself. The further you are, the closer you'll be to turning into a fond memory."

The ugly dyckling didn't want to believe Mildew, but she had no other choice. Just as the elder finished her presentation, a gang of the whitest swans broke into the bar, taking random shots at all ducks. With the wise one's words ringing in her ears, the ugly dyckling took flight before a broken bottle nearly claimed her. After days of flying, she arrived at a distant pond surrounded by grand brick buildings covered in ivy. There she found some strange ducks with long, round beaks resembling wooden spoons. Although somewhat cold and standoffish, the odd ducks came out to greet her: "You have a funny color and an even funnier accent. Where on earth did you come from?" The dyckling didn't quite understand the drawl of these ducks, but she understood their question and responded, "Pororico," the name of her now faraway pond. The ducks nodded, "Oh, yes, we visited that pond many years ago . . . before the last dump. It was lovely." One of the kinder-seeming northern ducks, with prematurely graying feathers and round Trotskyesque glasses, added timidly, "I was there when oil began to reach the shore and came down as rain. It could have wiped us all out."

The ugly dyckling would have liked to know more about this controversial event that occurred only a few months before her birth. But the conversation's climate changed from cozy spring to artic ice as the other queer ducks disapprovingly regarded the dyckling's instant conquest. The most influential of the group stealthily took over and shamelessly ended the exchange: "Hey, back off! It's the same to us. You can stay here or leave. As long as you don't steal any of our mates or interfere with how we run the pond, you can eat our crumbs." Upon hearing this, the dyckling felt a newfound shame. She remembered the priest's prophesy, "They are white and understand each other." This time, she would not test the waters or wait to be baptized by fire. The ugly one flew off and sought a different pond.

Flying south, the dyckling happened to come across friendlier if somewhat eccentric ducks. These "radicals" lived throughout the year on an island called Mannahatta that thought of itself as the world's queer duck capital. "Wow, you're so smart and interesting, I rather fancy you," said Barbarita, a duck in black feathers from head to toe who also had tropical roots. "What's your name?" "I don't know," said the ugly dyckling, wishing she would stop asking. "Strange," said Barbarita, "but it doesn't matter. I'll show you around." Barbarita and the ugly dyckling from then on became inseparable, gathering branches together, taking long walks along the pond, and engaging in frequent arguments about the dyckly life and the big world beyond.

But just as the dyckling daydreamed of how it would feel to kiss Barbarita on her beak, a messenger pigeon arrived with urgent news: "Your mother is probably dead." "What do you mean, probably dead?" cried the ugly dyckling. Although the pigeon did not mean to be indifferent to the dyckling's feelings, the courier spoke fast and matter-of-factly as she had so many other messages to relay. "She's been ill with flu-like symptoms for some time: blotchy feathers, no egg production, respiratory distress." Feeling empathetic stomach pains, the dyckling asked: "Where can I find my mother?" Already a few feet away, the veteran messenger responded stoically, "Around the pond. If she's still alive."

With sorrow in her heart, the ugly dyckling flew to Barbarita's nest, and they sat quietly side by side until the first light of morning. Barbarita then softly pecked the ugly dyckling in the neck, looked into her swollen little eyes, and said, "If you want, I'll come with you." But the dyckling feared for Barbarita. And she was even more afraid that Barbarita would see her through the pond's hateful gaze. "Everything will be fine," the ugly dyckling assured the only friend she'd ever had. "No worries. I'll be back soon." Terrified but determined to pay her last respects, the ugly dyckling took a few steps forward and felt her cold feet slowly leave the ground. Suspended in the air, her now-grown wings outstretched alongside her for what seemed to be miles, striking in their precision and strength. As she gained altitude, the ugly dyckling heard a harsh crackle followed by a loud pop that echoed faintly through the morning. Realizing she was unharmed, the ugly dyckling continued her journey.

This is how, after many years of living among all kinds of ducks and other fowl up north, the ugly dyckling traveled to her pond in search of her mother. Attacked by the small bacteria of nostalgia, she dreamt of the pond of her youth despite all the suffering it had imposed; of her brave mother and her weak father, who crumbled before social pressure; and of the space inside her now becoming a void. She thought that perhaps now, after seeing more of the world, her feathers would be sufficiently thick to shrug off pain and spit. But the ugly dyckling was overcome by questions.

How to return? How to go home with the ache of memory and without her mother's love and protection? For the first time since her childhood, she longed for a hollow tree trunk, wishing she could hide there. But the dyckling overcame this desire and instead picked out her finest armored feathers for transvestite travel. She packed black ribbons to elongate her neck and dyes that would bring out the darkness of her eyes and the grayness in her feet. She took into account everything she had ever learned from queer duck shows in all the ponds she had visited and from some dycklings who always surprise male swans, as they hide their genus well. If not at peace, at least she would be safe during her visit.

As she approached the pond, the dyckling became curious to see if anything had changed since her long absence. She passed by her mother's old neighbor Chiquita, whose main preoccupation since her most recent pairing was to remain watchful of her new mate's nomadic eyes. "Who could that be? I hope my Rover doesn't see her." The dyckling discovered how smoothly she could blend into the swan population with the right accessories. In many ways, swans and ducks are very similar, as are roosters and ganders, and ponds and swamps. But she also discovered the small ways in which they differed. So, she adorned herself as they did yet kept the memories of her ugliness in her suitcase. Despite all her efforts, the torrent came sooner than expected. On a cloudy morning, when the sun rays barely sliced through the clouds to illuminate her figure, the ugly dyckling dressed up and approached small groups of birds inquiring about her mother. She noticed, however, that the minute she got near, they would move away.

Fearing that the flock had discovered her, the ugly dyckling sped toward the pond, but before she could reach its edge, an angry Nico yelled out an old militant slogan: "Away with duck and foreigner scum." The minute he said this, a group of swans coolly waiting behind pulled at the ugly dyckling's black ribbon, displaying her duckish neck. The dyckling frantically tried to get her ribbon back but the swans circled her, daring her to take it from them. The swans would have likely continued taunting her if it wasn't for El Cotorrito, a day-glo green parrot with a loose tongue, flying over the pond frantically repeating, "It's bye, bye, birdy for you. It's bye, bye, birdy for you." Disturbed by the ominous message, the ugly dyckling broke through the circle and followed the parrot's lead until she saw several enormous trucks slowly driving in the direction of the pond. She thought that perhaps the humans had taken positive action against the pollution after all. But in less than a minute, the dyckling realized that the scene before her was of another nature altogether.

A truck as big as a building made a complete stop at the pond's ragged edge. Terrified, the birds ran as fast as they could away from the pond, abandoning the sick and the old. In a matter of seconds, the truck's discolored back opened like a gaping mouth, and it proceeded to vomit hundreds of glossy magazines copies with titles like *National Geographic*, *TV Guide*, and *People*. The ugly dyckling stared in disbelief at the unfolding attack until she saw a swan, too sick to run away from the human debris. Instinctively, she took a step to assist the swan, but then she hesitated. Why should she risk her life for a swan, even if she was ill? Hadn't they tormented her mercilessly since birth? They were white and understood each other, the pastor had said; she should never get involved in their games. But then she saw something that deeply disturbed her: that sickly white swan about to be flattened by the hostile drivers was none other than her mother.

The ugly dyckling projected the upcoming tragedy in her retina like a slow-motion film and let out an anguished scream as she ran to shield her mother from the racing threat. Her difficult life had served her well. She knew how to run fast, dodge moving objects, and hide away until the powerful and mighty had passed. She got there just in time, covering the mother's trembling body with her brawny wings. The clueless drivers, who had not noticed the birds but heard a loud cry, stopped the truck to see what all the commotion was about. When they didn't see anything moving on the pond, the men cheerfully went back to the trucks. They continued their work until the entire pond was coated with magazine covers, multicolored water lilies under the late afternoon sun.

After the drivers completed their long day's work, the ugly dyckling stuck her strong neck above the wreckage and shook the paper scraps off her. She looked down at Dolores's face, ashen and pale, and began to peck at her mother's feathers as the elder had done with her as a cygnet just out of the shell. Impressed by the scene, the birds who slowly emerged from the thicket, including Nico, did not dare to disturb them. The ugly dyckling continued holding her mother, for hours, until she heard a familiar crackle and pop, but this time it was closer and louder, as if the hunters from up north had finally caught up to her. She couldn't believe that she had made this journey, seen her mother for a brief moment, only for both to die where she was born and mocked. Realizing that life was coming around full circle and she had to take one last stand, the ugly dyckling looked straight on at the hunters in open defiance of the inevitable carnage.

Her heroic pose did not last long. The ugly dyckling had to quickly wrap her wings around herself and her mother to shield their eyes. As she looked up, dozens of blinding lights went off again, one by one, until she could no longer see. "There she is! There she is," said a human fast approaching with several others in tow. "This was the beauty that I was telling you about. I've been following her for days. What do you think?" "Wow," said another of the humans. "Never seen anything quite like her. Rare beauty, indeed. That's what she is." When her eyes adjusted again to the light of day, the ugly dyckling saw that these hunters did not have guns but some other dangling instrument with a long and hollow glass cavity.

Once they tired of shooting, the humans came down to the pond and caressed the ugly dyckling with their big hands. One of them then gently took the mother from the dyckling's arms and carried the bundle of disheveled feathers into a distant vehicle. The dyckling resisted this kidnapping as much as she could, screaming and pecking wildly at the humans' legs, but to no avail. The humans confidently got into their SUVs and drove away, leaving the bird behind on the foul dirt road. Crying, the ugly dyckling knew that she had once more failed her mother, being the ugly dyckling that she was. With sweat-soaked feathers, she fled to the pond's east side for the night.

The next day, the entire pond was afire with activity. Nico, alert and in his element, screamed orders to the others to push as much of the wet glossy paper out of the pond and to gather some food for the flock. As the day progressed, the swans, geese, and ducks cleaning up could not help but notice that some of the magazines featured a familiar-looking bird in the cover. The fowl tried to make sense of the scribbled words under the photo, but since none of them knew how to read, they looked and looked at the images until they became bored and returned to work. However, before swimming away, El Cotorrito flew over the pond, as he was prone to do, and gave them a clue: "Rare Beauty, rare beauty, indeed. That's what she is. Rare beauty, rare beauty." The confused birds did not know what to make of El Cotorrito's words yet they understood everything when they saw the ugly dyckling looking for something to eat before beginning her long journey back. "It's her! It's her!" said Señora Sofía, "I think I'm going to faint!" A nervous Puto ran to Señora Sofía's aid, bringing her special smelling salts so she wouldn't hit the ground, but the animals remained skeptical about the royal swan's conclusion. "Can't be!"

"But it is," said Dolores, making a grand entrance like a movie star, her neck long and white, her black legs perfectly hydrated, her face radiant with pride. "And you will soon be thankful to her. Her pictures have spawned a worldwide movement against water pollution." As if leading a parade, Dolores walked toward her daughter. Behind her, a long line of different kinds of trucks, without gaping mouths that heaved stitched-up papers, streamed by, imitating the mother's waddle. Out of these boxy vans came humans with rubber gloves and hoses and signs with big black letters that said, "Bird sanctuary. No dumping."

While the crew cleaned up the pond, mother and daughter spent long hours sharing stories about the time that they had lived apart and how the humans nursed Dolores back to health. The ugly dyckling told about the many ponds she had visited and her friend Barbarita, who had been so kind to her. Dolores encouraged the ugly dyckling to stay home for good, and she thought about it carefully. True, the pond was cleaner and the birds more accepting. Even Nico and Puto had come by to inquire how mother and daughter were doing, now that they knew how famous the ugly dyckling is. But she missed her other home, and she was eager to return. So, with some sadness and happiness too, the ugly dyckling closed her eyes and embraced her mother for a long time. Bringing the ugly dyckling's chin up, the mother kissed her daughter's forehead and smiled. "Come and visit me again soon, mi amor."

After leaving her mother's nest, the ugly dyckling was startled to see the most gorgeous duck that she had ever seen, quietly standing under a tree. "Hey, there," said the duck. The little dyckling could not believe it. "Barbarita? How did you find me?" Barbarita came out of the tree's shadow and invited her for a walk around the pond, like they used to do up north. "Come, I was born not far from here." That night, Barbarita again asked her name, so she could verbally ruffle her feathers. Despite the anxiety that the question provoked, the ugly dyckling felt the pleasure of another bird simply asking. She finally told Barbarita the name that everyone knew her by, the "ugly dyckling," even if she no longer felt defined by it. Barbarita laughed when she heard the moniker. Pointing to the black and white signs that now showed the ugly dyckling's silhouette everywhere around the pond, Barbarita could not help but object, "You aren't an ugly dyckling anymore! You're a hot chicky!" With that, Barbarita leaned in to kiss her mate. And as they both started the journey home, the dyckling could not help but laugh with joy, her cries heard throughout the land, "Quack, quack, quack."

MIA LEONIN is the author of four poetry collections: *Fable of the Pack-Saddle Child* (BkMk) and *Braid, Unraveling the Bed*, and *Chance Born* (Anhinga, 1999, 2008, and 2016, respectively). She also wrote the memoir *Havana and Other Missing Fathers* (University of Arizona Press, 2009). Leonin's poetry and creative nonfiction have appeared in *New Letters, Prairie Schooner, Alaska Quarterly Review, Indiana Review, Witness, North American Review, River Styx, Chelsea*, and other publications. She was born in Missouri to an American mother and a Cuban father and has lived in Miami since 1993. She teaches creative writing at the University of Miami in Coral Gables, Florida.

"How to Name a City" is nonfiction.

On a day like any other, it happens. You overhear a tourist berate your city's lack of "real" English. She calls your city "not really part of America." To your surprise, you're offended. You want to name this place for all of its intricacies, roll it into a spikey, multi-colored ball and hurl it at the tourist like your child's curse word. You want to blurt out a name for your city, a name that means "here" and "there," "them" and "us," but it occurs to you that all names are forgotten or never forgiven.

From "How to Name a City"

WHY I CALL THIS A TRANSLATION

Because my husband said arroz
and I heard Rolls Royce.

Because my dearest friend
calls me Palomita, Pal-o-mine.

Because my daughter has never said the word water
to me, only agüita. Because I was her first water.

Because in my neighborhood, if you're walking
toward a man, he says, "Good morning,"

but if you're walking away,
he sings, "¿Adónde vas, mami?"

Because in Miami, my tongue is not divided,
it is multiplied.

When my husband says eres mi luz,
I don't think light. I glide

through glass and slip through air.
I curl around wave and particle.

I think loose woman, Lucifer, and Lucy,
which always leads to You've got some 'splainin' to do!

I call these translations
because to carry across isn't a long haul.

It's a leap of imagination.

OFRENDA

After Nereida García Ferraz's painting *Travesía*, 2006

Yemayá, mother of all, dueña de todos los mares:

I trust your whirling skirts and rabia waves.
I trust your surfaces plácidas and your plummeting depths.

Yemayá, what if my offering is imperfect?

What if I only arrive at the bank of a river and not the sea? What if the river turns out to be a canal, and what if the canal turns out to be a puddle I stomped through, and what if the puddle is just my cupped hands under a faucet and the faucet is just me, a woman leaking a woman's fluids?

Yemayá, your altar swells into a sea garden.
Cowrie shells, blue glass, the echolocation of mar and mar adentro.

Yemayá, what if I am my only opening
and opening is my only offering?

HOW TO NAME A CITY

[Miami] is a profoundly American city—a place that reminds us that ideals matter more than the color of our skin or the circumstances of our birth . . .

—Barack Obama

You waver in the face of the word journey. This could mean more loss, but all the not-belonging has metabolized into longing, so you walk. You walk past the clump of fried dough huddled on the roof of your mouth. Past the fallen arch in your right foot and the hyperextended elbow that arches when you point. You walk past the dead poet's grave and the deaf gardener who tends it. You nod in agreement when the gardener smiles and shakes his head "no" at your request for directions. You walk past an old woman wrapping bruised mangoes in newspapers and past ancient, onion-skinned women who haul small houses and big-boned grandkids on their backs. You walk as far as you can and farther still. Cars race by, exhaust scorches your shins. Miniature flags from thirteen different islands wave at you from rearview mirrors. Wherever you stand, a new accent washes up from a far shore. Castilian, Creole, Patois, and Portuñol lap at your ankles. In this city, anyone claiming to be a native is laughed at or promptly interrogated. People put a hand on a stranger's shoulder. He thinks he's from here, they chuckle, offering a shot of strong, sweet coffee in a tiny medicinal cup. A woman wearing a neon bikini sells foot-long hot dogs from the median of a busy street. Your clothes have not yet unpeeled from the northern bitter. The long sheaths of your hippie skirts hover at your waist like attendant women preening and adjusting them against the city's prying winds. You've arrived. You don't realize it yet. You won't for weeks.

People stare at your hyperextended elbow when you point to "over there." You can't understand their directions anyway. Street names are carved into curbstones. Each street has an official name, a baptismal name, a nickname, and a number accompanied by court, place, terrace, and drive.

At night, you sleep through your own dreams. During the day, you listen. You stand up straight and crack open your sternum as if it were an ear probing a chest for a murmur. You cock your head forward. You listen with antlers and hooves, pawing at a flint of moon-colored bone in the ground. Idiomatic expressions flip from one language to the next like reversible gloves. Even university professors catch themselves saying, "Put attention" and "Te llamo pa'tras." In this city, one word multiplies like the word "carne" becomes meat, flesh, fruit, and sin.

You start varnishing yourself into this unfinished language, and after a few years, you're attuned to its subtleties. At the grocery store or the movies, you observe how this city's citizens elevate each other on a step ladder of ch words and cooing diminutives—oye chuchi, mi chini, cholita mía, chocherito de mi vida, only to be blunted by the augmentative insult—soplón, mamón, maricón. The speed with which the diminutive may be felled by the augmentative in no way negates its sincerity. In fact, the short-term memory of this city's inhabitants is virtually non-existent, which roller-coasters them into endless cycles of flirtation and bickering. They bark in media interviews. They grunt and hurl in post-election polling. The simple act of dropping a child off at school elicits a frenzy of prayers and blessings, shrieks and reproaches. You would think this speaks to their passion for family and community if it weren't for the pushy elbows and indiscriminate shopping cartwheels, the horn blaring and fist raising of daily life. They have vanished before. They have fled their country, or they've been kicked out. You suspect that they fear starting over again in a strange place where their right to belong is challenged.

Other notes on language: you nibble on the word for the crust of dried rice that sticks to the bottom of the pan (this word can be reshaped to compliment the sway of a woman's hips when she walks). There's a word for the last slosh of wine at the bottom of the bottle, a word for the little puddle of mamey milkshake left in the blender, a word for the few remaining drops of chicken broth. A word exists for precipitation that is neither shower, nor drizzle, nor mist. You sip from these words. You bathe in their non-rain.

Even after several years, you teeter on this city's skyscraper heels trying to fit in. You might even consider botoxing the worried furrows and under-eye angst from your face, but the duck-billed smile of this city's upper class frightens you. Instead, you tweeze your way past billboards for years without noticing they are human—unemployed men of all ages dressed up like Superman on Halloween and the Statue of Liberty at tax time. Hollow-eyed Tarzans and jittery life-size smart phones hop from one leg to the next and point arrow signs at the nearest strip mall without the slightest glance from you and other drivers. In bumper to bumper traffic, you don't notice the six men who meld into the rusted lattice of the enclosed truck bed in front of you. You don't see their glassy eyes staring at you among the machetes and leaf blowers. You do notice a woman who waits at the same bus stop bench at the same intersection every day, but by the time you realize that bench was her home, she's disappeared.

At lunch counters and sidewalk parks, you listen to exiles and immigrants shuffle the dominoes of their suffering. Exiles argue that immigrants don't suffer in the same way because exiles can't go back. Immigrants claim that without a path to citizenship, they can never go back or forward. You've listened for so long that one day you overhear yourself exclaim a Latinate "Ay!" instead of the Anglo Saxon "Oh" of your birth. When at a loss for words, you begin to emit an "Em" instead of "Um."

As your vowels ascend, so follows your solar plexus. Tuned to this multilingual frequency, something in you begins to open. A man speaks to you with a soft ch and a hard one, informing you that this "something" could be called unseen, vital points of energy (chakras) or small plots of hidden, fertile land (chacras). He calls himself zonzo alegre. He attracts iguanas, snakes, cats, rats, dogs, pigeons, and you. He rescues raspy flute breaths from a hundred-year-old Andean reed. The soft place perpendicular to your hipbone quivers in this city's smallest room. Your ovaries throb in traffic. You wear down the cotton heel of many socks, dancing this city's guaguancós and cumbias in your kitchen where you germinate, stew, and chop. You give birth to a girl of guava-sticky, croqueta-salted fingers, and panetón-pinched belly. You produce a susto water bearer and industrial grade manufacturer of mocos. In this city it's acceptable to call children creatures. Creatures of God that is. Fellow shoppers who previously pretended not to see you as they rushed to the front of the line now bestow your child with blessings: Que Dios me la bendiga. You would have once received such an affirmation with wry stoicism; however, the sweet heft on your hip drains you of all irony. You are grateful for any blessings that come your way.

This city lavishes its children with artificial snow in December, café con leche made with thick, steamed condensed milk, and thumb-shaped crosses pressed into foreheads daily. Your child will hurl her first curse word in this city, and you will be simultaneously tickled and horrified by the wriggling finger sound the word makes. She will learn to greet everyone with a kiss on the cheek. She will know how to dance, joke, and listen up and down the generational ladder.

On a day like any other, it happens. You overhear a tourist berate your city's lack of "real" English. She calls your city "not really part of America." To your surprise, you're offended. You want to name this place for all of its intricacies, roll it into a spikey, multi-colored ball and hurl it at the tourist like your child's curse word. You want to blurt out a name for your city, a name that means "here" and "there," "them" and "us," but it occurs to you that all names are forgotten or never forgiven. The land you stand on was once named for its natives, but the steady dorsal fin of road rage has plowed over the low-lying anthropology of the Allapatah, Okeechobee, and Mayaimi peoples. You your-self have globbed on sunscreen at the downtown red light that sits over a five-hundred-year-old Tequesta well. You've sped past the surnames of landowners and developers on the very streets named after them. A baby's scream at the Shwarma Mediterranean Grill on Kendall Drive could pierce deeper than the arrowhead from one of these lost tribes.

In ancient times, every city was named after God or a Godlike trait. Rome from the Greek word for strength. Jerusalem comes from Yeru (settlement) and Shalem (God). Perhaps a name like God would suffuse this city with rever-ence. It has taken so long to feel part of it. You don't want this city to be called by a nickname or slogan. Dueling pronunciations carved from socio-economic class will not do either. No grunting uh at the end of the city's name for those who eat dirt. No long eee for those who shop organic. No names of saints or industry, no etymologies or exegesis. You want a name pronounceable by hoodlum, hairstylist, hookah smoker, and hedge fund manager alike. You try it out. God, Florida; God, New Hampshire; God, Minnesota. When buttressed by a state, God sounds surprisingly ecumenical, atheistic, even.

If God is the name of your city, then silence is its gate. Belonging means you no longer think of it. You must know this city and forget it, breathe in its swells and digressions. This you have learned from your city and its inhabitants, who are named for no one and after whom no one is named.

RAÚL DOPICO is a Cuban writer, playwright, journalist, and theater and television director and producer. He is the author of the poetry collections *El delirio del otoño* (Extramuros, 1991), which won the Luis Rogelio Nogueras Award that same year, and *Estadios del espíritu disperso* (Atom, 2010) as well as the editor of the 1994 Cuban poetry anthology *Tras la huella de lo imposible* (Secretaría de Cultura de Jalisco, 1994). He has written two novels, *Dos gardenias para ti* (La Torre de Papel, 2005) and *Los gloriosos y los fuertes* (3 sílabas, 2014); a play titled *El sacrificio*, winner of the 1995 Cham de Literatura Prize in Mexico; and the feature film *La mala hora de Ramón* (Multivisión, 1998). His works have been translated into English and German. Dopico's theater work includes serving as dean of the State Theater School in Jalisco, Mexico, and directing a bilingual run of William Shakespeare's *Hamlet*; *La secreta obscenidad de cada día* by Marco Antonio de la Parra; *Morir de noche* by Roberto Ramos Perea; and *Los de la mesa diez* by Osvaldo Dragún. He has written, directed, or produced for major international media outlets such as Televisa, TV Azteca, Univisión, Telemundo, Caracol, América Teve, Mega TV, and Grupo Prisa. His contributions to journalism have appeared in *Uno Más Uno*, *Reforma*, *Siglo XXI*, *Etcétera*, *Encuentro de la Cultura Cubana*, and *Diario de Cuba*. He won Associated Press awards in 2017, 2018, and 2019 and received an Emmy award in 2017. He lives in Miami, Florida.

Please see translator ANDREÍNA FERNÁNDEZ's bio on page 38.

"Miami Is Cuban" is nonfiction, translated from the Spanish by Andreína Fernández.

"Cuban" became, then, a gerund that escaped into a participle. To be Cuban came to mean "to be an escapee, a fugitive," the uncertainty of the unknown world always preferable to the certain future of the known one. To Escape. To Escape. To Escape. To anywhere. But all the better if you could escape to Miami.

From "Miami Is Cuban"

MIAMI IS CUBAN

The only way to escape the
revolution was in a coffin.

Carlos A. Díaz Barrios

Miami was always, for me, a kind of promised land. The other face of Cuba, the one I longed to meet: the Cuba of pain, so brusquely transplanted to South Florida, where it had risen to become an economically, socially, and politically successful Cuba. In other words, Miami was a myth.

It was also where many of my childhood friends had gone to live, as had the life I'd known, lost to me when they left Cuba before I did (during the Mariel exodus) and were never heard from again, an acute feeling of loss forever in their place.

In Miami, then, lived a great deal of my past. And yet it was never just the house that held inside it the lost link to my nostalgia but rather a place of possibility, with a door that others had gone through before me, and that could open into the future at any moment. To be even clearer: it was the designated route of my getaway, land of refuge for Cubans who acted on the life philosophy that has ruled on the island for decades: escape. During my teenage years and early youth in Cuba, when you asked someone, "How are you?" the most common response was "Ahí, escapando." It was a phrase that defined an entire social sentiment. To escape. From what? From everything. From material scarcity. From lack of freedoms. From denied opportunity. For what? To survive. To forget the suffocating reality. To evade a present that went nowhere, going around in circles like a carousel forgotten by time. To where? Anywhere. But, preferably, toward "la yuma." Preferably, to Miami.

The image of success of the post-1959 Cuban imagination, Miami was an archetype quickly established by the Mariel exodus that, like a cyclical phenomenon, reappeared during the *balseros* exodus in 1994 and continued to transform until it became a complete escape, a collective jailbreak, a continuous bleeding that has lasted more than four decades.

Now Cubans escape regularly and en masse toward wherever. It makes no difference to them whether it is to frigid Alaska or to post-Soviet Russia. To the Spain of our ancestors or to insipid Switzerland. To successful Germany or to Nigeria, from where enslaved people were originally taken to the island. It's all the same. To escape. To escape. To escape. We used the gerund "escaping" as a metaphoric expression of our desire, transforming it gradually into the infinitive "to escape." Escape toward infinity. Even toward Nothingness. Escape as assurance of distance from imprisonment, from the danger of the idea that still burdens most Cubans: the possibility of not having a future, never mind that a future far away from the land that birthed you is always an uncertain one. "Cuban" became, then, a gerund that escaped into a participle. To be Cuban came to mean "to be an escapee, a fugitive," the uncertainty of the unknown world always preferable to the certain future of the known one. To Escape. To Escape. To Escape. To anywhere. But all the better if you could escape to Miami.

I escaped, not to Miami but to Mexico, which, in the late '80s and early '90s, became the preferred destination for Cuban intellectuals. To Mexico fled the painters of the new vanguard of visual arts, the writers, the academics, and audiovisual directors. Then the actors escaped as well. Then the ballerinas and musicians began to come too. And the jineteras. And the pingueros. And the engineers. And the architects. And then Cubans from all over arrived, from all places, from all professions, and all races. Mexico had become *the* destination for the Cuban escapee.

In Mexico I found love, marriage, heartbreak, and divorce. I found professional success and relative economic accomplishment. I say relative because Mexican society was politically and economically unstable, and what you made today was gone tomorrow when the currency was devalued.

But Mexico was never my home. It was never *mi* Mexico lindo y querido. I was never able to transplant Cuba, to bring it with me, to Mexico. The country is hostile to that kind of claim. The ruthless nationalism of Mexican society, the rancid classism and the racism, latent at all times against the overseas upstart and among the different races that form the nation, functioned like a barrier against anyone perceived as extraneous, unfamiliar. Foreign. At one point, we, the Cubans who lived in Mexico, numbered in the thousands, and yet we were too preoccupied with surviving to even think of creating a community. As a result, there were few safe spaces for Cubans to find solidarity, much less a reason to call the place home.

In the end, the vast majority of the Cubans I met in Mexico ended up emigrating to Miami, especially in the wake of the 2001 terrorist attacks, when fears that anti-Cuban President Bush would tighten immigration policies in the United States unleashed a stampede.

All that said, the Mexican experience was not wasted on me. Instead, I developed a career there, wrote plays, directed theater, did television, founded a school, and became a college professor and also a public official. Mexico gave me the space to finish several literary works and to deeply acquaint myself with a complex and rich culture, even as it tattooed the excruciating reality of uprootedness onto my bones and taught me what it meant to be an exile. The worst of it was spending twelve years there unable to see my parents, my siblings, or my daughter, even once.

I arrived in Miami in February 2002, after boarding a Mexico City plane destined for Matamoros, crossing the border to the United States on foot, and upon arrival, requesting political asylum from a Border Patrol officer. What followed were seven days in a high-security detention center in the Port Isabel Service Processing Center in Los Fresnos, Texas, followed by a long trip by bus to my promised land.

I had done it. I had escaped. Finally. I had escaped to Miami.

Once I arrived in my myth-city, my flight from the dark minotaur's cave that was Castro's Cuba became real, strangely enough, for the first time since I had actually left the island, and though it would be foolish to say I regret my years in Mexico (because without Mexico, I would never have had Miami), not a single day goes by that I don't wish I had come to Miami much earlier. Or that I don't bitterly regret arriving so late.

Setting aside the city I'd imagined, which was, of course, just an abstraction, the actual Miami really did turn out to be the city in which I'd be able to discover the Cuba I'd believed lost. The republican Cuba. The Cuba that my parents told stories about: young, vigorous, unruly, discontented, enthusiastic, imperfect, in development, virtuous, decent, fragrant, pithy, ambitious, dignified, lively. But also, wounded by loss. Resentful of distance. Tired of the wait. Worn from battle. Disillusioned with the new generations of Cubans.

In Miami I was once again able to speak Cuban without getting strange or mistrustful looks. Without catching a grimace of contempt forming on the lips of strangers. That is no small thing if we consider that strangeness and mistrust are part of the immigrant experience anywhere, really.

In Miami I once again felt at home, even after just arriving. I could breathe it in the air, in the body language, in the conversations in cafés.

I was almost an old man when I arrived in this dynamic city in vibrant flux, without mastery of the language and knowing I would never master it. But I arrived willing to do anything that would provide a calm and peaceful livelihood. And that was exactly how it went.

In the beginning I lived with an aunt and uncle in Hialeah. Every day I took the bus to work as a cook at a Pollo Tropical in downtown Miami. What I liked most about that job was that I was done by three in the afternoon and could walk from there to a public library where I could check out books and connect to the internet.

Later, a family friend found me something better: assistant chauffeur for a company that provided transportation for the elderly, taking them to doctors' appointments in clinics and hospitals throughout the city. I enjoyed that job because it gave me insight into Old Miami. And Poor Miami. And Black Miami. A full-immersion learning course into my new city.

One day, one of the drivers, a fat Cuban who knew I was a recent immigrant, asked me if I liked Miami. "I am still discovering it," I told him. In his fragmented inglés con barreras, he replied, "If you don't like it here, you are welcome to leave" and had barely finished the words before he was roaring with laughter. The phrase circled my mind all day. Leave Miami? Leave this country? And go where? Look for another city? Go back to Mexico? By day's end, an old Benny Moré song my mom used to sing to me had come to my aid, installing itself in my mind to the point I surprised myself singing it aloud. "Miami es la ciudad, que más me gusta a mí. Cuando a Miami llegué . . ." The fat Cuban, surprised, went into one of his fits of laughter. "Flaco, you learn fast. You're going to do fine here."

I never saw him again but wish I had. I would have liked to thank him for the words that had, at first, struck me as ominous but soon had the opposite effect of jolting my brain, of gifting me with the certainty that Miami, imperfect as it is, was home, that I was already where I needed to be. As José Lezama Lima said once, "Sólo lo difícil es estimulante." Only the difficult motivates.

Truth is, it hasn't been that difficult. Those who came before me had paved a path for me to follow.

I soon found a job in Spanish media, which allowed me to circumvent my shortcomings when it comes to Shakespeare's native tongue. My mother and daughter were able to follow me eventually and now live with me. Here, too,

I found love, marriage, heartbreak, and divorce. I have made few friends, but the ones I have are good ones, both women: a Boricua and a Cuban, my closest friends who have held my hand when I've needed it, as I have held theirs, and who appreciate what, they say, is my ability to listen as passionately as I debate. I have lost friends from my days in Cuba and Mexico. Reuniting in Miami did not revive the magic of past times. But that is also life. Encounters and escapes. Gains and losses. Something is claimed after something else is released.

On my journey I discovered that living in Miami is like living every day in Esteban Luis Cárdenas's poem "Ciudad mágica II" because they all "say that Magic City is a rural town/ they say that it is uncertain/ but they don't know of what they speak/ anywhere./ Magic City grows at its own pace/ and the people do not know why it grows./ The women smile, but say nothing."

And it's true that Miami is a vilified city, but maybe that is so because it is many cities that try to be everything to everyone but that in the end beats with a decidedly Cuban soul.

There's the Miami of high culture. The Miami of darkness, of depth. There is wealthy Miami. And poor Miami. Banal Miami. Political Miami. The souls of all of those Miamis are, in essence, Cuban, even when they, too, are diverse in their essence: Jewish, Catholic, Protestant, Yoruba, conservative, and liberal. The bourgeois and the rabble. The aristocrats and the working class. The middle class and the impoverished. The republican and the castrista. All coexisting, all slowly stewing in a new ajiaco. In a distinct Cubanidad, if not a new one entirely. A Cuban identity that, although similar in some ways, is nothing like that of the island. A Cubanidad that infuses (some would say, contaminates) everything it touches.

An example? Cuban has been spoken in Miami since the '60s. From the names of the businesses to the platitudes of politicians, the hurried words of waitresses, receptionists, public officials, public service announcements, news media, street names, and illustrious and less than illustrious last names. Everything. Absolutely everything in Miami happens in Cuban. This is why many older Cubans firmly believe that the only good thing that Castro's regime created was Miami. Others more sarcastic and caustic are sure that the only successful Cuban province is Miami.

These Cubans live in and are proud to have breathed life, economic, artistic, and otherwise, into this place that calls itself the Magic City. But that is not the Miami that is vilified. The one vilified is the one of the Cubans who took to the streets for days to protest the return to the island of a boy who arrived on a raft. The one that also belongs to the Cuban who dared destroy the records of an artist with a steamroller. And to the ones who celebrated with unbridled joy, before the eyes of an astonished world, the death of their would-be executioner. Those who believe that that Miami is the only Miami are usually the resentful ones, those who didn't live here when it was a swamp. They didn't suffer with Miami. Or grow with it. They can't understand it. Some, it must be said, be they Latin American or European, sympathize with that strange and perverse thing that they continue to call, even sixty years later, the Cuban Revolution. And sometimes they are Americans from all over the country who feel that Miami is not part of the United States but rather a strange cultural experiment they have no hope of ever understanding or changing. "It's a shitty little town, che," an Argentine friend who came to visit for a week told me. "It's a shitty little town, che," said the same Argentine three years after first overstaying his visa. "I'm going to miss Miami so much, che," said the same Argentine on the phone from Buenos Aires when he was deported after nearly eight years living in Miami, where he'd had a son and succeeded professionally as a television producer for various local channels.

That is Miami. The one Rodolfo Pérez Valero narrates in his essay "The Day That Simon, Garfunkel, and I Sang in Miami." The Cuba forlorn, the Cuba of the "complete exile" of Guillermo Rosales in *The Halfway House* and "The Magic Still," one that Pérez says can be "indifferent and superficial where the eye of God also deeply penetrates, and judges, and punishes, and forgives."

That loneliness, that ache, in Rosales's prose and life is what I have always felt is Miami. A city where the pain is sublimated by partying and rhythm, dancing, and ruckus, darkness, sexuality, and tragicomic melodrama, all boiling under a blistering sun.

Perhaps because of all that, the majority of people who arrive in Miami do not return to their places of origin. Because maybe the return would be more painful than the arrival. Or because when you arrive, the city shouts, "Welcome to Miami" and then runs from you, at full speed, as if inviting you to follow it in a hurry, to catch up with it and to hold on to it, which will take time, dedication, and much love because it is a surly city and will resist you. Make you work to dig into it, to discover it, until one day . . . you are an insider. A local. Ah, and then, then the love is fierce, and your myth-city will have become your reality, your home. But let me put it to you as Andrés Reynaldo says it in his poem "Americana 4": "I came to see the reviled Miami, that reunites the Cuban with everything else, and stayed forever. De todo Miami ya soy memoria."

Born in Miami to Cuban parents **CHANTEL ACEVEDO** is called "a master storyteller" by *Kirkus Reviews*. She is the author of *Love and Ghost Letters* (St. Martin's, 2013), winner of the Latino International Book Award; *A Falling Star* (Carolina Wren, 2016), winner of the Doris Bakwin Award; *The Distant Marvels* (Europa, 2015), a finalist for the 2016 Andrew Carnegie Medal for Excellence in Fiction; and *The Living Infinite* (Europa, 2017), hailed by *Booklist* as a "vivid and enthralling tale of love and redemption." Her essays have appeared in *Vogue* and *Real Simple*, among other publications. *The Cassandra Curse* (Balzer + Bray, 2020), in Acevedo's Muse Squad series for middle grades, was called "riveting and suspenseful" by *School Library Journal*. She is a professor of English at the University of Miami, where she directs the MFA program.

"Piercing My Daughter's Ears in Alabama" is nonfiction.

> My tía has already bought earrings for my daughter, tiny diamonds like the ones she got for me. Time spools itself around us, the patterns repeating.
>
> From "Piercing My Daughter's Ears in Alabama"

PIERCING MY DAUGHTER'S EARS IN ALABAMA

I do not recall the surprise of the needle when it pierced my earlobes so long ago. I was only a few weeks old, and the tiny diamonds had been a gift from my aunt. Not my real aunt, but the kind of tías that abound in Cuban families, family friends who have evolved to be more than that. My mother took me to the pediatrician, and I, two weeks old, was carried out of the appointment glittering, and likely, howling.

When I give birth to my first daughter, the question regarding the piercing of her ears comes up almost immediately among members of my family. One has to hurry, I am told. Before she can sit up, my mother suggests. Definitely before her baptism, my cousins urge. In a Connecticut hospital, holding my newborn far from the place I think of as home, with her azabache pin attached to ward off the evil eye, I add my daughter's ears to the long list of Cuban customs to worry about.

Those phone conversations in the hospital add to new and roiling maternal emotions in a way I am not prepared for. Truthfully, I'm always surprised when reminders of home strike. It is a pang in my brain, a dull thud of my heart, a brick sinking through my guts. No matter how long I live away from Florida (it was to be fifteen years of exile), no place ever feels quite like home the way Miami does. I lived in Pittsburgh, and New Haven, and then spent nine years in Auburn, Alabama. By then, I've amassed coats, bags of salt for slick sidewalks in the winter, and amnesia regarding hurricanes.

In Alabama, my six-month old baby in tow, I quickly adapt, allowing a twang into my speech when I am among strangers. It is a protective evolution. "Okay, y'all form groups and then discuss the text," I tell my college students, having excised the Miami from my palate, and they in turn do not ask me, "Where are you from?" Once, a graduate student, upon hearing that I am from Miami, asks me how many times I've been mugged. The answer is zero, but I'm not sure he believes me. The sting of the needle comes in many forms.

Other changes creep in, slow and encompassing as kudzu. Staring in my Alabama mirror, I simplify my jewelry. Anything beyond a pair of stud earrings feels like overkill here among the dogwoods, the First, Second, and Third

Baptist Churches, and the tailgates. Tank tops and tacones give way to blouses and sensible shoes. When visiting family back in Miami, they advise me: Ponte collares. Ponte aretes más grandes. Ponte anillos. And looking at my reflection in Miami, I see what they see—me, out of place.

I often feel out of place. Like when my daughter is invited to birthday parties, and there is one bowl of chips on the table, one juice pouch per child, and a plain vanilla cake. Parties are two hours long, and that is that. But when it is my turn to throw a party, we feed an army of friends, and my mother drives up ten hours from Miami with trays of croquetas, pastelitos, and bocaditos wrapped in bright yellow cellophane. My mother-in-law makes a piñata, the kind with the ribbons that dangle down, one ribbon per child, and loads the thing up with toys and candies. And Alabama friends come over, point at the tray of croquetas and ask, "What're those?" And their children eat, and bust open that piñata full of gifts, and go home exhausted.

Do I stand on my porch and wave those friends off, big hoop earrings that were gifts from my cousin back home brushing my neck, pride pulsing through me like lightning?

I do.

And when it is time to say goodbye to the family that loves us so much that they'd give up twenty hours to the Florida turnpike, in spite of creaky hips and aching knees, just to be with my daughter on her birthday, do I cry on that same porch?

I do, because it is only in those moments, surrounded by my family and our culture, that I am home.

I think of my grandmother often. She tells me that before she met my grandfather, a fortune-teller came to her house, took one look at my grandmother, and proclaimed, *There will be many miles between you and your mother for the rest of your life.*

So, it came to be. She married my grandfather, and together with their daughters, they moved to Los Angeles to start their life in the United States and like so many Cubans, ended up in Miami, where even the sunshine felt Cuban. They took only one trip back to the island in the winter of 1958, just as the Sierra Maestra rumbled revolution. They were meant to stay through Christmas, but my grandfather, weary of bearded men carrying guns and talking big, cut the trip short.

Did my grandmother resist the abrupt end to her trip home? Did she fight the prophecy regarding her mother and the miles of water between them with claws out?

Of course, she did.

Did my grandfather threaten to take his daughters with him, back to the U.S., where they had already become little americanitas?

He did. And so, they left. I am certain my great-grandmother, a woman I never met, cried on the porch as she waved them goodbye. As predicted, my grandmother never saw her mother again.

I think of these things and tell myself that I have no right to miss Miami so much, not when I can return to it without having to cross a border.

When my daughter is fourteen months old, I finally take her to get her ears pierced. "Aren't pierced ears on a baby a bit trashy?" a fellow mother asks at her day care, which only adds steel to my spine. The pediatrician looks at me with similar horror when I ask her to do it, and I feel the steel sloughing off as I slink away after the appointment.

On the way home from the doctor, my daughter points at the blue sky, and the wood-sided homes, and a stray dog sniffing along the side of the road. She has begun to speak, asking for leche, and her tete at home. At day care, the teachers correct her gently. It's called milk, and that's a paci in your mouth. She begins to prefer the shape of those words to the ones she first knew.

Later, I consider my choice as I feed the baby and rub her perfect earlobes. I struggle with the idea of injuring her on purpose. What if she hates them when she's older? What is the point? I wonder what her day care teachers will think, or her doctor. For one, they'll think, *Not one of us, then*, and it's this idea that firms up my decision.

Not one of yours, I think.

My tía has already bought earrings for my daughter, tiny diamonds like the ones she got for me. Time spools itself around us, the patterns repeating.

One of ours.

We end up in the mall, where a teenage employee does the deed. I choose a pair of the smallest gold spheres for my daughter. She'll have to wear them until the wound heals. A pair of older women watch the process from the other side of the glass storefront, and I can't tell if they are judging me or not. At least the store employee does it all with a smile and says, "Ma'am, your baby sure is cute."

She uses a gun-like device to pierce the first ear, and that's when my daughter starts to squall. I distract her with a red hair ribbon bedazzled with bells as the girl with the gun does the next ear. The ribbon costs $8.99, and I buy it when my daughter won't stop crying in the store. But she's over the shock of the needle in a minute, and the ribbon becomes a favorite toy, one she shakes in joy or fury as the mood takes her. I tie it to her stroller like a prize.

When my grandmother's ears were pierced, she was little, too, and so the story of this moment, which she passes down to me, must have been one she'd heard from her mother. As such, it feels like a gift handed down through the decades, and I hold it in my heart along with all the cuentos she tells me.

Back in those days there were no malls or monthly pediatric visits. There was only a mother's hands, a sewing needle made safe in boiling water, and a bright red thread. Someone held my grandmother, perhaps somebody cooed her name, María Asela, Aselita, mi niña, mi amor, she, the youngest of nine. A hand held fast the needle, pulled taut the earlobe, so small, like a button, and ran it through the sweet flesh, knotting the thread on either end until an earring could be inserted.

I've often wondered about the detail of the thread. Perhaps the earrings had not yet been purchased. Perhaps they'd have to save up for them. Perhaps my grandmother, or great-grandmother, invented it for its theatricality, the thread a dash of scarlet to accompany the blood, color in an otherwise banal tale.

Of course, the thread is not the point.

The baby had been marked, yes, for beauty, yes, but also for this: so that whenever she looked in a mirror she would know some part of herself, and in that knowledge, recognize home.

ARACELIS GONZÁLEZ ASENDORF was born in Cuba.

Her work has appeared in *TriQuarterly*, *Kweli Journal*, *Adirondack Review*, *Puerto del Sol*, *Acentos Review*, *Litro*, *South Atlantic Review*, *Saw Palm*, *Black Fox Literary Magazine*, *Hong Kong Review*, *Santa Fe Literary Review*, and elsewhere. Her stories have been anthologized in *All About Skin: Short Fiction by Women of Color* (University of Wisconsin Press, 2014) and *100% Pure Florida Fiction* (University Press of Florida, 2000). She is the recipient of the 2016 South Atlantic Modern Language Association Graduate Creative Writing Award for Prose and a 2019 Sterling Watson fellow and a 2019 C. Michael Curtis Short Story Book Prize finalist.

"Consuelo's Garden" is fiction.

Consuelo had bought a cow tongue and made a cut down the middle. She wrote Mateo and the woman's name on a piece of paper and tucked it in the middle, filled the fleshy crevice with black pepper corn and lemon rinds, then closed it with long sewing pins. Consuelo whispered an incantation to bring Mateo's union nothing but amargura y dolor—bitterness and pain. She slipped small pieces of cooked tongue into a beef stew she fed him and buried the rest outside their bedroom window. "You'll see," she'd said. "Their passion will rot with that tongue. And if traces of desire still linger, they'll have to make their way through the thorns of that cactus."

From "Consuelo's Garden"

CONSUELO'S GARDEN

Beba placed a dry towel around Consuelo's shoulders, tucking the edge inside her housecoat collar. She squirted a dollop of hair gel into her palm, rubbed it gently through her friend's hair, and felt Consuelo's shoulders drop as she relaxed. Then, Beba wrapped short strands of hair around a plastic curler. It only took a few minutes and ten curlers to cover Consuelo's head. She had more pink scalp than white hair. The style wouldn't last more than a day, but Beba knew Consuelo looked forward to the Tuesday ritual that left her feeling pampered and pretty, or at least as pretty as she could feel at eighty with the left side of her face drooping from a stroke.

Beba rolled the last curler. "There, I'll blow dry it in a minute."

They had been next-door neighbors for fifty years. Over decades, Beba and Consuelo had spent countless hours in one another's kitchen doing each other's hair, fashioning elaborate upsweeps like the telenovela stars, poufy perms, and countless frostings and dye jobs once they started to go gray. Now Beba came to the nursing home once a week and spent the day with Consuelo fixing her hair, giving her manicures, bringing her soups and smooth, syrupy flans.

Without turning around, Consuelo reached up for Beba's hands with her good one and said in her halting cadence since the stroke, "My . . . house . . . sold . . . yesterday." She continued, slowly, pausing after every few words, "Diego called last night. The realtor girl said the offer was good. Except papers, it's done, my friend."

Beba sat down across from Consuelo. The elastic band of her navy pants made a snapping sound as she adjusted it around her thick waist. "Who bought it?"

"No sé . . . nada," Consuelo shook her headful of curlers. She dabbed the left corner of her mouth with a tissue because, she'd explained to Beba, she often had the sensation that the edge of her mouth was drooling, even though it wasn't.

"Bueno," Beba said. "I hope my new neighbors aren't—you know," she rubbed her index finger up and down her forearm.

Two months back, Consuelo, with the aid of her son, Diego, had put her house on the market. The stroke had weakened the left part of her body and taken away the use of her left hand. She couldn't live alone the way she had since her husband's death ten years back.

With Consuelo directing from her moss-green recliner in the living room, Beba had helped Diego sort through drawers, closets and cabinets: things Consuelo wanted to take with her, things she wanted Diego to keep, things for charity, things that needed to be thrown away. And just like that, a fifty-year-old home ceased to exist. Empty rooms and bare walls.

"Are you sure Diego didn't tell you anything about who bought the house?" Beba asked again, because Consuelo now forgot things.

"No, he said . . . the offer was good . . . and the closing is Thursday." Consuelo reached out with her right hand and patted Beba's knee. "No te preocupes. It will . . . be fine."

Beba drove past the front of Consuelo's house slowly before pulling into her own driveway. The *For Sale* sign now read *Sold* across it in bright red. The realtor must have done it while she was visiting Consuelo. Had she been home, she'd have walked over and asked about the buyers.

Beba hoped it wasn't the family with four kids. She didn't want that much noise. And who can afford four kids these days? Irresponsible. And not the couple with tattoos covering their arms and legs as if they were wrapped in comic strip pages. Por favor, didn't those people realize it made them look dirty and cheap? Beba wondered who else had come to last weekend's open house. She'd driven to Miami to visit her cousin Estela. She could call Diego, but she didn't want to bother him. She knew he was busy. Consuelo said he was gone for work for a few days to one of those new states—Beba had trouble remembering which one—New York, New Jersey, New Hampshire.

The realtor's name was Cynthia, and the woman annoyed her. She hated the chirpy way she always greeted her and called her Miss Bee-bah even after she'd corrected her. *Beba like fella.* Was that so hard?

Beba always knew when Cynthia pulled into Consuelo's driveway because she gave her car horn three quick taps. The first time Beba heard the horn she thought she was being summoned and went outside. A superstitious habit for luck, Cynthia had said. *You know, the way baseball players have a routine before they bat. I want the house to know I want a homerun of a sale.* Qué jomerun ni qué carajo.

Beba walked to Consuelo's front yard. The towering royal poinciana in the center of the yard would bloom soon, ablaze with a canopy of bright orange flowers. She had a matching tree in her front yard. When the bloom petals fell, the lawns looked like they were covered with a dusting of orange snow. The trees had been saplings when she and Consuelo moved into the new subdivision built on what was then the eastern edge of Coquina Shores. Three bedrooms and one bathroom. Affordable. Dozens of Cuban families moved to the neighborhood. Many families were related, and she knew everyone. Now, many of those families were gone. Some had moved away to bigger, newer houses, and others sold when the elders, her contemporaries, passed away. Beba resented the way the neighborhood had changed. She hardly knew anyone anymore. Por Dios, even haitianos had moved down the street.

The soaring palm that grew at the right corner of the house was once a waist-high little thing Consuelo planted in memory of her father when he died in Cuba. Consuelo hoped her grief would diminish as the palm grew. They'd been neighbors for three years by then. Beba didn't care much for yard work, but Consuelo loved to garden. She'd filled the side yard with hibiscuses of every color and frangipanis that bloomed pink and yellow. Beba knew Consuelo planted the cactus that grew by her bedroom window sometime in the early eighties when her husband Mateo strayed. He'd picked up with an old girlfriend who'd come over during the Mariel Boat Lift. Consuelo said she'd worked too hard to build a life with Mateo to let some skinny-assed fletera take her man. She got rid of her with a strong trabajo.

Consuelo had bought a cow tongue and made a cut down the middle. She wrote Mateo and the woman's name on a piece of paper and tucked it in the middle, filled the fleshy crevice with black pepper corn and lemon rinds, then closed it with long sewing pins. Consuelo whispered an incantation to bring Mateo's union nothing but amargura y dolor—bitterness and pain. She slipped small pieces of cooked tongue into a beef stew she fed him and buried the rest outside their bedroom window. "You'll see," she'd said. "Their passion will rot with that tongue. And if traces of desire still linger, they'll have to make their way through the thorns of that cactus."

Beba was skeptical. But not six weeks later that woman packed up and left Coquina Shores for Miami.

She smiled at Consuelo's cactus. That thing had grown twelve feet tall. Mateo had never strayed again, and damn if that cactus didn't start giving red fruit and blooming twice a year with white, bell-shaped flowers.

The week had been filled with early Florida spring days with skies so clear and bright Beba felt she was living in a diamond. She opened her windows to the day's temperate weather. Spring weather was capricious in Florida, today's perfect open-window weather could change tomorrow to summer heat and humidity or conversely, dip low enough to make a space heater necessary in her bedroom. Beba was making fideo soup for Consuelo. She was adding pasta nests to the chicken broth when she heard the metal-on-metal screech of truck brakes, followed by the hissing of a stop. If she looked out the living room window, she'd see a moving van in front of Consuelo's house, and she wasn't ready to stop thinking of it as Consuelo's house. The noodle nests uncoiled and expanded as Beba heard car and truck doors open and close. She stirred, careful not to overcook the fideos, squelching her desire to look out the living room window.

"Diego sold the house to un chino," Beba said to Consuelo. "What was our boy thinking?" She placed a bowl of soup on the rolling tabletop she'd positioned over Consuelo's lap. Beba draped a napkin bib-like on her friend's chest.

"He didn't . . . tell me . . . anything." Consuelo brought a spoonful of soup slowly to her lips.

"They're moving in today." Beba had a napkin ready in hand in case of spills. Consuelo refused to let her feed her.

"Qué rica . . . your sopa . . . my favorite. And?"

"No sé. I saw a woman giving orders to movers. And an old man."

"We had chinos . . . lived on our street in Cuba." Consuelo continued slowly. "Well, he was . . . chino . . . she was mulata."

"Bueno, at least this one is with a white woman."

The next day, Beba awakened long before she wanted to be up. There wasn't anything she needed to do, but she wasn't sleepy, and she wasn't tired. All those years she was working and raising her daughter, what she wouldn't have given to throw her alarm clock against the wall and go back to sleep. Now, she was her own personal alarm clock, awake early every morning for no good reason. She stretched from her side of the bed, warm from her body heat, to the cool empty side and ran her palm along the sheet. *Mi bella Beba, hora de brillar.* She could hear her husband's voice singing his silly rhyme, all the mornings he coaxed her awake. Almost five years ago she'd lost Daniel, and she missed him every day. Thirty-three years since she'd lost Bebita, and she missed her daughter every minute.

Beba forced herself out of bed before she started feeling sorry for herself. Except for the achaques that came with age—coño, she'd be eighty-one soon—she was healthy. She kept that present in her thoughts as she lit the white candles she kept on her dresser for her husband and daughter. Beba lit a third one for Consuelo and began to pray a rosary for her friend. She'd looked pale last week.

Beba was lost in the trance-like repetition of Hail Marys when the clapping of boards startled her. She continued to whisper her prayers and walked to peek out her front door. Two men were unloading a trailer of fencing material in the driveway of Consuelo's house. Beba stepped out of the house, beads in hand, and saw the old man walk out and speak to workers who followed him to the side yard.

Even though it had been a week since they'd moved in, she hadn't met the neighbors yet. She kept her distance. You just never knew about people these days. She'd seen the woman leave in a silver SUV in the mornings. Off to work, Beba assumed. She hadn't figured out the man. She'd only seen him the first day. Maybe he was one of those old fools who married a young woman thinking it would make him younger—proof he still had what it took to be a man. That's why her cousin Estela's husband had left her six years ago. There he was, an old viejo chocheando acting like he was forty. And la boba Estela, still waiting, foolishly hoping he'd come back. Maybe she should've done that cow tongue trabajo like Consuelo.

When the workers returned to the trailer for another load of materials, one of them touched the brim of his green cap in greeting. Beba returned inside. She went to her kitchen window where, through the gingham café curtains she'd sewn shortly after she and Daniel moved in, she saw the men preparing to work. A fence. A wooden fence between her house and Consuelo's.

Throughout the morning, the men dug holes and planted wheat-colored posts into the spring grass. Every pound and thud reverberated through Beba. She watched as the man who'd greeted her turned the brim of his hat backward and bent down, closing one eye and squinting the other, following the blue twine he'd staked along the length of Consuelo's side yard, making certain the fence posts were aligned. With each post, Beba grew angrier. This wasn't going to be an idyllic picket fence; it was a privacy fence that would shield her view of Consuelo's yard. As Beba's anger intensified, her footsteps became heavier; she closed drawers, cabinets, and doors with emphatic smacks. She slammed the refrigerator shut with such intensity that it shook, making the bottles inside clink.

In the late afternoon, after the workmen left, Beba sat in one of the wicker chairs outside her front door and kept watch for the silver SUV. She walked to the edge of her property, waving to the woman as she drove into Consuelo's driveway.

"I'm Beba," she said, introducing herself.

"Tamara."

They exchanged a handshake of sorts, briefly touching fingers.

"Just moved in and already making changes," Beba pointed to the fence construction.

"No time to waste," Tamara said.

The woman was thin and much taller than Beba. When she looked up at her, Beba saw dark swags beneath her eyes.

"My friend, Consuelo, lived here. She planted everything. I see her garden from my kitchen."

"Well, I guess the fence will change that, won't it? Nice to meet you, Beba."

Beba was left with her words in her mouth. This woman, this Tamara, turned around and walked away. Just like that. With nothing, no I'm sorry, no nada. Pero, qué cosa?

Consuelo was in bed propped up on pillows when Beba arrived on Tuesday.

"A bad night . . . my friend . . . a bad morning. I won't be . . . good company today."

"No jodas, vieja. You need me more on the bad days than the good ones." Beba kissed Consuelo's cheek. "So, no hairdo today. Nails? Are you hungry?"

Consuelo slightly shook her head to everything.

"What is it, Consi?"

"You know . . . when you don't feel bad . . . but you don't . . . feel right? Like that." Consuelo dabbed the corner of her mouth that sagged like the rim of a melting candle.

"Do you want me to leave so you can rest?"

"I want company."

"Is Diego back?" Beba said. "Has our boy returned from his trip?"

"Llegó anoche . . . late last night . . . he'll visit later . . . and, new neighbors?"

"The woman is called Tamara. I haven't met el chino." Beba didn't want to tell Consuelo about Tamara being cold and rude, nor about the fence. "The cactus is blooming," she lied.

"This . . . early?"

"Remember when you planted it with the cow tongue? How that trabajo worked!"

By the end of the week, Consuelo's house was boxed in by a wooden six-foot fence that ran from each side of the house to the edge of the property lines and straight down to the back. When Beba looked out her kitchen window, she could only see the tops of the frangipani trees. They were in full leaf but not yet budding.

The rapidity of the fence construction didn't surprise her. Florida. Beba had seen whole houses go up in weeks and entire subdivisions developed in months. What stunned Beba when she came out of her house the day after the fence builders left was the pile of plant debris at the end of Consuelo's driveway. Cut and piled one on top of the other, their roots ripped from the earth, were Consuelo's hibiscuses. The yellow, pink, and red flowers wilted, their stamens drooped pitifully.

Why do such a thing? Beba rang the familiar doorbell, once, twice, multiple times in succession, but neither Tamara nor the old man answered.

Consuelo was in the ICU at the Coquina Shores Hospital. Diego called as the sun rose and birds began their chatter. Cardiac arrest, he said. His voice sounded tired, worried, and young even though he wasn't. Fifty-six, the same age as Bebita if she had lived. Fear can do that, Beba knew, bring out the child in us needing reassurance and comfort. Even at eighty, sometimes the only person Beba wanted was her mother. She'd longed for her when Bebita died. She'd ached for her mother's arms around her, knowing she'd never again put her arms around her daughter. She wanted her mother now. She wanted her to say Consuelo would be fine.

Consuelo was not fine. A machine with dancing lines beeped at her bedside. Fluids dripped into her veins, oxygen blew up her nose, and every few minutes a beast awakened, inhaling and exhaling loudly compressing her friend's legs. Beba touched Consuelo's forehead, smoothing her sparse, disheveled hair. Eyes closed, mouth crooked, bluish lips, gray age-mottled skin.

"She hasn't regained consciousness," Diego said.

She willed herself not to cry. "Take a break, mijo. Go home. Shower. I'll stay," she said.

Beba hated hospitals—hated this one in particular—where Daniel died after countless visits for the cancer that took him within a year. But worse, it was where she'd lost Bebita. In the emergency room right beneath her. The thin, gaunt Bebita she'd been unable to save. She'd overdosed weeks before her twenty-third birthday. The cocaine had been too pure. A life cut short and never-ending grief caused by purity. Beba whispered recovery encouragements to Consuelo and paced, praying her rosary. At Diego's insistence, she left the hospital mid-afternoon, exhausted.

When Beba drove up to her house, she saw Consuelo's cactus atop the pile of dead hibiscuses. Its thorny limbs amputated. Its trunk hacked to pieces. The tears Beba had kept in check at the hospital burst. What were they thinking? Beba rang Consuelo's doorbell repeatedly; she knocked on the door, then thumped on it with the palm of her hand, but she got no answer.

"You are killing her," Beba shouted in English and then in Spanish. "La están matando. Coño, me la están matando."

It was a clear night with an almost-full moon, and she was grateful. Beba waited until the houses on her street were quiet. No cars coming or going. No bedroom lights on, no televisions glowing through blinds or curtains. At the edge of her property, in front of the new fence, Beba bent her heavy body to her knees with some difficulty. She dug with a hand trowel, stabbing the ground, tearing apart the connecting roots of grass, exposing the sandy soil, breathing in the earth smell. The hole didn't need to be deep nor wide. She'd double wrapped the cow tongue in Publix bags. She'd filled it with pepper and lemon rinds the way she remembered Consuelo doing. On a yellow Post-it note Beba had written: *Tamara* and *El Chino*. She didn't know the words Consuelo used for her *trabajo*, but she knew how she'd felt. Now, Beba told the tongue her anger. She hated having Tamara and the chino living here. She hated the destruction they'd brought to Consuelo's garden. With every change they made, Consuelo became sicker. She wanted them to feel her pain. Beba spit into the hole and filled it with dirt, burying her curse.

The following morning, Beba walked into Consuelo's hospital room expecting to find her better, but she was the same. Still unconscious, gray skin, blue lips dry and chapped. She seemed frailer, smaller, thinner. "You have to hang on," Beba whispered. "Give the tongue time to work." She dabbed Vaseline on Consuelo's lips. "You'll see." The beast roared awake, compressing Consuelo's legs. Inhaling, exhaling. Consuelo never moved.

Diego came to the hospital late in the afternoon after work. They'd agreed that Beba would come early morning to stay with Consuelo while he worked, then he'd take over through the night. Consuelo wouldn't be alone. He was a good son, Diego. Consuelo's one and only, her heart, just as Bebita had been hers. He'd never give her grandchildren, but he never failed her. And Diego was alive. What Beba wouldn't give to have her child alive, regardless of her lifestyle. When Diego and Bebita were small and played together, years before the darkness swallowed her daughter, Beba imagined them grown and married. She and Consuelo, comadres forever, doting on shared grandchildren.

All Beba wanted to do when she got home was have a hot cup of chamomile and take a steamy shower. The hospital was icy. She knew the cold controlled germs, but por Dios, she'd spent the day in a refrigerator. Her body ached. As she turned into her street, even from half a block away, she could see the mound of gravel. A pyramid of slate-gray rocks and a stack of lumber in front of Consuelo's garage. Y ahora qué? What the hell were they doing now? Again, Beba rang the doorbell, knocked on the door, and again there was no one home. Those people. She stood over the tongue, "Rot faster, por favor, rot faster."

For the third morning in a row, Beba left for the hospital shortly after the sun rose. The early morning sun glinted off the pile of rocks in Consuelo's driveway. They almost look pretty, she thought.

The frigid, antiseptic-smelling cold of the hospital made Beba shiver as she waited for the elevator to the ICU floor. Prepared, she slipped on her long, thick cardigan. Diego, haggard and unshaven, greeted her.

"No change," he said. "They're worried about stress on her kidneys. Maybe I should stay, but that project? The one from New Jersey? Tía, it's wrapping up this week."

Diego was an architect. He designed big houses and buildings that, to Beba, always looked odd and futuristic.

"Go, mi cielo, I have her," Beba said. "You know, I always have her." Just like Consi had her when Bebita died. Back then it was Consuelo bringing her soup, coaxing her out of bed, convincing her that even though the grief would never leave her, she had to keep on living. For Daniel, Consuelo had said.

When Diego left, Beba took out the toiletry bag she'd brought. She dabbed Pond's face cream with the tip of her ring finger on Consuelo's face, careful of the oxygen tubes in her nose. She dampened her fingers with Royal Violets and brushed Consuelo's hair away from her forehead. "Much better. Now you don't smell like hospital," she said. She wanted to tell Consuelo about the things in the driveway but didn't want to risk upsetting her. Instead, she told her the poincianas were beginning to blossom. Then Beba took out the rosewood rosary she used for holidays, funerals, and hospitals, inhaled the beads' perfume, and commenced praying.

When she got home after five, most of the lumber was gone from the driveway. Beba rang Consuelo's doorbell to no answer. Again she pleaded with the buried tongue. The next several days followed the same pattern. Beba left for the hospital before the workers arrived, relieved Diego, sat with Consuelo, returned home to find the workers gone. She rang the doorbell, but no one answered; tried the side gates, but they were locked. Something with an unfinished roof had been built, but that was all that she could see over the fence.

By Friday, Consuelo was still unconscious. Diego returned after work, sat next to his mother's bed, looked up at Beba, and said, "The blueprints are finished. Sent. She's not getting better, Tía."

"It just needs time to work, mijo."

"What?"

"The . . . the rest, the care. You'll see. She'll get better. Have faith, mijo."

"Right." Diego ran his hand over his face. "I'm beat, and you're worn out. Go home, Tía Beba. Sleep. Sleep late tomorrow. I'll be here."

When Beba arrived home, Consuelo's driveway was cleared. No lumber. No rocks. A part of her wanted to knock on the door again, but she was exhausted—achy, stiff, sore—completely spent from the past week. She rested her forehead on her steering wheel and whispered, "Work your magic, lengüita, work your magic, por favor." She crossed herself, kissed her thumb, and went inside.

The alarm clock was ringing. Beba murmured for Daniel to turn it off and reached out to him. Her brain engaged and she awakened, having slept deeply and long. The ringing started again, and Beba reached for the phone.

Consuelo was dead.

She pressed the doorbell and banged on the door at the same time. She had thrown on her cardigan over her nightdress, her feet in slippers. No answer. Donde cono were these people? She banged on the door one last time before walking away. She stood over the buried tongue. Beba looked up and down the street. She spread her feet apart, took a deep breath to relax, and urinated. She felt the heat of her stream as some splattered on her legs. Malditos sean.

During the days that followed, Beba helped Diego choose the funeral flowers. She picked the memorial mass card, forgoing the traditional saints, crosses, and doves, selecting *The Heavenly Garden*: a paved path surrounded by blooming flowers leading up to the heavens. She picked out Consuelo's dress and led the rosary at the velorio. She held Diego's hand as they rode in the limousine to the cemetery and rested her head on his shoulder as they stood graveside.

Afterward, Diego took her home. She stood by her front door and raised a hand in farewell when he drove away. When his car turned at the end of the block, Beba walked next door and rang the doorbell in succession.

Beba was surprised when el chino opened the door. The knees of his khaki pants were stained with dirt. He was sweaty and had a smudge on his cheek.

"Do you speak English?" Beba crossed her arms.

"Of course, I speak English. My God, what's wrong?"

"She's dead, that's what's wrong. What did you do to her garden?"

"Who's dead? Should I call 9-1-1? How can I help?"

"It's too late." Beba covered her face and for the first time since learning of Consuelo's death, she began to sob.

He looked up and down the street, took her elbow, and led her into the house. Assuring her that everything would be alright, he guided her through the living room, around the kitchen to the laundry room, and out the side door.

The side yard was completely different. The ground was covered with slate-gray gravel instead of grass. A serpentine trail of round white stones ran the length of the fence, stretching to the farthest end of the backyard and swirling to border the side of the house. A narrower swath of polished black stones followed the curves of white ones, separating them from the gravel. In the center of the yard, a square wood deck had been built, covered by a lattice roof of thick crossbeams. By the deck, placed at 3 and 9 o'clock, were square, gray brick garden beds filled with soil and perlite mixture with assorted waxy succulents waiting to be planted.

He gestured to one of the wooden bench seats on the deck. "Sit, please. How can I help, Miss—?"

"Beba."

"Who's dead, Miss Beba?" he asked softly.

"My friend. This was her house."

"I'm very sorry. May I call someone for you, Miss Beba?"

"There's no one." She looked at him. Thick gray hair and black eyebrows, he wasn't as old as she'd thought. "A Chinese garden," she said, taking it in. "Because, you're Chinese."

He let out a sigh, ran his hand through his hair, and said, "No."

"Where are you from?"

"Delray Beach."

"No, I mean *where* are you from?"

"I was born in Miami. Jackson Memorial Hospital, to be exact. My parents moved to Delray when I was four. My mother was half-Japanese."

"And, this garden?"

"It's for my son."

"You and Tamara have a son? I haven't seen a boy."

"Are you sure there isn't someone I can call for you, Miss Beba?"

"Where is your boy?" Beba looked at him, "Bueno, where's your boy? This doesn't look like a good yard for playing. My friend's garden was good for playing. There was a swing set, back there, between the frangipani trees you cut down."

He shook his head, ran his hand through his hair again, and clapped his hands to his knees. "My son is not a boy, Miss Beba. He's a man, and Tamara is his wife. Her company transferred her here. He's still in Delray Beach. This garden is for him. There's a place in Delray Beach, the Morikami Japanese Gardens. Have you heard of them?"

Beba shook her head.

"Beautiful, sprawling gardens. My son loves them. He and my mother went there often together. Very peaceful, a place of calm and serenity. He's sick, my son, but he was getting better. Tamara needs this job, the health insurance, so we've been taking turns driving to Delray and making this for him. A garden a little bit like the ones he loves, that he could enjoy as he regained his strength. But, he's gotten worse the last few weeks."

Beba shivered.

"I know it doesn't make sense, but I feel like if I finish this garden, my boy will get better."

Beba covered her face and wept.

"I'm sorry about your friend, Miss Beba. What was her name?"

"Consuelo," Beba whispered, "It means comfort."

CARLOS PINTADO, born in 1974 in Cuba, is a writer, playwright, and award-winning poet who immigrated to the United States in the early 1990s. He received the prestigious Paz Prize for Poetry awarded by the National Poetry Series for his book *Nine Coins/Nueve Monedas*, published in 2015 in a bilingual edition by Akashic Press. His book *Autorretrato en azul* received and was published as part of the Sant Jordi's International Prize for Poetry, and his *El azar y los tesoros* (Bluebird, 2008) was a finalist for the Adonais Prize in 2008. He also contributed to the book *The Exile Experience: A Journey to Freedom*, edited by the Cuban American music producer Emilio Estefan. In September 2015, *New York Times Magazine* published Pintado's poem "The Moon," selected by U.S. Poet Laureate Natasha Trethewey. His work has also been published in *World Literature Today*, *American Poetry Review*, the *New York Times*, and *Raspa Magazine*, among other periodicals. In praising Pintado's work, the U.S. presidential inaugural poet Richard Blanco wrote, "The urgency and presence in Pintado's poems feel as if the poet's very life depended on writing them. They are possessed by a unique, intangible quality that arrests the reader and commands attention. His work is intimate yet boundless, moving easily between form and free verse, prose poems and long poems, whether capturing the everyday streets of Miami Beach or leading us into the mythic and mystical worlds of his imagination." In 2012 Pintado was one the judges in Gibara's Film Festival along with the Spanish singer and filmmaker Luis Eduardo Aute. Pintado's works have been translated into English, German, Turkish, Portuguese, Italian, and French and published in eight countries. In 2016, MSR Classics released *Of Love of You*, an album of classical music and musicalized poems including work by Walt Whitman, Emily Dickinson, John Milton, P. B. Shelley, and Carlos Pintado.

"Last Man on an Island" is fiction.

> Except for making love, most things turn out
> better when we do them alone.
>
> From "Last Man on an Island"

LAST MAN ON AN ISLAND

Why here? Why Florida?

It's taking me so long to answer your questions you've begun to fall asleep on me.

I guess that by "here" you mean Miami or Miami Beach, which is, perhaps, the same thing?

Well, not to me. I drown in my own gibberish, repeat "here, here," point to the floor with my finger, wanting to tell you about those places we arrive to as if fleeing from war. (I say war, but I could say family, country, government, lovers, instead.) I wish there was time to explain it better, but your eyes are closing.

I keep trying, go on with my monologue of disconnected phrases. I take a breath, a deep breath.

C'mon, babe. Stay with me, I say, shake you softly, kiss your lips, your naked body next to mine, your legs on my legs, white on whiteness.

I beg you to enjoy the day, the light, the life out there waiting for us, the blue of the beach or maybe of some bar miraculously open still. I repeat the word beach one, two, three times, to entice you. I improvise a karaoke with that Will Smith song:

Party in the city where the heat is on, all night on the beach till the break of dawn.

Absolutely no luck. I suppose the sound is as relaxing to you as those horrible songs they use in day care to turn the cute little devils into innocent sleeping larvae.

Total madness.

Welcome to Miami, bienvenido a Miami.

What can I do to keep your eyes from closing?

I've tried everything.

I've kissed them.

Set up alarms on my phone.

I've watched porn movies with the sound on.

I've masturbated next to you.

I have yelled, desperately, like a mad man.

I've sung too-loud songs.

I've hidden your pillows.
Tickled your toes.

I see them closing. Sleep is conquering you. I see them closing, your eyes, slowly; a huge curtain falling, leaving me alone in my room. An invisible man begging to be let out.
But, look, if you wanna stay here, you might as well stay. I'm leaving. I'm walking out. It's been thirty days without walking anywhere for me, without leaving this house.
I'll see you later.
Boom!

2

There's a 200-foot distance from my building to a restaurant called NEXT.
I walk to the usually coveted outside tables.
Being the last man on an island gives me the privilege of choosing any table I want.
I'm choosing this one.
A while ago, I used to breakfast here with my friend, the director Eloy Ganuza.

The table is equidistant from the restaurant door and the place where yesterday thousands of tourists came and went like crazy ants.
The table's empty like every other table, each one shaded by a huge orange umbrella.
I tell you, Anja: Being the last man has its charms.
I'm giving this a second thought.
I don't think I should be complaining.
I don't have to deal with tourists.
Nor street sellers.
Creams.
Perfumes.
Sunglasses.
Phones.
Key West trips.

Everglades excursions.
They sell you their soul.
I hate all that, Anja.

I hate it like I hate the false happiness of waiters.

(Wait: Should I tone this down? I don't want to sound like a sociopath.)

But who cares. It doesn't matter anymore: there ain't any waiters left. You can't find one in the entire city. You can't find anybody. Actually,

there's nobody left.

Only you and I.

But you're sleeping, Anja.

Meaning: it's only me.

No one else.

It's just me and these cute chubby Botero sculptures.

(Not chubby, but inflated, I once read).

One or two statues per block.

(Whose idea was it to put them here, all over Lincoln Road, in the middle of this pandemic?)

I grab a greasy menu from the table near me.

It's filthy.

Why don't people just clean their hands?

Fried squid and beer.

I go into the restaurant.

I throw some squid on the frying pan.

I heat the oil. I watch them fry while I drink a beer.

I have a Nazi patience for watching. Just a few minutes and they'll be ready.

I grab a plate. Some lemons. Some red spicy sauce.

I go back to my table with my plate of squid and my beer.

Squid and beer, an eatable version of happiness.

3

Except for making love, most things turn out better when we do them alone. Sleeping. Eating. Jumping. Walking the dog. Swimming in a river. Writing a letter. Dancing. Writing a poem. Walking naked. Showering. Skating. Falling asleep on a lavender field. Driving a car with the wind stroking your face. Holding a bird in your hands. Kicking a ball. Throwing a frisbee. Running. Relaxing. Sitting on a bench. Staring at things. Lying down on the grass, facing up. Screaming at the top of your lungs in a forest. Walking into a bookstore without being asked, How I can help you? What kind of book are you looking for? May we suggest this month's hottest book?

Except for making love, most things now turn out worse when I do them alone.

4

I am at Books and Books and I want to buy you this month's hottest book.
The one everyone wants you to buy. It's on display. It's everywhere.
I have the book in my hands. It's an orange book with a big bright black title.
Orange is the new color.
A spritz made out of a dream.
Orange . . . Orange . . . They call the president that.
I almost throw up.
I don't want this book any longer.
I pick others.
Thomas Bernhard's Cold.
Theodor Kallifatides' Another Life.
I sit down on the floor and I leaf through them both.
At the same time.
I like you and I like Thomas Bernhard.
Bernhard says that there's nothing he has admired more in his life than suicide victims.
So depressing. I know. Extremely depressing.
Kallifatides returns to Greece to regain his native tongue.
(How can you lose your native tongue?)
I'd love to sink into you now, Anja, and disappear.
And then go floating. Flowing with the tide until I reach a coast.
I don't care if it's a Greek coast, like that of Kallifatides.
I want a coast. A recovered language.
Only if that happens, Anja, would I be able to tell you why here, why Florida.
(When a woman sleeps, on which waters does she float?)

5

There's a poem by Emily Dickinson I recall now that I am about to watch "Portrait of a Lady on Fire."
You didn't want to come see it with me and I didn't want to put out that fire. Emily's fire. Emily's poem's fire. *You cannot put a Fire out/ A Thing that can ignite/ Can go, itself, without a Fan/ Upon the slowest Night . . .*

6

I have been inside this Starbucks for quite some time now. It's the one located on Lincoln Road and Pennsylvania Avenue. I'm still undecided about whether to jump over the counter, which is close to the cash register, make myself a Very Berry Hibiscus Lemonade.

The tables and chairs here imitate some kind of loneliness.

I look everywhere but I know no one will come to take care of me.

Still, I linger for a couple of minutes.

One minute.

Two minutes.

Three minutes.

I take a few steps back and then jump, come this close to hitting the cash register by mistake. I grab the Ice, the berry refresher base, a bit of sugar, some green coffee extract, freeze-dried Blackberries and lemonade.

It's $3.99.

I swipe my card.

A debit card.

I enter my pin number.

I confirm the amount.

Yes.

$3.99.

7

The evening light slides, untamed, over the awnings. The shadows gain space below; the edges of things have a luminous halo.   Heat is retreating.   From where I am, Lincoln Road is the closest thing we have to Champs Elysees or Fifth Avenue, the great boulevard of broken dreams, six blocks of shops and cafes, a catwalk for ghosts. Why do we choose one place and not another to live? Aren't we discarding thousands of cities when we choose one? Like in love, when we choose one, aren't we pushing all others aside?

AMINA LOLITA GAUTIER was born in Brooklyn, New York, to an Afro–Puerto Rican mother and an African American father. She is the author of three award-winning short story collections: *At-Risk* (University of Georgia Press, 2011), *Now We Will Be Happy* (University of Nebraska Press, 2014), and *The Loss of All Lost Things* (Elixir, 2016). *At-Risk* was awarded the Flannery O'Connor Award; *Now We Will Be Happy* was awarded the Prairie Schooner Book Prize in Fiction; *The Loss of All Lost Things* was awarded the Elixir Press Award in Fiction. More than 125 of her stories have been published, appearing in *African American Review*, *Agni*, *Blackbird*, *Boston Review*, *Callaloo*, *Glimmer Train*, *Kenyon Review*, *Latino Book Review*, *Mississippi Review*, *Prairie Schooner*, *Quarterly West*, and *Southern Review*, among other places. She has been the recipient of the Chicago Public Library Foundation's 21st Century Award, the Eric Hoffer Legacy Award, the Florida Authors and Publishers Association Award, the International Latino Book Award, the National Indie Excellence Award, the Phillis Wheatley Book Award, and the Royal Palm Award. For her body of work she has received the PEN/Malamud Award for Excellence in the Short Story.

"A Whole New World" is fiction.

> They say, "It's like being in a completely different country."
>
> They say, "The one time I went I thought the pilot had taken us too far out."
>
> They say, "It's not like it used to be twenty years ago."
>
> They say, "I almost forgot I was still in America."
>
> They don't have to spell it out—you hear them loud and clear.
>
> From "A Whole New World"

A WHOLE NEW WORLD

No one is going to miss you. After four years of teaching in the English Department at De Chantal, a Catholic university on the Northside of Chicago, you're leaving the Midwest for a major research institution in South Florida. For the past three months you've kept this news to yourself, keeping your lips sealed as you waited for the contract to be negotiated, the paperwork to be processed, your fall courses to be scheduled, and the whole thing to become official. You wait until the last day of finals at the end of the spring quarter. With teaching done and nothing but grades to turn in, your almost-former fellow faculty gather to shake off the school year. You attend the end of the year party to deliver the news and say your goodbyes in person.

The party's in full swing when you arrive. The conference room isn't big enough for all of the department's tenure-track faculty, admins, and adjuncts, so everyone attends in shifts, rotating in and out. As your colleagues crowd around the cold cuts, crudités, and cubes of cheese, you make the rounds to say farewell.

Even though you've been on sabbatical all year and you haven't seen anyone in ages, no one asks how you've been or says long time no see.

To your news, they say, "Nadia, it's all so sudden!" Which is true. You weren't even on the job market when you were recruited and made an offer you couldn't refuse. (Don't reveal the offer. Nobody likes a sore winner.)

None of your colleagues offer congratulations or wish you well. No one lifts their glass of wine and toasts. No one asks a thing about your new tenure clock or teaching load. Curiosity trumps academic social etiquette. How you will dispose of your property is what they are dying to know. "What will you do with your condo?" they ask. "Are you to going to sell it? Or are you renting it out?"

"Neither," you tell them. You're keeping it. You don't have time to put your place on the market, get it sold, go apartment hunting in a new city, design new courses and syllabi, and pack up your life and move everything you own in a mere six weeks. Even if time were not an issue, you wouldn't sell or rent your condo. True, it's nothing fancy, but it's nice, you like it, and it's all yours. There's no doorman, elevator, game room, gym, or indoor pool in the building, but from your place you can walk to a movie theater, a playhouse, a comic book store, a public library, and the lake. There are supermarkets in both directions, restaurants everywhere you turn, and a lovely wine shop three blocks away. If you don't want to walk, several buses run down your street and the CTA Red Line is just up ahead. Aside from some books, clothes, and shoes, you'll be leaving your condo just like it is. You'll return to it during semester breaks and university holidays when you're off from teaching. No need to sell it or have to deal with property managers and finicky tenants.

Your colleagues look at you like you're speaking another language. They cock their heads to the side, squint, and ask you to repeat yourself. They're not sure they've heard you right. "So you're just going to leave your condo?" they ask, unable to mask their accusatory confusion. It's as if you've left a dog tied to a post outside of a supermarket or placed a baby in a basket out on someone's doorstep and gone your merry way.

Baffled, they shake their heads and take bracing drinks from their glasses of wine. "I don't know how you can do it," they say. "I know I could never afford that." They expect you to behave the way they would, but you are not them and they are not you.

"And what about Miami?" they ask.

You say, "I'll probably just sublet or get a short-term lease and rent some furniture."

That's not what they mean. They clarify, asking, "Do you think you'll like it there?"

You shrug and say, "Sure, why not?" You've seen *Miami Vice*, *The Golden Girls*, and *Eve*. What's not to like? You say, "I'm actually looking forward to taking my talents to South Beach."

Only two of your colleagues catch the LeBron James quote. One jokes about the town not being big enough for both you and King James. The other predicts you'll score cheap season tickets since Lebron's leaving the Heat and heading back to the Cavs at the season's end.

Everyone else wants to warn you. "Prepare yourself," your colleagues caution. "It's nothing like here."

You assume they're referring to the beach culture, predicting that it will be hard for you to focus on research when everyone else is off sunning on the sand. Reassure them. "Don't worry," you say. "I won't become a beach bum."

But that's not what they mean. "Miami takes some getting used to," they say. "Really, it's a whole new world."

An image of Disney's Jasmine and Aladdin seated on a magic carpet and flying high above the city of Agrabah comes to mind. Assure them you can handle it. Academia keeps you on the move. For years you've followed dissertation fellowships, postdoctoral fellowships, and tenure-track positions wherever they've led. Each time it's been a whole new world, a whole new place to which you've had to become accustomed, a whole new city whose ways you've had to learn.

Speaking in hushed tones, lowering their voices to whispers, clutching the stems of their wineglasses, and holding their small plates close to their chests, they let you in on a secret. "Almost no one speaks English," they reveal. "It's a total culture shock."

They say, "It's like being in a completely different country."

They say, "The one time I went I thought the pilot had taken us too far out."

They say, "It's not like it used to be twenty years ago."

They say, "I almost forgot I was still in America."

They don't have to spell it out—you hear them loud and clear. What they mean but will never come out and say is that Miami isn't white enough for them. A majority-Latino city with seventy percent of its population classified as Hispanic, there are too many black, brown, and indio Latinos running around the city, and running the city, to suit them. It makes them uncomfortable to be in a place that's not predominantly white. They don't know how to be a minority. They like their Hispanics fumbling through phrases of broken English, not speaking three or more languages with ease. They like their Latinos picking fruit, bagging groceries, and driving taxis, not treating patients, managing condos and hotels, and approving or denying reverse mortgage loans.

They don't imagine they are offending you. If anything, they believe that they're preparing you for the culture shock that you are sure to feel; they assume that their misgivings are yours. How quickly they forget that Latinos come in all colors—even black—and that you can still be Latino without looking like Jennifer Lopez or the guy from *Saved by the Bell*. They know that you're African American, but they've forgotten that you're also Puerto Rican. Here, in the Midwest, you pass without intending to, all because of what others fail to see. At home in your native New York, it only takes one glance for people to know what you are. In Brooklyn, there are so many ways to be Puerto Rican that no one ever bats an eye at your special blend, but in Chicago, no one recognizes you're Boricua unless you show up for salsa nights at Sangria's or The Cubby Bear. Hopefully, when you get to Miami, you won't have to carry pictures of your abuelo and tíos everywhere you go just to show that you belong.

Two months later, in August, when you leave for Miami and fly over a city whose condos and casitas nestle alongside one another, the culture shock commences. It begins in the airport. As soon as you land, get your bags, hop into a taxi, and the driver asks for your destination and nothing else, you know it's true—you really have come to a whole new world. In Chicago, all the taxi drivers are nosier than a bochinchera hanging outside her window all day, bothering you with intrusive small talk about where you're from and why you're here when all you want is to get to your destination. In Miami, the drivers mind their business and allow you to ride in peace.

There are seven staff working in the condo building where you are renting an apartment, a Colombiana property manager from Medellín, two Cuban housekeepers who are old enough to be your abuela, and two maintenance men: one Cuban, the other Colombian. At the front desk, two older men, one Cuban and one African American, take turns signing in guests and recording package deliveries. It takes three months before you even notice that only the property manager and front desk men speak English.

It turns out that your former colleagues were right, after all. Miami *does* take some getting used to. In the Publix supermarket, there is more than one kind of sofrito, so now you have to choose. Goya or Badia? Either way, you can leave your pilón in the cupboard—you don't have to pound garlic, onion, green pepper, and culantro to make your own. You no longer have to buy masa to make your own empanadas. In Miami, empanadas are everywhere—in the bakery section of the Publix, in the airport's food court at Versailles or La Carreta—they're even sold on the university's campus in a food truck near the building where you teach.

It's not all dulce de leche, though. Some of the ubiquitous empanadas don't measure up. The chicken ones are drier than what you're used to; they're missing that good Boricua sauce that spills out on the first bite. When you go to dinner at Lario's, singer Gloria Estefan's South Beach restaurant, your arroz con pollo is served to you in a skillet, the rice wet and soupy, with not an aceituna in sight. What's worse is that when you order arroz con pollo elsewhere, it comes slathered with a horrible thick white cream across its top. Even though Cuba and Puerto Rico are two wings of the same bird, you'll just have to fly alone in this case and stick to what you know. These problems take some getting used to, but these problems are your biggest ones, problems you can easily tolerate in a city that offers maduros as an accompaniment for almost anything you order, problems you can put up with from a city that awakens the flavors on your tongue that have been napping for so long.

Hardly the whole new world your former colleagues predicted, Miami's more like a place you've almost been to before whose ways you remember.

Force of habit makes you acknowledge the viejas you see standing outside the Metrorail station all morning hawking *The Watchtower*, and you've always known better than to leave an occupied room without first saying buen día before you go. Maybe your Spanish isn't perfect. Maybe it's rustier than an iron nail and as broken as a shard of pottery. Maybe it's as unfinished as the poem it's always writing in your heart, but it's enough to make yourself understood, get your point across, and move through the city without difficulty. It's true that you hardly ever hear English once you leave campus at the end of the day, but you don't feel like you're in another country. No, you don't feel like you're in a foreign land at all. You're in the country beneath this country, the land beneath this land. You know exactly where you are.

ACKNOWLEDGMENTS

My first heartfelt thank-you goes to you, dear Person holding this book (or digital reading device). May it fill you, teach you, help you remember things about yourself. May you feel me with you, reading, commenting, sharing what my heart knows about this incredible adventure that is uprootedness.

My lovestruck gratitude and admiration go to the writers in these pages. Thank you for trusting me with your beautiful works, with your histories, with your hurts and your triumphs. Thank you for working on deadline and for writing when you didn't have the time and were as afraid of all the death happening around us as I was.

Thanks to the translators, especially to Andreína Fernández, but also to Anna Kushner and Mariana Lentino. How would our words travel without gifted translators like you?

And now I want to thank the special people I call magic book helpers. Helpers are more than mentors. They love what you are doing, want to help you make it happen. They listen and give you what is theirs but also work to convince others to give to you so the book goal can be accomplished. Even those who said they were just doing their jobs went high above and way beyond. Thank you, Esmeralda Santiago, Silvia Matute, Rafael Ocasio, Angela Willis, Luis de la Paz, Perla Rozencvaig, Isabel Allende, Thomas Colchie, Bárbara Pérez Curiel, Hernán Vera Álvarez and the amazing students of his now legendary writers workshop, Ladislao Aguado, Rita Jaramillo, Verónica Cervera, Mia Leonin, Richard Blanco, Jaquira Díaz, P. Scott Cunningham, and Lynne Barrett along with the lovely, dedicated faculty of the Florida International University Creative Writing Program led by Les Standiford. Thanks also go to Lawrence Wong, Cristóbal Pera, Julia M. Balestracci, McKay Keith, Chloe

Firetto-Toomey, Abby Muller, Frederick T. Courtright, Stacey Hayes, Farwah Haider, Alexander Smith and Lauren Ricci of the *New York Times*, Christopher Wait, Nicolás Kanellos, Leticia Gómez, Sandra Guzmán, Jimmy Smits, and Nilo Cruz.

Thanks to Michele Fiyak-Burkley, Rachel Welton, Brandon Murakami, and the entire team at University of Florida Press for all you do to create and publish beautiful, relevant books, year after year. You are all amazing.

Gracias, Dany, mi vida, and thanks to my daughters, Vanessa and Verónica; a mi mamá, Lucy; my sister Yadira; my favorite niece, Solange; and my best friend and vital organ, Migdalia.

And then there is one person who is like no other: my dream editor come true in Stephanye Hunter. Stephanye, thank you for being boss, friend, sister, mentor, agent, office manager, counselor, reader, editor, book godmother, accountant, financial adviser, cheerleader, and badass book mistress all in one. Working with you is amazing. Just amazing. Thank you for being the one person who loves this book even more than I do.

With love and an abrazo,

Anja

CREDITS

ABOUT THE EDITOR

ANJANETTE DELGADO is a Puerto Rican novelist and journalist whose work in both fiction and nonfiction focuses on heartbreak and social justice. She is the author of *The Heartbreak Pill* (Simon and Schuster, 2008), a 2009 winner of the Latino International Book Award, and of *The Clairvoyant of Calle Ocho* (Kensington and Penguin Random House, 2014), an Indiefab finalist for best multicultural book of the year. Her work has appeared in numerous anthologies as well as in *Kenyon Review, Pleiades, Vogue, New York Times, Hong Kong Review*, NPR, Boston Review, HBO, the Women's Review of Books, and elsewhere.

Anjanette is a Bread Loaf Conference alumna and the recipient of an Emmy Award for her feature writing; she served as a judge for the Flannery O'Connor Short Fiction Award in 2015. The following year she was a Peter Taylor Fellow in Fiction, and in 2020 she was nominated by Pleiades Mag for a Pushcart Prize. Anjanette has taught writing at the Center for Literature and the Miami Book Fair at Miami Dade College, Florida International University, and writers conferences from New Jersey to Mexico City and Puerto Rico. She holds an MFA in creative writing from Florida International University, where she also teaches, and lives in Miami.